D0638309

Advance Praise for The Next 15 Minutes

When I read memoirs or listen to a speaker, I want to learn and I want to be inspired. Kim and John's story does both. Their lives will inspire all readers and allow us to pull lessons learned from their lives and struggles. As readers, we gain strength and hope through the sharing of their story.

~ **Phil Ershler**, AMGA Certifitied Alpine Guide, author of *Together on Top of the World*

Kim's positivity and grace under pressure is incredibly inspirational. Her story is a joy to read, and it reminds all of us to get outside with the ones you love.

~ **Ingrid Backstrom**, Professional Skier

As a transplant surgeon, I witness the immense physical and psychological challenges facing patients with a life-threatening illness. Ms. Kircher weaves her experience as a ski patroller high in the Cascade Mountains with the current battle against her husband's liver disease with intense emotion and heart-wrenching detail. As she draws on her prior high-adrenaline experiences to face the current challenge of her husband's illness and pending transplant, it leaves the reader feeling breathless, as if they are standing on the edge of the mountain with both husband and wife...This book is a fascinating memoir for any reader, and especially one who may be in the midst of or recovered from their own major adversity.

~ **Julie Heimbach**, Transplant Surgeon, Mayo Clinic

A profoundly courageous and honest exploration of Kim and John Kircher's journey together during John's nearly fatal battle with liver cancer. Their lives together in the mountains they love so much are the backdrop, and the lessons Kim has learned as a professional ski patroller give her the strength to make it through a harrowing year.

~ **Dan Nordstrom**, President and Owner of Outdoor Research

In the year leading up to her husband's liver transplant, Kim Kircher triumphs over the long wait and harrowing diagnosis by drawing lessons from her life in the mountains. As a ski patroller, she witnesses tragedy and triumph, dark storms and sparkling beauty, and learns how to fight for her husband's life, offering him the support and partnership necessary to weather the storm. ~ **Chris Klug**, professional snowboarder, Olympic medalist, liver transplant recipient, author of *To the Edge and Back: My Story from Organ Transplant Survivor to Olympic Snowboarder*

THE NEXT 15 MINUTES
Strength From the Top of the Mountain

by
Kim Kircher

Behler™
PUBLICATIONS
California
USA

Behler Publications
California

The Next Fifteen Minutes: Strength From the Top of the Mountain
A Behler Publications Book

Copyright © 2012 by Kim Kircher
Cover design by Cathy Scott – www.mbcdesigns.com

All rights reserved. No part of this book may be reproduced or transmitted in any form or by any means, electronic or mechanical, including photocopying, recording, or by any information storage and retrieval system, without the written permission of the publisher, except where permitted by law.

Some of the names have been changed and some conversations have been condensed in order to retain the flow of the narrative.

Library of Congress Cataloging-in-Publication Data

Kircher, Kim.
  The next 15 minutes : strength from the top of the mountain / by Kim Kircher.
     p. cm.
  Includes bibliographical references and index.
  ISBN-13: 978-1-933016-11-5 (pbk. : alk. paper)
  ISBN-10: 1-933016-11-6 (pbk. : alk. paper) 1. Kircher, Kim. 2. Skiers--Washington (State)--Crystal Mountain--Biography. 3.   Avalanches--Control--Washington (State)--Crystal Mountain. 4.   Skiis and skiing--Washington (State)--Crystal Mountain. 5. Husband and wife--Washington (State)--Crystal Mountain. 6. Cancer--Patients--Familiy relationships. 7. Bile ducts--Cancer--Patients. 8. Liver--Transplantation. I. Title.
  GV854.2.K53A3 2011
  796.93092--dc23
  [B]
                              2011018718

FIRST PRINTING

ISBN 13: 9781-933016-11-5
e-book ISBN 978-1-933016-77-1

Published by Behler Publications, LLC
Lake Forest, California
www.behlerpublications.com

Manufactured in the United States of America

For John

Foreword
By Ingrid Backstrom

Crystal Mountain is one of my favorite places on earth. Located an hour and a half drive from Seattle, out thirty miles of deeply forested, elk-trodden roads, then up a steep windy final six miles, Crystal holds many surprises. While it might not look like much from the bottom — a cluster of quaint buildings, a church and clock tower, and several lifts stringing up into the clouds — once you get off the lift at the top, with 14,410 ft. Mount Rainier just across the valley, the mountain's splendor comes alive. If the view doesn't take your breath away, there's the ski area itself — wild and rugged, long and steep. The terrain here is like the place itself in that it rewards those willing to give a little bit extra. A mini hike or a short traverse offers some of the best gladed skiing in the US, and a 20 minute hike in a different direction puts you on top of the King, a legitimate big mountain peak of the kind people usually travel a long ways and spend tremendous effort to stand atop, let alone ski down.

Lucky for me, my parents loved this place, too. They went on their first date at Crystal Mountain over 30 years ago, and did everything they could to ensure our family skied as much as possible. Growing up with parents on the volunteer ski patrol, the mountain was our playground, our babysitter, a place we could explore and be free while learning valuable lessons — mainly, that a little effort gets you the fresh pow; don't duck the closed ropes or you'll have a long walk back; and if there's free time while you wait for your parents to be done working, it goes a lot faster when you play in the snow.

Ski patrollers in general have a difficult, admirable, and thankless job — and the patrollers at Crystal have always been an exceptional group of people. Tight knit and very hard-working, they think nothing of countless morning wake-ups at oh-dark-thirty to make trail in deep snow and throw bombs to open the mountain. The lift-accessed backcountry here is some of the most unique in the country in that it is controlled—they bomb it for you and monitor access through gates—but not patrolled, effectively giving a wilderness skiing experience to many who otherwise wouldn't have the opportunity.

I grew up idolizing the ski patrollers. They were the strong, good-looking ones who skied hard, laughed a lot, and could casually launch a 20-foot cliff pulling a massive red safety toboggan. They climbed Mt. Rainier all the time and sometimes Everest, they talked about summers skiing in New Zealand, and if you were lucky, you got to hang out in the shacks with them and eat your lunch while listening to their stories.

Kim always stood out to me even from her first days on patrol. Sure, she was tall, lean, and gorgeous, but it was more how strong and capable she seemed; pulling sleds and throwing bombs were all just taken in stride with a smile. Every time I get a chance to go back to Crystal, this is still what I see—a smiling Kim, blue eyes shining, telling me that she just did a route in the Southback and they are opening it any minute! She is genuinely stoked on adventure and life and wants others to enjoy these too.

Perhaps her experiences on the patrol have made her a stronger person, more able to deal with the adversities that have come her way; but perhaps also it is her strength and grace that, along with so many other remarkable people who chose it as "their mountain," help to make Crystal such a special place. I for one am very grateful for Kim's bravery in keeping Crystal a safe place to ski, and also for sharing her story.

~ **Ingrid Backstrom** – Performed freeskiing scenes in skiing films *Yearbook, The Hit List, Impact, Steep,* and *Claim.* Backstrom was the only female to be featured as one of *Powder Magazine's* Future Big Mountain Heroes in 2002. She won "Best Female Performance" and "Breakthrough Performance" at the 2005 *Powder Magazine* Video Awards.

Prologue

Leaning out the open helicopter door, I sighted my target. A thousand feet below our position the snow-covered spine gave way to a black cliff. Ribbons of ice covered the cracks in the rock where the snow had melted and refrozen. I would drop my bomb below these rocks. "A few feet to the left," I said into the mic, waiting for the pilot to maneuver the A-Star into place.

"Ready?" Paul, another ski patroller sitting at my right, placed the bomb in my lap. Half a bag of ANFO with a ninety-second fuse, the explosive would surely rattle the slope. ANFO, ammonium nitrate mixed with fuel oil, came in 50-pound bags, and when detonated with a boosting agent, could produce a pretty large "boom."

Avalanche control at Crystal Mountain didn't usually include helicopter bombing. As ski patrollers in an avalanche prone ski area, Paul and I usually threw explosives by hand, hiking the ridges and traversing the slopes with our payloads carried in backpacks. However, sometimes the snow piled up so fast and so dangerously that we had to call in a helicopter and throw bombs from above.

"Iggie on." I slipped the igniter over the fuse, signaling Paul to start the countdown. John, my husband and the General Manager of the ski area, sat beside the pilot and turned his head to watch me pull the igniter. The helicopter hovered in place, the noise of the blades thwapping against the cliffs.

Dropping explosives from a helicopter let us reach hard-to-access chutes and slopes without venturing onto them ourselves. The raging winter storms of the previous few days had forced us to close Southback, an inbounds "sidecountry" at Crystal, allowing four feet of snow to cover a layer of surface hoar. While beautiful when it first forms with its feathery crystals catching the sunlight, surface hoar, once buried, becomes a dangerous sliding layer for avalanches.

"Fire." I pulled the igniter string. With my earphones on, I couldn't hear the fuse sputter and spit—one of the indications of a lit fuse. Instead, I pulled off the iggie and inspected the fuse, aiming the shooting sparks out the door.

I leaned out again, my feet resting on the doorsill. I would need to throw the bomb out and away, so it didn't get caught on the skids. The tether attached to my harness was just long enough for such an eventuality—so I could step out of the helicopter and free the bomb if the fuse wrapped around any part of the helicopter.

Earlier, during the pilot's briefing back in the parking lot, I'd gotten a chill visualizing a bomb getting hooked on the landing gear struts. John had made a dismissive gesture for my benefit, as if to reassure me. A pilot himself, John was no stranger to pre-flight safety. The pilot had asked John if he wanted to join us for this mission, and he'd agreed. We could use his eyes in the front seat, leading the pilot to the Southback bowls, while Paul and I arranged our explosive cargo in the back seat.

I pressed the bag of ANFO to my body, and then hurled it with both hands as far away as I could; it cleared the struts and sailed towards the slope. I smiled. "Bombs away."

I'd always wanted to say that.

The helicopter veered to the right and hovered in the middle of the basin, a safe distance from which to view. I checked my watch. In avalanche control, time was both a martinet and a comrade. If all went well, our mission would take less than fifteen minutes.

Once ignited, a shot exploded in ninety seconds, but it felt much longer. Leaning my whole body into it, I waited for the explosion, every follicle and skin cell ready for the concussion. While waiting for the bomb to explode, each minute crawled by, and I second-guessed the ignition. Did I see sparks? Had the fuse really crackled and spit? Was the cap seated in the shotwell securely enough?

In the mountains, time had its own tempo. In these intervals between repose and the exciting punctuation, when I was forced to watch the clock, time crept like a thief. But when fixated on a task, such as placing an igniter over the end of a fuse, pocketing the metal safety clasp, and finally pulling the string on the end, time flew by.

Mountain tempo lapsed not in hours and days but in smaller fractions of time. In life-threatening emergencies, caregivers called the first hour of care, in which the outcome was often determined, the "golden hour." In my experience, it was more like the "golden fifteen minutes." Whether administering CPR, driving an injured skier in a toboggan, or hiking a steep slope; if I looked too far ahead, I lost my sense of perception. Instead I broke it down into smaller segments, sometimes just fifteen-minute intervals.

The cadence of the mountains differs from the city. When faced with the immutable dictation of glacial time and death's knocking hand, we can focus so intently as to change our perception of time's passing. Fifteen minutes could blink by or else drag on, depending solely on the intensity of our focus. Ski patrolling taught me to adjust the volume, to turn it up or down based on the direness of the moment.

It would be six months before I used the lessons I learned in the helicopter that day about time's changeable nature and applied it to my husband's illness. Waiting for my explosive to discharge on that clear windless day, waiting for the concussion to rock the helicopter, the windows bowing in just slightly with the boom, the avalanche spreading and cracking, bringing down the new snow in a powdery cloud, I looked at John and smiled. This was fun. Dangerous and strange, perhaps, but we'd both learned to lean into the mountain's steep slopes and trust they would hold us. Like a season's snowpack stacked up storm upon storm, we'd bridged over our weak layers to form a strong slab, which held fast to the slope. After only a few years together, our bond was strong. It would take quite a payload to shake us loose. We felt secure in our life, our marriage, our mountains.

Maybe it was the whir of distant helicopters, or the

1

The Virtues of Being Tough

"Nice one." John's pensive voice blended with the glowing sky.

For a moment we were surrounded by darkness, and I held my breath. There must have been thousands of people there on the grass. We had found a small spot to lie down, our bodies tight together. "This one's good," I said, the twinkling lights falling beside us. The grass felt cool beneath my body as I stared at the night sky.

"Wow," we both said at the next explosion. A flower of tiny red lights gave way to green dots transforming into purple streamers that whistled to the ground. "Those are my favorite," I said. "The ones that start off as one thing and change into something else." Another pinwheel burst open and cascaded around us. So this was Fourth of July in the Midwest: Rochester, Minnesota's big night.

I saw John's profile lit by the flashes. I knew it so well—the length of his nose, his thick brown hair. In the darkness, I could see his yellowing skin or his bloodshot eyes. Inching closer to him, my head against his ear, I felt his hair tickle my forehead. I imagined how we must look—two tall bodies stretched out together; his feet crossed, my knees bent up.

Later, I would look at this image like a photograph and study it for the signs of terror that lay ahead, wishing that his lean body had more heft—like a life preserver to buoy him in the months to come.

At the time, I didn't know any of this. I was blissfully unaware that my rule in the mountains of the "golden fifteen minutes" would apply right here, in this land of cornfields and medical specialties. That soon I would pray he could survive even these short increments of time. Nor did I know how I would sift through my past like an archeologist, searching for tools to get through the terrifying year before us.

Instead, I was almost optimistic, lying there with my new husband. Here was our first major hurdle as a married couple, and I could help him get through it. Feeling his lanky, muscular leg through his jeans, I ran my finger along the groove on the outside of his thigh, clenching the grass with one hand and touching his leg with the other.

This wasn't where I thought we'd be that night. After twenty years of living with a mysterious liver condition, John's odds had run out. We'd come here for the Mayo Clinic. John's appointments started in the morning.

Four years earlier, when we first met and shared our "secret medical histories," I'd told him about my diabetes. He'd wanted to know all about it—what happened if I had a low blood sugar in the middle of the night, who'd take care of me? How did I manage my blood sugars while skiing? Did I ever think time would run out? I suppose we both had chosen adventure in spite of our diseases.

Or perhaps, *because* of them.

Then he told me about his, Primary Schlerosing Cholangitis, another autoimmune disorder. *See, we have that in common already. What are the odds?* He would need a liver transplant someday. He shrugged as if it was no big deal. He could survive anything. But I figured he would need someone when it finally happened, a Florence Nightingale type.

Earlier, when we checked into the hotel, the clerk had recommended the fireworks while John stood aside, his yellowing eyes downcast. And it wasn't just the fireworks. Minnesotans celebrate summer. In the weeks to come I would witness a town drunk on sunshine, BBQs, and softball games. And in spite of it all, I would grow blind to the joy around me.

Rochester was a lovely little town plunked down in the middle of cornfields—like Kevin Costner's *Field of Dreams*—but John and I would never truly enjoy it. As we walked back to the hotel with our hearts in our throats, we talked about his appointments the next day, afraid of what the doctors would find.

John's skin had changed color overnight. The whites of his eyes were now the color of lemons, and his beautiful skin, once olive, was now almost green. I tried to convince myself there was an easy solution. I imagined the doctors smiling humbly when they told us that a stent as small as a toothpick inserted into just the right spot would forestall any major disaster. Walking amongst the Independence Day revelers, I began to have my doubts. Other people's certitude had that effect on me.

"It could be just one single blockage."

John walked silently beside me.

"Or it might be time for a liver transplant." I tested the idea aloud.

John took a deep breath and nodded, his sign that he heard me but didn't want to talk. I wondered sometimes if it happened to him, too. Did his throat close over like he had a tennis ball stuck in there, too deep to cough out, but too shallow to swallow down?

We arrived at the hotel.

"It's probably time. It's been twenty years since I was diagnosed. Most patients need a transplant after just a few years."

"Maybe not." Now that I heard it coming from him, I wanted to take it back. I didn't want to have this conversation right before bed. "Let's not think about that right now."

"I'm sure of it, actually." John pressed the elevator button in the lobby. "I hope I have a transplant. It beats this kind of thing—slowly getting worse until who knows? Better to just get it over with."

"I don't think a transplant's an instant thing." We walked onto the elevator and waited for the door to hiss shut. "Isn't there a long waiting list?"

"They can put me on it tomorrow." He bounced a little bit on his toes, and I realized he was excited. He saw an end in sight before the battle had even started. He could tell himself, just like that, how this would end. I looked at him as the elevator slowly rose towards our floor with warm tears pooling in the corners of my eyes.

~~~

After our first date, John never talked about his disease. Instead he collected adventures, always cramming in another one, just in case. During the ski season, he worked and played in the mountains. Born at a ski area his father had built nearly forty-eight years earlier, John's psyche never whirred too far from the slopes. He was spontaneous and greedy with his time. Confronted with a few unscheduled days, he would suggest a ski holiday, or at least a visit to one of the other ski areas he and his siblings now managed. He simply couldn't sit still. It wasn't the doing of the thing that mattered so much. It was the small moments of appreciation he found through his adventures. One day early in our relationship, John and I stood on Sunnyside, a run at Crystal right under the chair. After a two-day storm, we had awakened to a day as bright and calm as a postcard. Snow mist the lightness of fine dust hung in the air and sparkled like tiny diamonds. Bouncing a little on his skis, John asked if I knew what formed the beautiful halo.

"It's ice crystals, right?"

"When it's cold like this the crystals refract the sun like tiny prisms."

I slid my skis forward, and the snow halo moved with me like a dance partner. Inside my glove, the large diamond engagement ring pressed against my finger, and the moment felt wonderfully clichéd.

"It's beautiful isn't it?"

I looked at John when he spoke, his chin lifted a little to the sun, his lips parted in a smile. Here was a man who racked up transcendent moments. Instead of a list of accomplishments, John catalogued these fragile, charmed memories.

One such day occurred on a snowy Christmas morning at Crystal when John and I uploaded the chairlift early. Since it was the busiest time of the season, we worked on holidays. But that year I had the day off—being married to the owner had its perks. It had snowed a foot of fresh, light powder the previous night, and we were alone on the chair. On rare occasions, John would give himself the bonus of "early ups" before the chair was cleared for public. He could speak to the patrol director on the radio and stay away from the areas they were still bombing. I hadn't yet seen this rule-bending side to him, and frankly I liked it.

Skiers waited patiently while the ski patrol finished blasting the mountain. The bombs were going off, and John nodded at the lift operator who let us through the closed gate. I glanced at the waiting skiers and smiled, too, feeling a little bit like a rock star, or at least a pro skier.

But it wasn't always glamour. Owning a ski area sometimes meant getting to the top first only to turn around and welcome those behind you off the chair. Often it meant helping lift operators shovel their ramps or set up their lift mazes in preparation for the crowds. At other times, it meant driving a snowcat or selling lift tickets or flipping hamburgers in the base lodge. John had learned from a very young age that ski areas are built on the backs of hard working souls eschewing better pay for a great view and the chance to ski. And John understood hard work.

But today was Christmas.

All around us the snow clung to the tree branches on either side of the chairlift, bowing their limbs into mute toy soldiers.

We sat quietly on the chair, afraid to break the spell. Perhaps John intended to merely watch the first riders unload the chair and drop in twos and threes into the steep powdery face below. Maybe he simply wanted to witness the joy of his customers as the whiteness of Christmas exploded into their faces as they plunged down the mountain. It could have been that John only invited me along as a bystander for the spectacle.

John lifted his radio to this face. "Ski patrol, this is John."

"Go ahead." Paul's voice came over clearly through the speaker.

"Do I have permission to drop into the Frontside while you guys finish up?"

There was just a slight pause before the ski patrol director answered. "Should be good skiing. I assume you have a partner?"

John glanced at me. "Kim's with me."

Paul chuckled on the radio. "Of course she is." He told us about the results from the morning—that a few teams had released small pockets, but nothing big. Then he said, "Have a nice run."

I pressed my cheeks into my collar and breathed into the closed space, warming my chin and hiding my smile. John clipped his radio to his belt loop and bounced twice on the seat. "Frontside it is, then."

The Frontside referred to the broad, curving face stretching out below the chairlift. Wedged in between two groomers, the black diamond run rarely saw big avalanches, due mostly to the heavy number of skiers and snowboarders hammering the snow into moguls. If you happen to ride one of the first ten chairs on a powder day and reached the Frontside before it got tracked up, not only were the turns amazing, but the envy of those still on the chair sweetened the run. Starting off as a shallow slope, the run quickly tipped forward, through gullies and trees, each with names and stories reaching back to the first days of the ski area.

We passed near Gregg's Gulch, named for a now-retired ski patroller who got caught in an avalanche there.

Straight ahead of us was Sunnyside. Each year as the winter edged into spring, the comfort of corn snow, breakaway bumps and slush that hissed with each turn could first be found here. An early cadre of ski bums, known as the Sunnyside Sliders, having reigned over the ski area decades earlier, would take this steep face without turning, barreling down the mountain at frightening speed. While the Sunnyside Sliders predated me, many of them still worked and skied at Crystal. But nowadays everyone made turns across the mountain. It was just too suicidal not to.

The slope mellowed and we approached the top. John could still pull us back, playing the responsible ski owner. And I suspect if we had encountered anyone else — a shoveling lift operator or a ski patroller returning from his route — he would have done just that. But the ridge was quiet. The snow below was marked by only a few tracks; two teams had headed down the valley on their way to throw bombs on Exterminator and Rock Face. It had probably still been dark when they dropped in, and they would have gingerly turned into the dark powder. Now the snow fell in fine flakes, filling in their turns.

We veered onto the cat track toward Sunnyside. Our jackets rattled against the silence of the crisp air and we sped towards the lip. John bounced a little and I mimicked him, as if testing the strength of the snow. Flakes hit my face and turned to slush. I lifted my arms to catch a little wind and slow down, but the slope slanted towards Sunnyside, and I followed.

Paul had already given the lift operators clearance to load the chair, and at the top of Sunnyside John stopped to look at the lift. A long chain of unloaded chairs met a string of beaded gems, each wearing helmets and light-lensed goggles and swinging their skis as if to usher them up the hill more quickly. John looked at me and smiled. "Ready?"

"You first." In the past few weeks, I had skied powder more times than I could count. At the end of an avalanche route, I often enjoyed twenty or more untracked, unhurried turns. I was pretty sure it was those runs that kept me coming back every season. John didn't always get out first thing in the morning. And when he did, it was usually to work, not ski.

He pointed his skis downhill, his tips disappearing as he broke through the surface snow. I stood for a moment longer. The upcoming traffic almost reached John's downcoming turns like a finger reaching towards an electrical current. I felt the pull too, but made myself wait just a moment longer. The lift line at the bottom now pressed out of the fences, spilling onto the adjacent slope. There wouldn't be another run like this today. The crowds had arrived. John's back flew over the lip of the steepest section of the run and the snow swirled over his head like thistledown. I imagined that he must have been smiling, the snow melting against his cheeks, freezing them in place. I lowered my head and turned downward.

I didn't ski on top of the snowpack, but rather inside it. Like a light-as-feather mask of snow moving with me as I turned, the snow cracked open, allowing me passage before closing behind me. I had skied plenty of powder before, but this was different. Light and creamy and the consistency of dryer lint covered in sheet rock dust, the snow ruffled like a bed sheet, just high enough to accept me under it's flapping sides, wrapping around my skis and boots, slowing me down enough to check my speed as I tipped forward over the steep section. The crowd of loaded chairs met me when I came up for air between turns. Curious looks, some smiles and a few catcalls followed me. But I didn't care. Let them rage. I'd envy me too.

Another forty blessed turns awaited me. The snow hitting my face had freed itself from gravity, from its layer within the snowpack, and floated up, suspended. I wriggled into my collar, breathing strategically when the snowpack released me from its gentle grip. Down into the white snow, up unweight, breathe, breathe, and then down again. Wait for the splash of brilliant kisses. Smile. Let your cheeks freeze into place. A tinkling hiss followed behind me, the sound of disturbed snowflakes settling back into place, forever changed by the pressure of ski tips and edges slicing the wings of stellar crystals and starting the process back towards water. I was an agent of change. Lifted by angels and ushered by fairies, my transient turns had already started hardening the snow, breaking the arms off the light fluff and marshaling it towards the hard, round balls it would eventually become.

Powder doesn't last. And there isn't enough of it to go around. Fanatics might spend years in search of the kind of run John and I enjoyed that Christmas morning. Unlike the skiing hoards that would soon unload the chairlift, our run had been unhurried, unfrenzied by the tidal wave of others at our heels. A good powder run, like any of our best moments, flees too quickly. We regret its end even while it still continues. The mountains are full of these ephemeral flashes.

Perhaps John sought these moments with more fervor than most because he foresaw his demise. His diseased bile ducts pinched his capacity for patience and blasé acceptance of life's fleeting divinity. He wanted it all, right now. He hadn't yet gotten his fill. But just like all hallowed moments, the trick is to enjoy it while it lasts.

~~~

While I knew John had a serious condition, I didn't suspect his liver was failing. Life was just too good. His flu-like symptoms became more common, especially in the months before we left for Rochester. Even then, we never saw it coming. Later, the doctors would name this particular malady: cholangitis—an infection in the liver. We didn't realize it at the time, but it was the inevitable build up to PSC's final stand. Come spring, the disease was winning.

Earlier in the year, it happened while John and I had skinned to the top of a backcountry peak to camp under a full moon. By attaching skins to the bottom of our skis, we could hike uphill. Being the second full moon of February, technically it was a blue moon, and John wanted to take advantage of that. Camping under a full moon was romantic enough, but camping in the snow under a blue moon? That was typical John, all romance all the time, as if he had a secret manual called *101 Ways to Woo Your Woman*. Halfway to the top, John stopped in the fading light. He couldn't go any further.

"Are you injured?" I asked, my EMT training kicking in.

"No. Just bad."

"Bad how?"

"Sick."

"As in puking sick or just blah sick?"

"Neither. But it's painful."

"Should we turn around then?"

He kept hiking, slow and steady, ignoring me. He was determined. Also, he thought it would go away. The same mysterious nausea that had plagued him before had always passed. By the time we arrived, he felt fine again; the pain vanished. I told him I'd set up the tent while he cooked dinner over our camp stove.

"What tent?"

"The tarp, the Megamid. You know. My floorless tent." I smiled at him. I loved my Megamid. Like a circus tent without a floor, the "mid" was perfect for winter camping. Allowing you to shovel platforms for sleeping and an opening in the snowpack for the entrance, the mid didn't need a floor. Plus, it was roomy and lightweight.

"I didn't bring that thing."

He had to be kidding. What kind of romance could we have without a tent?

He smiled, anticipating my thoughts. "Look at how beautiful it is." He glanced at the big moon rising over the ski area. Tiny lights from the snowcats dotted the runs, which were visible even from across the large valley. "It's warm. Besides we have our bivy sacks."

"It's not warm." I zipped my down jacket to my chin and shivered, anticipating the cold night ahead. I was diabetic dammit. My circulation wasn't all that great.

"Plus I feel better now. Whatever that was has vanished." He handed me a mug of hot tea laced with a shot of whiskey.

I wanted to ask him more about it. Perhaps he was just getting older, unable to push himself as he once had. I supposed I didn't need to remind him of that by discussing it. I sipped the whiskey tea and tried not to shiver. Shoveling two platforms separated by a hole that would allow the coldest air to sink below us, I warmed up a little while John cooked dinner and tried not to grumble. I wanted to say something about how even cavemen knew the importance of providing shelter, but I dismissed it. I couldn't play both sides of that coin. John's manhood wasn't diminished one bit being with a strong woman. Nor did he protest when my backpack was heavier than his. I'd spent years working as an Outward Bound instructor, hiking through the Cascade Mountains laden with several weeks of food supplies, ropes and gear to climb the mountains. John was far stronger, but he chose to pare his gear down to the barest of essentials because he was long used to a school-of-hard-knocks style of camping. I wasn't a sissy; I just wanted to be warm.

"I'll make you a hot water bottle."

I opened up my second Nalgene and emptied the contents into the pan. "You can make me two." Once filled with boiling water, the two bottles would heat me inside my sleeping bag and keep me from freezing to death.

"You worry about the cold too much." It was easy for him to say. His body worked. It regulated his temperature and utilized every last calorie for energy and warmth. Without insulin, my metabolism slowed to a thick ooze. Fifteen years of diabetes takes its toll, especially on blood vessels and fine nerves. I was a rock star diabetic, always keeping my blood sugar within the "normal range," but still. Having children was out of the question; I'd made that decision early on. Pregnancy would cause swings in blood sugar, which could damage not only me but also a fetus. I never wanted that kind of responsibility. But I shouldn't have been thinking about my own disease. Shivering made me do it. Instead I should have watched John, studying his actions like a scientist, inspecting the little ways his body was already betraying us.

John smiled at me, dismissing my fear of the cold and my excuses. I also forgot about his strange pain. There had to be some other explanation.

Life just couldn't be that cruel.

That was how it was for a while. Off and on. If we had really been paying attention, we could have been more proactive — mapping out the liver's demise with MRI's, maybe taking vitamin supplements, or finding some kind of guru or prayer group. I would have slept every night out in the cold if it would keep him from getting sick. Maybe we could have forestalled some of the outcome. We could have, at the very least, padded our hearts a little in preparation.

~~~

Ensconced in Dr. Alexander's office in Rochester, I watched him settle back into his chair and look at the computer screen on his desk. His demeanor had changed. A moment ago he and John had been talking about a mutual friend — small talk really. The image on the screen was why we'd come. He leaned back in his chair and put his hands together, forming a steeple with his index fingers and focused on a picture of John's liver. He pointed to a blank space within the image and began talking.

The rhythms of his voice floated above me for a moment, and I tried to concentrate. He talked about strictures and the procedure to open up the bile ducts, using the term Klatskin tumor, which made me straighten up as if pulled by a marionette string. "Of course we also need to take brushings," he said. I imagined tiny paint brushes skimming the surface of the stricture, picking up cells like fish scales to be put under a microscope later. Then he said, "to be sure it isn't cancer."

"Do you remember the story about Marty's fall underneath the Mad Wolf chair?" John had asked Dr. Alexander just a few minutes earlier. They had been talking about physical toughness, and now I realized why. Dr. Alexander wanted John to remember Marty — tough, hard-as-nails, Marty Pavelich — when he discussed the diagnosis. John had brought up their mutual friend, the retired NHL Hall-of-Famer, who played for the Detroit Redwings on a $7,000 contract, rode trains to games and never missed a match. A sick or injured player would be cut from the team. Perhaps John knew, too, that he needed to be tough, just like Marty, in order to survive the next few minutes. Like me, John needed a way to get through small increments of time. And for him, he conjured images of exemplary resilience.

I didn't want to think about the word *cancer*, knowing that once we started down that line, there'd be no turning back. Small pieces of lint floated in front of me as I shredded the tissue in my hands. The doctor had placed the box of Kleenex on the corner of the table in preparation. I stared at it now, thinking back to John's story of Marty. His tone was light and filled with awe, and I could see that John was trying to channel him. The sound of my breathing cracked the room's silence. The word *cancer* echoed against the fluorescent lights and wafted in the paper sheet stretched across the examination table. I stared straight ahead and remembered John's story of Marty.

"The guy busts his chest right down the middle, which had to hurt like holy hell, and then he wouldn't let them put him in a toboggan." John had bobbed his head up and down as he told the story. "He skied all the way to the bottom," he'd said, raising his eyebrows and motioning with his long fingers to mimic skiing. "Rode the chair back up to the top of Andesite, then skied down to the base. The guy was 70 years old at the time. At the end of the day, he's the toughest guy I know."

Dr. Alexander nodded. "He's tough." He had narrowed his eyes a bit, driving home his point. It helped to be strong and resilient. Sometimes that's all a person had. Remembering that, I turned my gaze towards the doctor now, his lips having just formed the word cancer; he seemed to be studying his knuckles, rubbing each ridge with a contemplative forefinger.

I had met Marty at Big Sky where he shook my hand ferociously and patted my shoulder, asking me *how ya doing, how ya doing*. His smile was strong and hard as a bullet.

I raised my eyebrows now and looked at the doctor. "Cancer?" I willed myself into the dark shadow of the moment, like stepping from the bright light of a playground into a dark, cold cave. I'd already looked up the term Klatskin tumor and dismissed it as a possibility, as if enough Google searches could ward against the worst possible outcome. It was true that sometimes PSC caused cancer, but not this time. Or so I had thought. I believed we had prepared for the worst. Cancer just wasn't part of the game plan.

I glanced at John as he sat in the chair beside me. His lips were pursed in concentration and his face had turned to stone. All the earlier animation had vanished. Maybe John didn't understand it. Possibly he didn't hear it. Perhaps he already expected this and just wanted to get the messy diagnosis part over with and move on to conquering it. Or conceivably his throat had gone too dry to speak.

In the next sentence the doctor waved his hand, and said cancer was "unlikely." He explained the endoscopic procedure, known as an ERCP, in which they sent all the equipment through a tube down John's throat and threaded through his small intestines, up his bile ducts to his liver. I placed my hands on the cool cushion of the built-in couch, fingering the grooves in the gathered folds of the fabric, trying to commit the doctor's words to memory. I tried to listen, to remember his exact terminology, so I could scrutinize it later and turn it over in my head until somehow it made sense.

Cancer.

"Unlikely," I repeated.

A few minutes later John and I stood in the elevator while my mind formed a hypothesis. "Do you think it could be cancer?"

"Of course not," I said.

"Well, they're testing for it, aren't they?"

"You're jumping to conclusions. PSC constricts the bile ducts. That's all this is."

"But it can lead to cancer." John appeared to accept this fate. Maybe he wasn't taking the diagnosis personally. Something shifted in his face and he looked at me sadly. "This is cancer, Kim."

"How do you know? You're not a doctor."

"I know my body."

"No you don't."

He looked at me sternly.

"You don't know this is cancer." I insisted.

That was one thing that bothered me about John. Once he made up his mind, he wouldn't listen to logic.

2

Shearing the Weak Layers

As John and I moved further along the clinic conveyor belt towards diagnosis, I searched for stories of my own to buoy me. John had Marty Pavelich; I had my experiences, though I never played hockey without a cast or skied down a mogul field after breaking my sternum. John found strength in Marty's courage and stoic resolve; Marty once played hockey with a broken arm, convincing the doctor to cast the uninjured limb as a ruse to fool his opponents. Missing a game meant losing his spot on the team. John admired that kind of grit. On the mountain, I had learned to expose and alleviate weak layers. It had been my job for twenty years.

On snowy mornings at Crystal Mountain, ski patrollers headed out early for avalanche control, in which we blew up the mountain to save people. We carried explosives, throwing them one by one on the steep slopes, and started avalanches. That way the snow slid when we wanted it to, not when an unsuspecting skier took his first turn.

We called it avalanche control, but it was more like mitigation. We tempered the slides. Getting the slopes to fail wasn't always easy, even with the heavy firepower we carried in our packs. The fastest way to stabilize a snowy slope was to ski it. By working the snow until it was a field of hard moguls, it became safe. But in order to get there, we had to reduce the avalanche hazard for the first few skiers.

Crystal Mountain is in avalanche country. Given the right conditions of heavy snow over a weaker layer, any slope over thirty-degrees can produce avalanches. Most of the upper slopes are well over thirty degrees, and some even reach twice that. Explosives aren't our only defense, however. We also have dogs.

Rocket was my avalanche rescue dog. He was a black lab, small enough to carry over my shoulder to any disaster on the mountain. He was trained to find avalanche victims buried in the snow, seeking out human trace in the snowy wreckage and alerting me with a bark or rapid digging to tell me he'd found something. Sniffing the air and then burying his black, glistening nose in the chunky avalanche debris, he never knew the real game — that someone's life hung in the balance.

When I pictured him someday finding a real victim, he would be heroic. Scratching at the snow frantically until the quarry, alive and whole, emerged from the snow, Rocket would be victorious. But life didn't always follow my precise planning, not on the slopes or later when John got sick.

One January morning, the wind gusted to 100 mph at the top of the Rainier Express, the chairlift leading to the summit of the ski area. According to the Beaufort scale, anything over 70 mph is considered hurricane force. This wind, combined with fresh snow overnight, formed stiff Styrofoam-like drifts called wind slabs that created high avalanche hazard. With the strong wind making it impossible to run the chairlift, we rode to the summit in snowcats for avalanche control. High winds could blow the haul rope right off the sheeves (the rubber-lined wheels that held the cable in place), or blow a skier sideways.

We called it "nuking", which it did as I hiked up Exterminator Ridge. The wind pelted my face (only the tip of my nose and upper lip was exposed). I leaned into the wind, carrying my skis on my shoulder. Each time I lifted my leg, the wind blew it off course a little. After a while I had to lower my skis and carry them by the tips, dragging the tails in the snow behind me.

My avalanche partner and I were to control Exterminator Ridge, and we had brought along extra firepower to do the job. In addition to the small explosives we normally carried, we also lugged two extra "party packs"—simple explosives made by filling empty milk jugs with ANFO. The colored pellets looked like candy and smelled like gasoline. These explosives had a higher burn rate, which meant a larger boom—often tripping off the alarms of cars parked two thousand feet below. Party packs were the go-to tools in conditions like this. Wind slabs needed a little extra *oomph* to get them going, but once they started, the results could be devastating.

We carried our heavy backpacks up the last few feet to the top of Exterminator Point. From there I looked down at Exterminator Proper (as opposed to Exterminator Ridge, the route just to the left) and called Doug, the Snow Safety Director. "You're definitely going to need another team for the Proper," I said into my radio.

"How does it look?"

"Fat." I pressed my ski pole into the snow surface, punching through the stiff top into the soft snow below: hard slab over a weak layer—perfect conditions for big avalanches. "The wind rolls are huge. I can put one of my parties on that, but I can't go any lower." Doug understood my dilemma. The Proper Route was going to need its own team, and the closed lift made it hard to get teams back to the top.

"Got it," Doug's voice cracked on the radio. "It doesn't look like the upper mountain's going to open anyway."

"Do you want us to control the Proper instead?" Exterminator, a double black diamond run, hung far above the ski area. Our assigned route, Exterminator Ridge stood above a cat track that the snowcats would use to exit the upper mountain after grooming the slopes that morning. Doug was weighing his options. He had one team in place to cover two potentially hazardous slopes. If the upper mountain was closed, no one could get here anyway. The snowcats, however, needed a safe exit.

"No," Doug answered. "Stay on the Ridge. And be careful."

We got big results that morning; stiff fracture lines like erratic EKG readouts zig-zagged along the ridge. The edges of our skis barely carved tracks in the stiff wind slabs. Rigid and hollow, the snow echoed beneath us, making the tips of my fingers sizzle. Of all avalanche conditions, I liked wind slabs the least. To the uninitiated, stiff snow might seem safe, sequestering its weaknesses in shallow pockets. But ski across one of those weak spots and the entire slope could release as a stiff, punishing slab. That day we lowered our explosives on string to keep them from sliding to the bottom before offering their payload; the wind hammered our backs and poured driven snow into our packs each time we opened them. We were doing the best we could.

As it turned out, Doug did send another team towards the Proper. The route leader called in from his hike up to Exterminator Point. The wind blew across his radio mic, nearly scratching out his words. He had to abort; the wind was too strong. Doug agreed. You just couldn't hike through stiff Styrofoam snow in hurricane-force winds.

Even in the extreme conditions with the upper mountain closed, two skiers hiked up from the bottom of Rainier Express. Perhaps they hadn't planned on hiking all the way to the top of Exterminator. Maybe they just wanted to ski a few untracked turns, thinking no one would notice as they hiked past the closed signs. I later learned that they owned avalanche beacons (a radio transceiver used to find victims buried in the snow), but were not wearing them that day.

When the call came in from Dispatch, I'd already been back from my route for a few hours. "Code 2, Exterminator," the voice on the radio blared. There'd been an avalanche. After a moment, another call: "Where are the dogs?"

Rocket slept under a bench, just below where I sat.

"Top of Chair 9," someone answered.

I was already up and putting on my jacket. This was it; this was what we'd trained for. I skied fast, carrying Rocket over my shoulder. We quickly reached the snowmobile that would give us a ride to the summit. The wind had increased, and it was still too dangerous to run the lift.

It didn't take Rocket long to find the guy. The two skiers, who had hiked from mid-mountain, headed straight for Exterminator. The first skier triggered the avalanche, while the second man watched his friend get swallowed by it. How his heart must have knocked against his eardrums as he watched it all unfold. The stiff slab would have broken apart slowly, moving as one piece for a while like a single white dinner plate flying down the slope. As the slab gained momentum, it would have slid through the trees, breaking limbs and ripping against the smaller trunks. A powder cloud would have led the charge — the suspended snow crystals and wind roaring down the slope in front of the churning slab. Then the slab would have broken into smaller chunks, like shards, pressing into the victim's side, ripping off his hat, goggles and skis. He would have tumbled, helplessly rolling in the debris, smacking against the trees, one after another until he couldn't feel it anymore.

The witness would have fumbled for his transceiver, ready to turn it to *receive* mode to find his partner's *transmit*. Then it would have hit him. *Shit.* They left their transceivers in the car. They hadn't planned on backcountry skiing that day. Who'd ever heard of an avalanche in-bounds at a ski area? Ever since ski patrollers started using explosives to control them, in-bound avalanches fatalities had all but vanished. Not that day, however. Given enough snow and heavy winds, sometimes avalanche control just wasn't possible. Sometimes skiers broke the rules, thinking the closed signs were meant for someone else. He must have stood there for a second as it all unfolded, the three-foot crown spreading to either side of him as he watched his friend disappear. It could happen that fast.

A physical description of the missing skier had just been broadcast on the radio. "Black parka, gray ski pants, black boots." The search had extended into a Missing Person; perhaps the victim had dug himself out already and had made it back to the base area.

That's when I noticed Rocket alert: hunched over, his body full of purpose. He dug ferociously and I skied over, probing in the snow between his paws. I gasped. Maybe a foot deep, my probe hit something spongy. "I think I have a strike," I radioed and began shoveling. Two scoops and I saw it: a gray pant leg and a black ski boot. Rocket tugged at the cuff of the pant, trying to pull the body from the thick, cement-like snow.

Five or six rescuers jumped in with shovels and probe poles. I pulled Rocket away, and we watched from a distance as they began CPR. I held Rocket's reward toy—the one he played with only after finding someone. Until now, it had always been practice; the "victim" would jump out of a hole in the snow with the toy and play with him, and he loved it.

This was different, and Rocket knew it. Even as I waved the toy in front of his nose, he ignored it.

"You're a good boy, Rock." Taking off my glove, I placed my hand on his smooth head. I rubbed my fingers over his soft ears; it felt like dipping my hand in a bowl of flour. He looked at me momentarily, his eyes glistening. "You did your job. Let's go." But I couldn't pull him away. A doctor on scene had already called off the resuscitation efforts. It was no use; he'd been pushed through the trees at a tremendous speed. He must have died instantly.

Rocket wouldn't budge. He watched them draw a blanket over the body. The wind howled in the trees, dropping clods of snow from the branches that left craters in the snow all around us. It was just a small circle of us by then, each staring at the snow beside the blanket, waiting for the toboggan. Only Rocket kept his eyes on the victim, the gray blanket spread over the twisted limbs and geometric scar left in the debris from where they pulled him out. Even as they lifted the corpse into the toboggan, Rocket kept staring, trying to make sense of it all.

Years later, sitting with John in the hospital, I wanted to go in the operatory with explosives and control the hazard—blow it up to start the slide so it happened when the doctors could watch over him, scalpels poised in the air. I wanted to bring Rocket in there with me, have him alert on just the right spot. *Here, right here. If you poke your instruments in right here, then the trouble will go away. Problem solved.* Like Rocket, I still wanted to believe the body would come back to life—jump out of the hole with a toy.

But that's not how it worked: in the hospital or on the slopes. This situation wouldn't respond to avalanche control, and a rescue dog couldn't fix it either. I would have to learn some other technique of survival, hoping the hidden layers in the snowpack would prove strong enough to withstand whatever heavy weight lay ahead of us.

~~~

"Fifteen Mississippi," I whispered to myself. It was very quiet while I waited. The cold snow pressed against me as my breath filled the small space, turning the slick walls to ice. A sheen, like a freshly groomed ice skating rink, now glistened on the walls. Drops of ice melt dripped onto my parka and seeped into my ski pants. I covered my face with my gloved hand, wiping away the thought of the ice mask that could grow so quickly, cutting off my oxygen. After being tumbled in an avalanche, the victim often died of suffocation, the snowy debris melting and refreezing with each breath, sealing her in a tomb of her making. Sometimes the force of the slide pressed the snow into her throat, which quickly formed into a tube of hardened ice, one she couldn't spit out. It would be an awful way to die.

Maybe I should just relax and take in the tranquility, I thought. Wasn't that how people died, just closed their eyes and let themselves drift away? On the other hand, the more I breathed the more quickly the snow would melt and refreeze, cutting off the supply of fresh oxygen that could only get here through the tiny gaps between the snow blocks.

Instead, I wanted to stay busy, buried here in the snow. I'd been counting, and already I was up to fifteen Mississippi. If I panicked, I'd breathe faster, my exhalations warming the air. I couldn't panic. I recited the alphabet backwards, getting stuck on p-o-n-m, so I started again at z. This wasted more time. I pushed away the thought that I could wait forever here in this snowy grave.

In my line of work, I had imagined getting fully buried by an avalanche, how I would try, at first, to keep myself on the surface of the debris, avoiding trees and other obstacles as I was catapulted down the hill. Then, if I tumbled, losing my sense of up and down, getting thrown around like a sock in a dryer, I would wait for the debris to slow. I'd feel for it. The sides would start to press against my body, locking my limbs and neck into place. At this moment I would form an air pocket around my face before the slide stopped completely and solidified into a heavy casket. I would paw frantically at the snow with my other hand, trying to find a way to the thick, easy air of the surface. A hand on the surface would tell rescuers where to find me. Plus I might be able to move some of the heavy chunks away. This dreadful fantasy always made me shudder, but here I was subjecting myself to it again. I had even imagined submitting to the slow, cold death. But in those terrible visions I never considered the tranquility. It was precisely this quiet that frightened me now. If I didn't keep my mind occupied, I might panic. And I must not panic.

The melting walls of snow made ticking sounds as they settled around me, and I started to quake. It was too cramped to change positions. I wish I hadn't been so hurried earlier; now I just had to be still and try not to breathe. Six feet above me, the air was crisp-fresh against the gray sky. I wondered if it was snowing again. Maybe the wind was howling up there; but inside it was peaceful. I just had to slow down and breathe, compress the waiting into only the next moment ahead of me. Then the next. That was the trick. I wondered if it had been fifteen minutes yet—enough time for my scent to percolate through the snow to the surface. In actual avalanches, victims found within the first fifteen minutes have about a 90% chance of survival. Double the time under the snow and the rate drops to 30%. Just like with critically injured patients, avalanche victims also have a "golden fifteen minutes."

I heard a dense sound, like a cracking. The walls could collapse around me, and I had my radio close to my mouth just in case this happened. But the roof of the cave stayed intact. Listening intently, I heard the sound change to a rhythmic scratching. The scratching grew louder, and I knew what it was. Rocket's paws broke through the ceiling of the cave, his head framed against a burst of light. I could see only his head and wagging tail behind him. He seemed to be smiling. The drill was complete, and Rocket had found his victim.

At least once a week, I dug a snow cave and buried myself in it so my dog could find me. Sometimes the caves were too hastily built and the narrow and cramped confines made me want to press the snow-blocked mouth open and breathe again. But I always waited, trusting my dog's nose. It was supposed to be training for Rocket, but it had taught be something too. With this new disaster brewing in Rochester, Minnesota with John, I realized I had trained myself to stay calm in the face of hardship, taught myself to quell the panic by occupying the smallest moments with distraction. That was how I would have to get through John's diagnosis—whatever it may be. Even if the doctors found cancer, even if they told me John would die, I wasn't going to panic. I promised myself that. Instead, I could squeeze time into smaller increments, and not try to conquer it all at once. I would try to get through it just fifteen minutes at a time.

3

Please Remain Calm

The afternoon of John's diagnosis, I allowed myself to cry for fifteen minutes, convincing myself this was a necessary release. Back in the hotel room, waiting for the results of the endoscopic procedure, I researched Bile Duct Cancer, also called cholangiocarcinoma, and learned all the terrible ways it killed. Its victims, once diagnosed, usually lived nine months. A few hours earlier I hadn't heard of it, and now I wondered if it would kill my husband before the year was over.

It didn't grow as a tumor exactly, more like a thickening inside the ducts—like tentacles stretching out through the vessels. It clogged the liver, but the really deadly part was how it wrapped around the hepatic vein and spread its cells into the abdominal lymph nodes. Like any cancer, it killed by multiplying.

I found another piece of information; the cancer was treatable if it hadn't spread—the only cure was an entire resection of the liver and all the bile ducts.

My armpits stung, like tiny needles pricking my skin, and I felt a nervous spasm through my spine. If the stricture was cancer and it had spread, then he would have about nine months to live. I pushed my chair back from the desk and held my hands in front of my face as in prayer. Shaking somewhere in my arms or my abdomen, I tried to hold against it, my fingertips pressed to my forehead.

I looked over at John's clothes on the bed, which I had started to pack. His pants were folded neatly and his long sleeve gray t-shirt lay over them.

For a moment I couldn't recall what he wore that morning. I searched my brain, trying to visualize him, as if his image was already slipping. Then I remembered that I'd helped him change into his gown in the pre-op room. He wore a black shirt, jeans and his black shoes. I had stashed those clothes in the closet of his room, and they were still in there.

Nine months. I walked over to the bed and knelt in front of it. I touched his shirt, putting it to my nose and inhaled his scent. I began to pray.

I rocked back and forth, begging to God. The carpet was scratchy on my knees and my elbows rested on the smooth bedspread, its bright floral pattern fanning out like blood stains. I squeezed my eyes shut and concentrated. I tried to bring all my energy into this one plea.

Please don't let it be cancer.

The tears were faster now and I gave into them, allowing myself only a few minutes for this. I figured that if I let go a little now, I could maintain my calm later, like pressing a pressure release valve.

My body convulsed, and I dropped to the floor. I bargained with God, creating a story that I could live with and asking Him to play along. *If it's cancer, it hasn't spread. They'll get it all out and he'll survive. He'll be okay.* My knees and elbows rubbed on the carpet and I cried into my hands.

~~~

As a diabetic, I didn't like feeling out of control. Even in the midst of a low blood sugar reaction I tried to maintain an outward calm, as if just the power of my mind could hold back a seizure. It was as much for my own safety as it was for my pride. If I held it together long enough to drink some orange juice, I would be fine. No one would have to know. Like the lesson waiting for Rocket, I just had to get through the next few minutes until the juice kicked in. But if I gave into the adrenaline rush, I could lose myself in it, walling off my sugar-starved brain.

That had happened before. Once I had a diabetic seizure in front of a group of ski patrollers. We were training for our avalanche blasters test, studying the book of regulations, memorizing the table of distances and the components of our explosives for recitation in a few weeks when a representative from the state arrived with the tests. I had been talking—all eyes in the room were focused on me. The conversation had veered a little into general avalanche control. It had been an excellent snowfall year at Crystal, earning even the first-year patrollers enough hours of blasting to sit for the test.

Looking at my hands, I had thought they belonged to someone else. They shook violently. I began to sweat little droplets of acid that pricked against my temples. Someone asked me a question, and I looked at her apologetically. She wanted me to finish my story about the time I hung a bomb from the Reynolds tram before realizing the retrieval line was knotted and wouldn't allow me to release the now-lit explosive. I had been making some point about preparedness and planning.

I might have asked for a glass of juice. Another person may or may not have asked, "Isn't she diabetic?" Voices echoed around me. I blinked my eyes hard, trying to stay conscious.

I was sure someone ran to the kitchen. I could still fake my way through this and save myself the embarrassment. All I had to do was drink some juice. I turned my head left and right, searching for it. Instead I saw only the inquisitive faces of my friends as medical caregivers. Someone held my hand. Another one touched my forehead. I couldn't make out their words.

I was slipping. Grabbing the bottom of the chair to keep myself from falling, I twisted my head around to find the juice. My knees bounced violently in front of me and I looked at them harshly, willing them to stop. I had to lie down before I fell. I tried to ease myself onto the floor, but someone's hands held my arms behind me like Superman.

That was when my mind and my body lost contact with each other. I lay on my back, shaking violently. I clawed at the floor with my fingernails, trying to avoid slipping sideways. I thought someone put a pillow behind my head. Maybe I screamed. I might have wriggled under their probing fingers as they searched for a medical alert tag, my body bouncing on the hard floor.

When I emerged from the seizure, my mouth was sticky sweet, my lips tasting like orange juice. I sat up as if nothing had happened. The others talked quietly, having already returned to their seats, and avoided my gaze. The conversation had moved on to other "learning experiences" the new patrollers had undergone that season—not seating the iggie far enough down onto the fuse; not checking to see if the thing was lit before throwing it down the slope, where it disappeared beneath the new layers of fluff; tossing a charge onto a wind-blown surface without first tying a string to the bomb, that would keep it from sailing all the way to the bottom of the hardened slope. It seemed like there were more opportunities to screw up than succeed.

I excused myself to the bathroom, where I sorted my thoughts as if patting down my pockets looking for my keys. I wouldn't let this happen again. I'd pay better attention next time. I'd check my blood sugar levels on my glucometer more regularly. I vowed to be better.

But that's not exactly how it turned out.

It would have been easier if I wasn't so physical. A ski patroller's job required calories, which insulin helped to metabolize. But I had to time the shots just right. If I started the day with a hearty breakfast, I might not burn it off until noon, thus causing my blood sugar to skyrocket—inviting long-term vascular complications. Conversely I might eat light, expecting an easy morning, and end up on a rescue or an explosives mission.

Being a diabetic ski patroller required flexibility.

~~~

And just like on the mountain, the circumstances shifted like an approaching storm back in the hotel room in Rochester, and I allowed myself the flexibility to cry. After fifteen minutes, I stopped, holding it in like an oncoming seizure. I walked into the hotel bathroom and looked in the mirror. *You have to do this.* John may have already accepted his fate, but he didn't know how serious this was. *He didn't really appreciate the situation here.* I filled my hands with cold water and pressed them against my eyes. *You can do this.* My face in the mirror looked older. My jaw muscles flexed hard, braiding ribbons along the edges of my face.

I had been through worse dangers than this. This wasn't a wind slab ready to slide or a storm depositing battered snow crystals onto an already tenuous slope. This didn't require that I act immediately. Besides, he was getting excellent medical care. The best. I took a deep breath and brushed the hair out of my eyes. John needed me to be strong.

You can do this.

~~~

As ERCPs go, doctor shorthand for the endoscopic procedure to open John's bile ducts, John's had been a doozy. They succeeded in opening the stricture (his bile ducts were now flowing), but they also irritated the pancreas. Now he lay in the hepatology wing of the hospital, the pain in his side a ten out of ten. I thought of him back in his room, a few doors down from where I sat, and wondered if he'd finally fallen asleep, the television washing the room in an eerie blue.

After four days in Rochester, I needed to inform our family and friends of the situation here—about the complications caused by the procedure. I sat at the computer at the end of the hallway. It was a small room, just for visitors of patients on the ninth floor of St. Mary's Hospital. The keys on the ancient keyboard wobbled under my fingers. I wanted to portray strength: John gritting his teeth through the pain of pancreatitis;

me, the stalwart in the midst of the storm. I wasn't ready to make an all out plea for help and support. That would mean the situation was dire, and I didn't want to admit that yet.

Since we'd arrived in Rochester, I had scrubbed myself raw with research, as if the hours in front of the computer and the colorful hospital pamphlets could sanitize us. The United Network for Organ Sharing (UNOS), the clearinghouse for organs, decided which of the 17,000 patients waiting for a liver would receive the next one. Meanwhile, every day eighteen people died waiting for organs.

Getting on the list was our first major hurdle. It wasn't like putting your name on the ski patrol glove order list. *I'll take two size mediums please.* Dr. Gores, John's hepatologist, first had to present his case to a panel. He'd be given a MELD score (model for end-stage liver disease), determining his place in the queue. I whispered the words *end-stage* aloud, testing it out, in case I had to get used to saying it. Those closest to death got the first livers, I knew that much already. But first John had to get through the pancreatitis.

On the computer, I wrote: *John is strong, as always.* I explained where to send flowers, telling everyone not to worry. *I will keep you posted as things develop.* What I really wanted to say was how scared I was. I wanted to write that my husband was acting like his usual stubborn self, that he thought it was cancer already, fitting it into a neat diagnosis for the doctors to solve. But he didn't get it. A cancer diagnosis was a death sentence. Instead of relying on a thin promise of recovery, I denied it.

This couldn't be cancer.

~~~

On the mountain I carried a Barbie lunchbox in my backpack. Plastic and pink, it smelled faintly of peanut butter and synthetic shavings. Barbie stood on the cover, her arms taking in the scene of swirls and hearts surrounding her like snowflakes. With a black Sharpie, I added skis and poles to her body and covered her blond locks with a ski hat. In block letters, I wrote Outdoor Barbie at the top of the box.

I never used a lunchbox in grade school, and perhaps now I was making up for lost time. Barbie watched over my sandwiches, and I introduced her to the world of skiing. We had an understanding. She still had her flowing hair and her hourglass shape, but I'd added stiff boots and a sensible pair of ski pants.

She showed me that even tough girls could be cute. It didn't have to be one or the other. As a kid, I was a tomboy and would never have used a pink lunchbox. More often thought of as a boy than a girl, I embraced my tough side. Even as an adult in my ski patrol uniform I had been mistaken for a man. As a strong six-foot tall woman covered in baggy layers, it was easy to see how this could happen. Barbie taught me to braid my hair and wear it on the outside of my jacket and to find better fitting pants that showed off my long legs.

Not until I met John did I realize I could be both sexy and outdoorsy. He held a new mirror in front of me, altering my self-perception, allowing me to contain my Barbie side. He gave me a diamond ring that sparkled in the sunlight, and I fused together disparate parts of myself, soldering the tough woman I'd had to become in my job to the softer, less certain, one. Sitting with John in the hospital I could do it again. I had never thought of myself as the type to take charge, to beat cancer and a scary diagnosis with attitude and vigor alone. But maybe I was. I could almost stand above myself and watch as I made phone calls to his mother and urged the doctors to explain it to us one more time, trying to hold all that scorching love inside.

It would be easy to fall back into my old pattern—the monster-under-the-bed mentality of dealing with my own personal crises. Other people's I could handle; my own emergencies were another thing entirely. If I didn't look at the bad things, choosing a lifestyle that kept me in the moment, I could avert my gaze from bad news. If I couldn't see it, it couldn't see me.

But here I was facing down a steep, curving chute that could end in a rocky cliff or an avalanche, burying me in a morass of sorrow. And I wasn't flinching. I was taking the dissimilar sides of my personality and putting them to work. The boldness I'd cultivated on the mountain could be brought to the hospital.

I could sit at the computer now and research the disease, teetering back and forth on the lip of a cornice. If I dropped over the edge and felt the wind on my face, I knew I would land one way or the other. I could hold John's palm between mine as the doctor said the word *cancer*, the walls of the chute might shudder and settle against the added stress. If the slope gave way, if the diagnosis ruptured the smooth skein of our constructed lives, tumbling me inside until it battered me against whatever lay below, I could fight to stay on the surface, using my strength and skills to climb out. Patients survived cancer. If he had cancer, we could fight it. We didn't have to just give up. And if it, like an avalanche, slowed to entomb me, I could teach myself to breathe slowly, squeezing the terrible future into manageable intervals until there was no sound or air to scream into.

~~~

I couldn't remember the last time Mom came to my aid, but now I needed her. We'd been in Rochester almost a week, and this was too big. Even as a child I sought independence, wanting to prove my capability, searching for risks, and proving myself against them. My adventures became a reservoir, something I could tap into during a drought. Always helping others as the EMT, the teacher, the Outward Bound instructor, I found purpose in making a space for others to grow. Mom always wondered who watched over me. I scoffed, reminding her that I was an adult. I didn't need tending. Of course, I never truly wanted to admit that I needed help. That would mean directing my gaze at my own weaknesses.

Now in Rochester, I had to admit it. I couldn't do this alone. But I was afraid that around Mom, my mask of strength would fall. She'd find a chink in my armor. She'd reach into that small entry with her slender fingers and extract handfuls of my sorrow, holding it for herself, as if by harboring my pain, she could keep it from me.

"I just can't take any more bad news." I spoke quietly with my hand cupped around my cell, wondering if I might be going haywire. It felt like a confession.

"Honey, I'm coming out there. I already made a plane reservation." My mother's voice was like a beacon through the phone. "Can you make it two more days?"

The pancreatitis had gotten worse, and John was still in the hospital. "It'll be good to have you here."

I walked back to John's room, hoping for a better scene than earlier that morning. A nurse had been drawing blood after John's CT scan and x-ray. A tube poked out his nose, and he looked terrible. "Honey," I'd said, touching his gown, "I'm here."

"Thank God." He opened his eyes. "It was the worst night of my life." The skin on his face looked thin, papery. He told me how the naso-gastric tube was shoved down his nose. The vomiting had been the worst part. I silently vowed to sleep in the room with him from then on.

Every fifteen minutes he pressed a button that automatically administered pain medication. The docs had started him on Demerol, but quickly graduated to Dilaudid, a fast-acting morphine derivative that slurred his speech and made him sleepy. All that, and it still didn't ease the pain. Hospital medication was strong stuff, and yet it wasn't working for him.

Health care workers use the ten-scale for patients to describe their pain. I'd asked my patients on the ski slopes many times — *Describe your pain on a scale of one to ten, ten being the worst pain you've ever felt.*

For John, his pain hovered around ten, and for him that was saying something. Waiting fifteen minutes for the next dose of Dilaudid seemed like hours. Pushing the "pain button," as we called it, before it was time caused the machine to shriek three quick warnings. John's life was reduced to fifteen minute intervals, and he got through it one push at a time.

His sisters, Amy and Kathryn were coming that afternoon. John could use the support and I couldn't do this alone — not anymore. I could admit that now. For a while I thought if I was a good enough wife, I could do this on my own. Needing to show strength above all else was ridiculous. No one expected me to handle this crisis alone. I needed to conserve my energy.

"Have you been awake long?" I asked when I walked in.

"Off and on."

"How do you feel?"

"Like an elephant is standing on my stomach." He held his palm against his right side.

"Have you pressed your pain button?"

He pressed it again, and it shrieked. He had to wait.

4

Double Blacks and Toilet Paper

I decided that our expeditions in the mountains were like dress rehearsals for the real thing. We had sought out these ordeals and called them "adventures," even if we didn't know at the time how they would toughen us up for this later trial. Now, as we faced the fearful labyrinth of hospital stays and diagnoses, while John fought against his pain on the ninth floor of St. Mary's Hospital, I could turn my denial into a force of optimism. I'd survived other adversities—I'd skied high mountains and saved lives, so I could get us through this.

There was something else, too, about our past. Perhaps we had thought that if we kept moving, kept adventuring, maybe those bad things would never find us. If we filled our lives with these chosen risks, then there'd be no room for the unwanted ones, as if each life had a danger quota. For years I convinced myself that by taking calculated risks I was actually forestalling calamity. But that's not how it worked. Even when we chased adventure, disease followed us. Now we were on the edge of the biggest double black diamond run of our lives. Still, sitting at his bedside, my heart fluttered remembering the adrenaline rush of voluntary risk, and I wondered what it could teach me.

I searched our adventures for sandbags to add to the jetty. Forming a sort of wall around the ninth floor of St. Mary's Hospital, I sifted through our past. While John eked out his existence in fifteen-minute gasps, I looked further back. Seven months after we met, at the tail end of our first winter together, John and I flew to Chamonix, France for the famous ski mountaineering traverse known as the Haute Route, connecting it with Zermatt, Switzerland. John had concocted the idea after a brief conversation with someone in the Snorting Elk — Crystal's après ski bar. Two months later we were in the Alps, hiking and skiing along the route we'd traced on the map.

On our second day of the climb the group reached a narrow pass, called the Col du Chardonnay. Beyond the col, a steep face descended quickly to a glacier below, which we would have skied had it been better conditions. The bergshrund, the top of the glacier where it separated from the mountain, gaped open at the bottom of the cliff. Our guide rigged up a multi-client belay in which two of us were lowered at once, separated by a tail of rope that would supposedly keep our crampons out of each other's eyes. I should have told the guide I didn't like the configuration; the belay points were too close together. I, for one, didn't want someone else's crampons swinging just two inches from my jugular. However, I could see this was the Achilles' heel of the day—a choke point that everyone had to get through, so I let it slide. If the guide knew what he was doing, we'd be fine.

Another group, probably trying to save time, didn't use a rope. They free-climbed down with ice axes and crampons digging into the ice. Instead of waiting for them to get out of the way, our guide belayed John directly through them. The rope caught on the backpack of one of these down-climbers, pushing the guy sideways and threatening to pull him off the ice. John watched it from below, knowing that if that climber lost his grip he would slide down onto John, his ice axes and crampons wheeling in circles. John kept his cool. He gained some slack in the rope, flicked it upward, and freed it. That was John—taking his first pilot lesson at age twelve—the man was calm in a crisis.

The climber had sworn at John in an Aussie accent. "The fuck're you doing? Why don't you watch out?" John calmed him down by explaining the situation.

John was confident and determined. It reminded me of the first moment he learned I had diabetes. Without any hesitation, he asked if he could inject my insulin. He'd never tried it before, but he knew he'd be good at it. I'd trusted him too. Undaunted, he steadied the needle above my thigh, willing to stab me on our very first date. On the second day of the Haute Route ski tour he had proved it once again. He had nerves of steel.

I reminded myself of that as I sat on the ninth floor of the hospital, watching the blue lights of his IV machine fade and return like a shimmering planet. John could handle this.

The austere beauty of the Alps—stone, ice and snow merged together—became a sort of crucible for our new relationship. We lived on raclette cheese, French baguettes and chocolate bars. We snapped photos of ourselves (to be added later to the collection on the fridge). He watched me for low blood sugars while I double-checked his climbing harness, and we learned to rely on each other. The trip became something against which we could rest, like a point of reference.

John skied at the front of the group, just behind the guide. The corn snow hissed beneath our skis as we turned. Consolidated into tiny grains, the snow offered a measured resistance to our skis, allowing us to sail across the slopes. At lunch breaks, during the climbs John declared, "this isn't so bad." While he'd hiked and skied before, he'd never done anything like this, yet he was a natural. Approaching fifty years old and still strong, John drew in the other members of the group. He recapped the day's events in the huts at night, and now his stories included them. That was the thing about John. You felt lucky to be around him.

The bathrooms along the route had been tricky, but the facilities at the last hut had a double black diamond difficulty rating. On our last night in the mountains, the wind blew ferociously at the Vignette Hut, which was perched atop a rocky outcropping just below the Pigne d'Arolla, a nearly 4,000 meter chunk of rock and ice. The thick cables holding down the roof should have been my first clue. When we arrived in the late afternoon wind, we had to claw our way horizontally along the catwalk that led to the front door and hung several thousand feet above the glacier. I noticed the outhouse then. It was perched above the glacier, and the hole dropped into the windy back eddy screaming up the cliff face. Bits of wadded toilet paper flew around beneath it, getting hung up on the guy wires. The unlatched door yawned open and slammed shut. Toilet paper sailed up through the pit and back out the door. John laughed when he saw that. *Isn't that hilarious?*

While trying to sleep in the top room that night, with the cables screeching in the wind, I didn't want to get out of my sleeping bag to make the long trek outside to the outhouse. Truth be told, I had a wind phobia. Strong gusts unhinged my universe. My fear could strike anywhere, but the wind singing through the cables felt sinister that night. Maybe if I had been a windsurfer or a sailor, I would have learned to like the wind – to harness its power instead of fear it. But as a skier, wind only ruined the snow. And in my mind, the wind stripped away my veneer of courage and bravery, revealing a shivering puppy. That night, I imagined that each new gust would snap the thick cables and peel the roof off.

Eventually I slipped into my down jacket and headlamp and padded to the door, where I put on my cold ski boots. The wind had increased. I inched along the catwalk to the outhouse, scraping the rock wall as I avoided the thousand-foot drop a few feet to my right. If this place were in the States, the railing would be reinforced with rebar, concrete and two-inch cable. Big signs would enumerate the dangers and liabilities: Stay Back from Edge, Do Not Throw Material Off Bridge, Watch Out for Flying Objects. Instead, there was a single, frayed cable between the icy ledge hacked out of the rock wall and the glacier below.

Alone on the catwalk, I didn't have to pretend to be brave, and that made it worse. I could descend into my fear and let it catch hold. Who was I kidding, acting so strong and brave all the time? I thought about crawling, but I would have to look down. So I shuffled and whimpered. The wind pulled at my jacket, snapping it against the gusts, forcing me to freeze in my tracks. I clenched the rocky wall caked in ice and felt around for handholds. It was only a few more steps, but my feet wouldn't budge. I wondered how they'd find me in the morning. If, when I finally collapsed, would I roll onto the glacier below, or land on the catwalk in an ignominious end? It gave a new meaning to the term *frozen by fear*. This was crazy. I waddled forward a few steps, then a few more. The door gaped opened and snapped shut on its own—the sound only now audible above the screech of the wind.

When I held the door open, bits of toilet paper flew into the beam of my headlamp, probably the same shreds I noticed earlier. They had floated all this time like flotsam just below the toilet seat. I had gone to the bathroom in some challenging places, but this was ridiculous. Reluctantly I closed the door. My headlamp darted around inside and illuminated the toilet paper falling about me like snowflakes. The wind subsided once the door was closed, and I avoided looking into the hole, down at the dizzying expanse of the glacier below.

Avoidance was my tried and true technique for overcoming panic. As I quickly did my business, I knew I'd learned two very valuable lessons. First, pack an FUD—a feminine urination device—essentially a plastic funnel that would allow me to pee into a bottle in the safety of the hut. Secondly, I learned not to panic in the midst of fear. When crisis strikes, keep moving forward. In the mountains or in the hospital, I couldn't panic and freeze. Nor could I stand aside and let someone else do the work for me.

~~~

The doctors had decided to try chemo and radiation, even if they didn't find cancer. No matter what the pathology report said, they would treat him like a cancer patient. The doctors explained to me that bile duct cancer was hard to detect. If their tests missed it and he got a transplant and started on immuno-suppression, the cancer would grow like hoar frost on a clear cold night, poking up like little shards of tinkling glass into the hood of the night sky.

While I wanted to freeze on the ledge of this new information, I knew I had to keep moving forward. Only at Mayo Clinic could a cancer patient receive a liver transplant. The work here was cutting edge, and I had to trust the doctors. They had scheduled another ERCP to place more tubes down his throat and all the way to his bile ducts. John's liver counts were up and they thought the stents (the ones that caused the pancreatitis in the first place) were blocked. Not only could that further irritate the pancreas, but it also delayed the real treatment. Plus, John still couldn't eat.

Instead of panicking, I would have to move forward. That was the way. Channel strength (be plucky!). It was pure acting. Just like in the outhouse, if I didn't look down at the dizzying expanse, maybe it could never reach up through the toilet paper-swept wind, up the hole of the outhouse, and grab me. I just hoped that like some heat-seeking missile, it couldn't find me anyway, regardless of the tricks my mind employed.

5

Doomed Glaciers

Six months before John noticed the first hint of his illness, we climbed Mt. Kilimanjaro, the tallest peak on the African continent and one of the largest volcanoes in the world. The surrounding plains shimmered dramatically from atop its 19,330-foot summit. On a brilliant morning in September 2006, John and I stood together on the crater rim at Stella Point and watched the sun rise over the continent. The view was magnificent. We had first talked about skiing the doomed glaciers, seeing the trip first and foremost as a reconnaissance mission. But the trip would have to be guided, a regulation of the Tanzanian government, and no guide company in their right mind would let us ski.

Turning back towards the mountain itself however, the scene was more disturbing. The glaciers that once draped the mountain now barely clung to its side. The ice cap within the crater had shrunk dramatically, no longer feeding the glaciers. Those rivers of ice would continue to slide towards the warmer temperatures below and eventually melt.

John and I climbed past walls of vertical ice on one side and the crater on the other, our route tracing the disconnected expanse between the ice cap and the doomed glaciers. I had climbed among plenty of shrinking glaciers in the Cascades, but never as dramatic as this. With some scientists predicting the glaciers would melt within the next decade, we were drawn to the mountain. We wanted to see the last of the frozen rivers before they were gone. Upon our arrival, I had given up the idea of skiing the glaciers, but John still only half-joked about doing it anyway, "before it was too late." His plan made me laugh nervously because deep down I knew that he was serious. He really did want to ski it.

From our early camps, he mapped a ski descent of the glaciers that would end in either a long climb back up or a squirrel suit scream into a BASE jump (essentially an extreme type of parachuting and something that Mom *definitely* would not have approved of). Squirrel suiting had recently become the new "extreme" sport, where a wing-like suit of Lycra extended a BASE jumper's glide, allowing one to sail away from the rocky cliff before pulling one's chute. It was essentially flying through the air like Superman, and it was just as dangerous. The glacier terminus ended just as abruptly as the top, in an icy cliff. We were familiar with glaciers since the view from the top of Crystal looked squarely into the eye of Mount Rainier and the gaping crevasses across the valley. Yet these glaciers on Kilimanjaro were starving orphans—no longer fed by snow at the top and crumbling at the bottom, like a few swipes of white frosting on a chocolate cake.

Climbing Kilimanjaro was a cultural experience. The locals, known as Chaggas, portaged our loads up the mountain. Due to a government mandate to capitalize on tourism, no one could climb without them. Many of the porters made the six-day trek in bare feet. Guided groups provided boots for their porters, but they were often sold for cash before the climb started. Our group, *International Mountain Guides*, required the porters wore the provided boots for the duration of the trip. The Chaggas carried our packs on their heads, bearing tremendous weight over slippery and steep terrain. Once, while I clung to the side of a nearly vertical wall, carefully navigating the low fifth-class terrain, a group of hardy porters carrying nearly one hundred pounds on their heads passed me at a run. Amazingly, one carried ten plastic chairs (the stackable, plastic kind you find at Kmart) on his head, and never once lost his balance or even looked down. His toes clung to the craggy rock while his head supported his ungainly load.

One afternoon we rested at the top of a hill, warming our backs on the sunny rocks. Normally the porters reached camp hours before we did and would have our tents already set up. Instead, they came up behind us having stopped to carry water up the hill for the evening meal. I snapped a shot of three of them just as they crested the long, grinding hill. Small white clouds like puffs of smoke hung above the African plains behind them. Two of the porters carried our bright yellow duffel bags on their head, while another one balanced a large red cooler.

Years later, that framed picture sat on our mantle above our fireplace. These men carried our gear for mere pennies (well not exactly, but definitely cheap). And when I compared our current situation—John's illness—to the hardship that sculpted their lives, I knew that a soul could endure much worse, if necessary.

It was the same in Rochester. As John's illness grew progressively worse, I searched for sources of strength. The doctors stood in his room each morning, their clasped arms revealing nothing. I could hear their whispers in the hallway before they entered our room, and I strained to capture the scent of their words like an avalanche rescue dog searching debris. I knew they were talking about the dire situation and the still-pending results of the brushings that would tell us if he had cancer. Regardless of the results, John would still undergo chemotherapy and radiation. I knew this. But still I prayed it was just a precaution.

Not wanting to give into fear or even a good cry, I demonstrated toughness as if to armor us against the onslaught of this disease. Crying always came easy for me; I even teared up at Coke commercials. It was a release, my way of letting feelings pass through me without taking hold. When other people got angry or irritated, I just cried. After a good, private cry I felt washed clean on the inside, able to go forward. Publically, I never let on. It didn't match my tough girl persona.

Afraid now to give into my tears—concerned that once they started I wouldn't be able to turn them off—I walked some kind of dusty line, scared to cry and yet worried that if I didn't my feelings would separate from my core like orphaned glaciers inching toward a steep terminus. I felt a rough sadness, like glacial deposits gathered in the corners of my heart, a sort of gritty scree that scratched at the soft folds of skin. Against such abrasiveness, my tears could get caught, snagged inside me instead of gusting through like a fierce snowstorm, blowing into the crevasses, rendering them smooth and less treacherous. A natural flow had been interrupted, like the way that snow, with enough time and pressure, can turn to glacial ice and course slowly back towards the rivers that fed the land. Without a bond to the ice cap covering the top of the mountain, like a sort of hub from which the glaciers originated, the rivers of ice on Kilimanjaro, like my emotional release, were marooned and vanishing.

That was the thing really. I worried that this ordeal with John was changing me—that I would lose the link to my central core. A vast sandy wasteland cleaved the once instinctive stream from my heart to the glacial tongues of my outward actions. A gulf had risen between the healing storms of emotion, my crying jags that once washed me clean and covered over the land with a fresh blanket of spotless snow, and my sense of duty to be strong and fearless in the face of steep cliffs and dizzying falls. I wasn't sure how long I could last like this, but I knew it wasn't sustainable.

~~~

The sky blushed above the summit cone of Mt. Baker, the northernmost volcano in Washington. Of the five major volcanoes in our state, we'd already skied two of them that season on our quest to climb and ski them all. A few weeks earlier we had ticked off Mt. Adams by carving turns through perfect inch-deep corn.

Baker proved a different story. The previous week had been hot and sunny, melting much of the snow in the first few miles of the approach. After the ski areas closed for the season, those wanting a little more skiing turned to the volcanoes, where the snow might last well into summer. Even with a heavy snowpack a few weeks of blazing heat could quickly shrink it down. We had hoped to skin up from the parking lot, making fast time to the campsite a few thousand feet below the summit. But the snow, which we had heard started just up from the parking lot, didn't materialize, and John hiked in his ski boots.

Ever the lightweight backpacker, John surrendered his hiking boots, figuring he would only need them for the first hour. Instead, he clomped up the trail in ski boots, and I followed in my hikers. The steep dirt trail dug into his heels, and he gritted his teeth. By the time we reached camp several excruciating hours later, his feet were killing him.

The tough part was behind us now, I told him. From here on it was just a conveyor belt of snow-covered glaciers all the way to the top. We probably didn't even need to wear our rope. Since we would untie our ropes on the way down, I figured we could dispense with them on the way up. I'd carry it along just in case we came to a particularly crevassed section. But I could see the route from where we stood sipping whiskey tea, and it looked perfectly safe.

Above us, the summit cone turned to strawberry ice cream and then orange sorbet as the sun set over Puget Sound to the west. We positioned the opening of the tent to take in the view of the mountain and the Easton Glacier rising towards the alpenglow.

Located in one of the snowiest places on Earth, even Mt. Baker's glaciers were receding. Baker is the second most heavily glaciered peak in the state, behind Mt. Rainier, with ten main glaciers. The Coleman glacier covers 1,280 acres while the Easton is nearly half that. Below our tent, where the glacier ended, supplanted with snow-covered rocks and then just rocks, lingered evidence of the once larger glacier. In the bowl below our camp, fine silt slid down steep runnels like snow into the river we had crossed on our hike up. Drawing in on themselves, it seemed all glaciers everywhere could lose contact with their source. It was only a matter of time.

We woke the next morning at 2 a.m. and started up, our headlamps illuminating two puddles of light as we negotiated the rocky rib towards the summit. When we reached the glacier, we tied into the rope, since I'd given it a second thought and figured it was better to be safe than sorry. We readjusted the climbing height on our bindings, which allowed us to ascend the steeper sections without tiring.

A few hours later, John stopped and looked back at me. "You want to unrope?" The sun had risen enough to see the route, revealing small undulations that could be crevasses.

"Not yet." The going was easy, so I figured we might as well be safe. Not that I could do much if John fell into a crevasse. The best I could do would be to self-arrest and dig my ice axe into the snow to stop my slide and hope that I could build an anchor. Then I'd find something from my harness to bury into the snow to transfer the weight, and that would allow me to get up and tend to John. All this would be quite a trick since I wasn't carrying an ice screw or pickets, and the snow surface was rock hard.

But the rope made me feel a little safer when we crossed, one at a time, over the large depressions, each one bridging over an icy fissure of infinite depth. As the sun climbed, wetness oozed between the snow grains, large and shaped like rock salt, and threatened to melt the snow bridges. I hoped the bridges would hold.

Above our heads, the summit deceived us by casting the illusion of proximity. I stared at my feet and breathed while

counting to a hundred. Looking up, I tinkered with our direction
and pointed the line formed by the rope between us towards
some distant feature. As before, I looked down at my feet for
another count. It was easier when John led, because I could just
follow his tracks.

We reached the Roman Wall and smelled the strong sulfur
wafting up from Sherman Crater, reminding us that just thirty
years earlier the volcano had awakened and sent plumes of
steam into the atmosphere. While it wasn't as spectacular as its
southern cousin, Mt. St. Helens, Baker still smoked and churned,
reminding the tired climber that even a skein of snow as tall as
three stories can't ever really cover over that kind of inner
turmoil.

In the last few hundred feet of the climb, the slope inclined
and the boot pack turned sloppy and hard to follow. Stepping
outside the track meant sinking to our knees in slush. The sun
now baked us and the snow bridges below turned into warm
goo.

At the summit, we discussed our descent. The bridges were
collapsing, but I figured that if we could pass over them in the
uptrack, where the snow had been work-hardened, they'd be
more likely to hold. John wanted to rope up, but I scoffed. We'd
come here to ski, not down climb. The advantage was we'd be
off the glacier in a matter of minutes, not hours. Sure, the other
teams on foot should stay roped up. But the length of our skis
and the condition of the bridges would keep us safe. At least
that's what I wanted to believe.

Of course what I didn't know was the rescue going on at
that very moment on Mt. Rainier, the tallest volcano in the state.
I might have been more cautious had I known that a skier on the
Emmons Glacier fell into a crevasse because the snow bridge
gave way, leaving him with massive injuries. I might have
listened to John had I known it would take rescuers hours to
yank him out of the crevasse, and that a guide had to be lowered

into the narrow fissure in order to stabilize the patient's injuries before he could be hauled up with ropes and pulleys and the muscle of several guides.

I might have made the prudent choice if I knew what lay ahead for the fallen skier—hours of uncertainty in the emergency room, a fractured pelvis and broken ribs, and the long struggle back through rehab to be able to walk again.

But I didn't know these things.

Instead, I looked down at the long descent, nearly 5,000 feet of vertical fall line, and pointed my skis toward the orange tent, a tiny dot on the ridge far below. My skis slid over the creamy snow I shifted from one edge to the other. I glided across the crevasses, careful not to press too hard, not asking too much of the snowpack and the bridges on such a pristine day. Making myself as light as possible, I skimmed over the snow, which melted into twin tracks behind me. Perhaps those tracks would hold it together long enough for John to cross too.

I stopped below the most heavily crevassed area and watched John. If he fell through, it would take precious minutes to hike back to where I'd last seen him, and I hopped a little in anticipation. But John was smart and glided even more gingerly across the crevasses. His skis hardly touched the surface as he levitated across the depression. He turned slightly to avoid the next depression, and then he was through. I sighed, the noise of my exhalation matching the hiss of his skis as he skimmed past me. I turned to follow him down the mountain, ignorant still of the warming snow bridges and the other, more dangerous, storm gathering itself like seeds brought to one's breast, ready to cast us into the wind.

Looking back on it as I sat in the hospital, I wondered who spotted the skier on Rainier. Had he been with a partner, or had the guides and their clients come across him on their way up to the summit?

Had he lain there, alone on the ledge that broke his fall, thirty feet down into the maw of the glacier and figured this was the end? That he might as well just fall asleep? Or had he yelled up to the sliver of blue sky, lamenting the lost heat of the sun and cried until he was found?

That is the moment I fear most, after the initial impact but before the outcome is determined. We knew now that John was sick and the doctors were wringing their hands each time they walked out of his room. I could almost see them shake their heads in regret. But I wanted to know the results of the tests. Was it cancer or not? Would they come for the injured skier, alone in the crevasse, or would he be a witness to his own descent towards death?

6

A Mountain I Couldn't Blow Up

John wasn't in his hospital room. Fresh sheets curved around the edges of his mattress, and I sat down on the tightly tucked cotton blanket and looked around. A blue parallelogram of light spread out towards the quiet hallway. Our mothers had gone back to the hotel.

The bathroom was empty. I wondered where he could have gone. The night shift had arrived, and nothing happened after-hours on this floor. Not unless it was an emergency.

I peeked down the hall and saw an orderly carrying a messy tray, her figure moving in and out of the blue light. I would just have to wait. I decided to crochet, having already made five hats since that first appointment. Was it only two weeks ago we first noticed John's yellowing skin? I pulled a hank of red yarn from the pile and began a foundation chain.

Twelve days ago we cut our vacation short in Sullivan Bay, where we had flown with John's kids for 4th of July, and boarded the first floatplane home to see about this liver problem. These past days had been like quicksand, sucking and heavy. Yet even when the doctors tried to throw me a rope, raving about John's strength and his chances for survival, I didn't let it drag me out.

Instead, I pulled apart the separate strands of sorrow, worrying them into a frayed edge. It seemed easier this way—to curl up inside myself and refuse to be soothed, letting my body be numb. It was another way of keeping the lurking beast at bay. The rough yarn slid through the fingers of my left hand. The hook in my right hand plunged into the stitches and pulled through a loop.

I examined the quality of my tears, imagining that if I recognized each way to cry then I would be prepared. My six-year-old stepdaughter, Evelyn, teased me for crying at children's movies. "What are you, a two-year-old?"

What if I cried when the doctors gave the diagnosis?

What if I couldn't ask the right questions, squeaking like a cornered mouse?

What if I fell apart?

I inspected the top of the hat. The stitches curved into a circle and spread out nicely across the crown. I changed colors, choosing a vibrant orange, and began a row. This would be a rainbow colored ski hat with a bright pom-pom on the top. Mom used to wear one like this, except hers was orange and yellow. I remembered it vividly, how I'd seek out her bouncing head just ahead of me on the ski slope. The hat matched her belted orange ski coat, which I could easily spot in the lift line.

I decided that if I couldn't control my tears, at least I could see them coming by putting my ear to the tracks and sensing the vibration of the crying fits as they approached. Aha, I could say. Here comes the five o'clock cry. Right on time. Then I wouldn't be blindsided while riding the elevator with a stranger, or walking across the street.

I glanced down at the stitches in my hand. The orange yarn looked nice next to the red and I continued around, satisfied with the result. I tightened the tension by wrapping the strand around my left pinky.

I decided to catalog my tears. Like a scientist, I could categorize them, and, perhaps, gain some objective hold over them. Some tears were sneaky, falling unannounced. My cheeks would be suddenly warm and streaked, like a toddler not yet potty trained. The droplets would stick to my eyelashes through repeated blinking, forcing me to wipe them away and reveal that I'd been crying

Other tears brimmed over my eyes and I'd try to suck them back into my pupils before they landed like huge, warm raindrops on my cheek. These tears tried to defy gravity, hanging there, teetering on the edge of my eyelids. If no one was watching, like in a movie theater, I could lean forward and drop them unnoticed in my lap.

Then there were the Greek Tragedy tears, the ones I feared the most. They rumbled towards me like a locomotive. These were the mourning wife's tears, the mother-being-held-back-as-she-reached-for-her-dying-child tears, the rocking-back-and-forth-on-your-knees tears. They would interrupt me on the way upstairs, forcing me to grab the banister before I doubled over, my body heaving from the sheer terror. They fired out like lava, all sound and fury. These were the ones that all other tears were afraid to become, like the out of control drunkard at a Christmas party, slurring his yuletides. They were one step away from the wino clutching his brown paper bag for dear life. Looking at them from a distance, with the methodic clicks of the crochet hook sharpening the air, these tears squinted their eyes and stared at me, while I held my breath.

I put down my crochet project and walked out into the hallway where a woman in dark blue scrubs sat behind one of the computers scraping her spoon on the bottom of a small yogurt carton. I asked her if she had seen my husband. "I'll page his nurse," she said and dropped the container in a small garbage can beside her.

I returned to the room and sat back down. His IV pole was gone, so perhaps he felt like taking a stroll. I doubted it, though. When I left earlier, he couldn't even walk to the bathroom.

Earlier that afternoon I had cried from the bottom of my soul, screaming and pulling my hair like Helen of Troy. It was too hard to hold it back any longer. At some point, it just had to go. I allowed the *what ifs* I'd tried to suppress.

What if this was cancer?

What if it had spread?

What if he died?

I worried that I couldn't stop. It felt like an addiction that I briefly welcomed. Let it roll through me. *Go ahead, do your worst.* A few minutes would pass and I would step aside, watching myself from a distance. My body heaved and sobbed, rocked and swayed. There was fear too, and I grasped at it like the rope I had held on the mountain. I felt along its frayed edges. *This is what sadness feels like. Here, right here, this is anguish.* I noticed my sobs, counted my inhalations, licked my lips. *This is what fear tastes like.*

Now, sitting in John's room, I ran the yarn along my fingers letting it slip through. Perhaps I was holding onto the fear now, keeping a vigil over it, like a tenuous flame. Earlier, when the tears had finally played through I sat up and looked around. A light on the telephone blinked. My computer sat open on the bureau. The fluorescent light in the bathroom flickered like a feather. You can do this, I told myself, those words having become like a mantra.

You can do this.

John's nurse walked into the room and interrupted my reverie. "We had to take John for a CT scan."

"Oh?"

"He was in quite a bit of pain," she waved her hand through the air.

"It seems so unusual at this hour."

The nurse wrote her name on the wipe board and erased the previous one. Her back was to me, and I noticed her take a slow breath.

I waited for her to explain. Getting nothing, I said, "Is it unusual?"

She turned around and shrugged. "Not really. He should be back soon."

Once she left, I lay down in John's bed and took off my shoes and stretched out on top of the sheets. I saw my reflection in the gray television screen. In the curved monitor I looked like a tiny raft afloat in a white ocean. A bouquet of flowers sat on the windowsill, its greenery already turning brown. Standing in the corner like a dour orderly, the white cabinet held extra pillows and a meager promise of comfort. My chair, with its hard cushion, sat beside the cabinet. I pressed my head down on the pillow and looked at the chair—the hard-cushioned one I'd sat in—making sure he could see me without craning his neck.

This was how his days passed. Pressing my hand to my right side, I imagined his pain; I could almost feel it, a hot brick just below the ribs. I put my nose to the sheets, which smelled faintly of bleach and photographic developing fluid—sharp smells that lacked the softness of human touch. The sheets themselves were rough, and I ran my hand along the side, smoothing them down as if just the friction of my palm could keep them from scratching John's skin later.

~~~

When we had sick and injured patients, we brought them by toboggan to the ski patrol aid room at the bottom of the ski area. The beds were wrapped in plastic and lined up against a wall. The wool blankets we draped over patients helped with warmth and privacy. Most of the time I took blood pressures and splinted broken limbs, but sometimes the injuries were more serious and required intervention in order to save their lives.

Once, a patient—I'll call him Jerry—hit a tree while skiing fast. I had reached into the trunk of the tree and felt for a pulse. Jerry had been awake at the time. His voice was strangely calm as he answered my questions in slurred monosyllables. The snow blossomed in a red bouquet as his head injuries bled into the tree well. The extrication went quickly. The patroller's limbs and fingers worked in unison towards the goal of strapping buckles, grasping ski clothes, and breaking tree branches for better access. We brought him down in a toboggan where the paramedic took over.

While waiting for a helicopter ambulance to land in the parking lot, the medic started an IV in order to give him meds. I handed the medic the IV start kit and brought over the metal tray with a bag of fluid and medication.

Jerry didn't look good. I paused while trying to access his radial pulse. I couldn't find it. "Go for the carotid," the medic reminded me. He still had a pulse but it was thready and weak. We were losing him. The medic slipped the needle into Jerry's arm and hooked up the bag and pushed the meds. The room was a scene of measured chaos. Patrollers worked quickly over the patient; drawers were opened and slammed shut, the proper equipment was found and extracted. Minutes ticked by on the clock on the wall. The helicopter should have been here by now.

Jerry was probably bleeding out internally, and he needed to get to a hospital fast. Lucky for him, the weather was good for flying. Otherwise, he would die in the two-hour ambulance ride. I still couldn't get a radial pulse, but I tried for a blood pressure. His arms had grown stiff, and my stethoscope slipped a little when I listened. I could only hear the systolic pressure, which measured at 90. It had clearly fallen.

The air ambulance nurses arrived and whisked him away in the back of a truck to the waiting helicopter. I peeled my rubber gloves off as they wheeled him out, wishing there had been more we could have done. I wondered if the nurses would hear a blood pressure at all.

We later found out Jerry had ruptured his spleen and had been in emergency surgery for hours. Miraculously, he lived. Perhaps we had stabilized him just enough to keep him alive. Or maybe our quick action and the good weather had allowed the chopper to land, giving him precious time to let the surgeons save him.

Sitting in John's room, I thought about Jerry's loved ones. He must have had a wife, or family, or someone who arrived at Harborview Medical Center in time for the surgeons to tell them the news. As an EMT, I'd often thought of the patients—and even their families—but I never thought I'd be one of them. I never imagined myself in the hospital waiting room, clutching tissues and trade magazines, anxiously anticipating the news.

~~~

Dr. Williams said, "We have the test results back."

I inhaled quickly, my lungs nailed to my ribs.

The doctor placed his hand gently on John's forearm. "Is everyone from your family here?" My throat burned like I had swallowed a tiny medusa jellyfish.

The other doctors stood around John's hospital bed. One held her hands behind her back in fists as if playing a game with a child. *Guess which hand I'm holding the diagnosis in.*

Tiny needles stuck into my armpits, and I started to sweat. If he was asking this question, he must have bad news. He wanted John to gather his family like armor to shield him. Mom stood beside me, her shoulder brushing my arm. John's family members stood beside his bed. We all leaned closer.

"Yes." John smiled as if to ease the doctor's discomfort. That was just like him. I glanced up at the nurse, watching her swallow hard as she concentrated on the tiles at her feet.

John's hands were still on top of the sheets.

"It's cancer," the doctor said.

I breathed it in, letting the slithery word wrap itself around my sternum. I rolled it around in my mouth. It started by sticking to the back of my throat and had a hiss in the middle. *Cancer.* I looked at the doctors, each one with his or her arms crossed behind their backs, except for Dr. Williams who gestured and talked about the next steps. I knew I had to listen, and I tried to concentrate on his words. He spoke of radiation and chemotherapy. He mentioned staging surgery, *to make sure it hadn't spread.* His words fell like coins dropped into an unplugged jukebox, producing no clinking sound of metal as it found the right slot. No music.

John bit the skin on the inside of his cheeks. I closed my eyes for a second and wondered what it would feel like to have a doctor touch my fragile hand and say, "It's cancer." I imagined my whole body reacting to the news before rejecting it like poison.

I watched his face, studying it for a grimace or a look of fear. I read an article once about the language of facial expressions, how emotions are revealed in split-second shifts — an eyebrow slightly raised, a nostril flared, a bottom lip pressed against teeth. John's features were steady; he kept his eyes on the doctor's face and nodded at the appropriate times while avoiding my gaze.

My own body shook, and I felt Mom's finger touch mine. I let her hold my hand, but I didn't have the heart to press back. Instead, my fingers folded on themselves like crooked match sticks. I forced myself to look at the doctors standing there with their thin lips and downcast eyes. It would be easy to hate them. I wanted them to leave, even though I knew they would be my lifeline in the weeks to come.

How could John be taking this so well? It's cancer. It really is cancer.

~~~

This was a mountain I couldn't blow up — an emergency I couldn't solve. I wanted to take the radiation gun myself and start aiming at the offending bastards — to kill the cancer cells and get on with the transplant. Instead, this was a slow crusade that required vigilance. I wanted to know right away about staging surgery. Had the cancer spread or not? If it had, all bets were off. But the pancreatitis came first. If we didn't solve that problem, the rest would be moot.

Now that the doctor's orders had been dispensed, the family had broken for dinner, the hospital was now quiet, and I was alone with my thoughts. I was not ready to write to our entire group of friends yet. I could try one out on my friend

Beth, ferreting out some of the fear and pain, spreading it out like a smorgasbord, picking which version of the story I wanted to portray and turning it into the truth. In the few hours since the doctors stood like stone figurines in John's room, a chasm had grown between what actually happened and how I imagined it.

While John slept off the words of the diagnosis like a hangover, I'd told Mom that it didn't really matter. The diagnosis was just a formality. They planned on doing chemo and radiation anyway. Spraying down the messy conversation with a verbal germ killer, I now had a more sanitized version of the ordeal. I let it buoy me.

I looked around the small waiting room. The television was off and the room was dark except for the small puddle of light at the desk. I squinted at the pale blue screen. How could I write *my husband has cancer*? I wanted to temper it with some shred of good news, to reveal my plucky fortitude.

A few lines in I wrote about the diagnosis, my throat closing over as I typed. I told Beth the doctors thought it was localized. *But I'm not so sure,* I wrote. I straightened my back and cracked the knuckles on my right hand, making a fist and covering it with my left palm. I deleted the last sentence. I was terrified.

I imagined myself standing at the bottom of a stepladder that disappeared into the sky like an illustration from Jack and the Beanstalk. I just had to keep taking small steps. This was the story I told myself. I couldn't look around and get dizzy, thinking too much about what it meant. The key was to just keep moving. Even when I thought I couldn't. I'd been doing the same thing for decades—on steep ledges overlooking dizzying glaciers, on the flanks of mountains, within my own low blood sugar-addled brain.

This was no different.

7

Bad Weather in the Mountains

Our second ski season as a married couple was a disaster for the ski industry in the Pacific Northwest. Crystal Mountain opened and closed three separate times. The season started innocently enough — opening late November with several feet of snow falling in a single storm. In December it all changed. It rained until the snowpack was fully saturated, then the temperature dropped, freezing the ponding water into ice-glazed slicks. On the steeper slopes, the snowcats tilled in the deeper, drier snow each night, but each day it grew harder and more translucent. The holidays brought once-a-year skiers that slipped on the ice and left unsatisfied, and by January we realized we would have to close down — something John had never encountered in his thirty-five years in the business.

One night, with the sky as nondescript as vanilla pudding and not holding the promise of even a few snowflakes, I asked John how he managed the stress.

"I can handle the big disasters," he said. "No snow, rain, road closures," he gestured towards the window. "It's one thing after another around here. I just deal with it. But my cell phone losing reception, that's another story entirely."

It was true. John's DNA wrapped perfectly around huge crises. In his job, he prepared for these inevitable downturns by planning for them. He figured that every third year would bring the wrong weather — too much rain or not enough snow, or even too much snow at the wrong time. He anticipated the weather like a farmer, and he knew it wouldn't always go his way. He expected this. In the Washington Cascades, where the weather was extreme in both quantity and temperature, he was usually right. And when he wasn't, he was pleasantly surprised.

"But why does it have to be that way?" I asked.

"It's better than freaking out."

"But you do freak out. Just not at the big stuff."

"It's like this. I have a bullshit quota. And it gets pretty full just from what goes on at work. I can take the weather. I can handle the snow. The fact that we might have to close *down*, for God's sake. But it all adds up. It fills my allowance. So when I come home and the little, piddly things aren't working right. I don't know. I'm just over it."

"Right." Of course, I got it. A quick little rage was like a brush fire for him. It burned through swiftly and left nothing behind. It reset his quota. Emptied his trashcan. Drained the bilge. The problem was, I couldn't stand by and not get burned. The heat of his anger blew past me, and I still smoldered long after he'd moved on.

So I trimmed back the fuel supply like Smokey the Bear: *Only YOU Can Prevent Forest Fires*. It played into my need for acknowledgement and my role as a fixer. Daily he gave me new problems to fix. I bought him a Blackberry. We got laptops and got rid of the desktop. I picked out a new dishwasher (one that didn't hiss during the rinse cycle) and streamlined his inbox. I took on projects around the house. I thought that if I could solve these small problems, then maybe our lives would get back to how they were that glorious first year, when the snow fell in just the right quantities, never too much to cause problems, and always enough to fill in the previous day's bumps and holes. The more I tried to solve these problems however, the worse they got. While I found a space for my do-it-yourself skill set, John was losing places to harbor his anxiety about the Big Stuff. Other things started bothering him. His list of annoyances grew.

When the Little Stuff stopped working, John blamed the world. Every detail about his life was egregiously wrong. Life as he knew it was untenable, clinging just barely to the tenuous civilization to which we claimed to belong. It was as if the entire world had turned its back on him, and he bristled at the slight. It offended him. It bruised his sense of autonomy. And it was unfair. The world was ganging up on him.

The ski area closed in mid-January that season. The icy base had melted away. In February, we bravely opened for a week after a little stormlet dropped just enough snow to promise hope. But it was a hollow pledge. The storms refused to blow through. A blocking ridge sat stubbornly off the coast of Washington deflecting the oncoming storms like a tai chi master, pleasing only the non-skiing residents of Seattle who probably thought this was a wonderful winter we were having. The small February disturbance proved futile and again we closed. Almost a month later, we opened again. Winter had finally arrived, but it was too late. The skiers had switched to golf.

John and I weathered our storm too. I couldn't fix his cell phone (the thing he hated the most about it was that it worked— it rang all the time). Besides, he needed those little brush fires to control the fuel supply. I just had to learn how to stand back and let them burn through. And I learned something about myself. I simmered. My reactions were delayed; even joy took a minute to register as if I didn't quite trust it. In a moment of crisis, though, it could be a handy trait. I'd used it in first aid calls, when emergency required I postpone my emotions. And I had learned to use it with my husband.

The thing was now, when we were faced with the biggest crisis of our lives, I wondered how simmering would help me cope. Maybe it was best to just let it all out—give in to the self-pity and the debilitating tears. But it felt like there was more there and I didn't really want to look too closely for fear of finding a monster too big to quell with just one crying jag—that pacing beast lurking in the dark, ready to pounce as soon as I drew near. My dark forest was overgrown, and a fire licked at its edges. Too late, I was wishing I'd cleared out the brush and been more like John with tempering my fear and anger.

Trying to convince myself that staying calm in the face of danger and even irritation, I looked at John, our ski season melting away into dirt and rocks. "I guess that's your strategy. I have my own."

He raised his eyebrows a little. "You don't react."

"That's right. I don't."

"How nice that must be for you."

I sucked in a breath. "Yes and no." I had to admit, it didn't always help to postpone my emotions, setting them aside to grow unsupervised, like a tuft of mold growing in a leftover Tupperware in the back of the refrigerator. "But sometimes it helps."

"Like when?"

I had to think about it for a moment. "Like when I almost got struck by lightning."

~~~

Over a decade earlier I was in the southern interior mountains of British Columbia skinning out of a basin with my three friends: Susanne, Martha and Anne. We had just skied a glorious thousand-foot descent on snow the consistency of iced gelato. The snow had melted like butter on hot pasta beneath our turns. My life was about to turn dramatically, and I could feel the change simmering beneath the earth's surface like a fault line.

"Hold on," I said. "There's a bee in my hood."

"A bee?" Martha asked.

I unstrapped my backpack and placed it in the snow between my skis. "Whoa. Check it out."

The others looked back over their shoulders, each in a line. "What?"

"Look." I pointed toward the tip of my shovel, which poked out of the top of the pack. "It's glowing."

It was true; the buzzing I had heard wasn't a bee, but an electrical charge emitting from my shovel tip. I reflexively touched the back of my hat feeling for burn holes.

The four of us were staying in a small cabin at the base of Kokanee Glacier. The cabin sat in a high basin within the Selkirk Range. Ringing it were tall peaks whose north-facing slopes held snow well into spring. We had arrived the day before by helicopter and would stay a week ski-touring all the accessible peaks and would be helicoptered out in six days. In other words, it was paradise.

"St. Elmo's fire?" Anne asked.

We all glanced at the sky. Less than an hour earlier, we had skied down in sunshine, hardly noticing the clouds building up nearby. Nor had we seen the thunderheads that now crept across the valley like thieves.

"Okay everybody, lightning drill." We had talked about this earlier. With lightning common in the mountains, even this time of year, you had to be ready. "Leave everything metal right here. Skis, poles, backpacks. Just drop them and spread out." My instructions were unnecessary. The three others had already scattered. Anne ran uphill with her shovel, dug a little trench to squat in and tossed her offending metal objects back into the pile.

People think lightning strikes from above. They imagine an electric bolt slithering in the sky like a wooden toy snake just looking for a place to strike. However, a lightning bolt usually starts in the ground. Clouds, just like the ground, contain both negative and positive ions. They live in harmony—attracted to each other in that peculiar and predictable way taught in high school physics.

Everything changes, however, when clouds build up excess electrostatic charge. Think of it as the seven-year itch. The negative ions migrate to the bottom of the clouds and form a sort of inverted layer of frosting. For whatever reason, they no longer find their positive ion-mates appealing and now want to search elsewhere. Namely, the ground.

That's precisely what happened while we climbed back up that slope. Positive bachelor ions lined themselves up along the surface of the snow, their arms waving wildly in the air. *Pick me. Pick me.* Those bachelors glommed onto the metal edges of my skis, crawled up my legs into the aluminum stays of my backpack, found my shovel and thrust their arms into the air. Luckily for me, the negative bachelorettes in the sky were being fickle.

I crouched in the snow, my hands held out in front of me, my knees touching slightly. Since victims are usually struck from the ground (unless of course you get struck by a direct bolt of bachelorettes taking things into their own hands), your best bet is to give it an escape route that doesn't include your heart or your head. If it enters in through one foot, and your knees are touching each other, it just might cross that bridge and exit out the other foot. I'm not saying that a lightning strike entering and exiting your feet and traveling through your shins wouldn't be terribly painful. It just wouldn't be catastrophic. I looked down at the metal buckles on my ski boots. *Damn.* I considered removing them, and standing barefoot on the snow, but decided against it. The pile of metal nearby had started to buzz and tick, like a car engine in the hot sun. At this point I figured I should just keep my head down and hope that pile of ski equipment gave the ions something to do.

"Maybe we should've just skied back down," Susanne called from her spot in the snow.

I looked up at the top of the peak. We had only a hundred yards left until we reached the top, where we would cross a small col and descend down the glacier to the cabin. The already black and white landscape had turned gray and grayer; granite spires seemed to poke tentatively above the ceiling of clouds, as if they, too, feared lightning. It had been a long, though not

terribly strenuous, hike out of the basin. Being so close to the
top, none of us wanted to retreat and wait it out only to retrace
our steps after the thunderhead passed. Besides, it happened too
fast. My shovel was already glowing. Better to jettison the most
conductive materials (which also happened to be our fastest
option for descent) and crouch like bandits.

The buzzing grew louder, and I repositioned my arms. You
don't want to touch your arms to your knees (the most obvious
and comfortable crouching position) because they'd beeline that
current straight to your heart. I put my hands on my head and
pointed my elbows down in a sort of modified crash position.
You also don't want to be any closer to the sky. Those
bachelorettes up there could change their minds any minute
now and call up their new beloveds right through my precious
heart.

I thought about my mother and was glad she couldn't see
me now. While my father's DNA passed down to me, Mom's
bursts of emotion mirrored John's, and she would get it all out
with a quick brushfire. What would she say if she saw me now? I
had promised to be careful before I left, nearly belittling her
request. "Aren't I always careful?"

"Well, no. Actually you do so many risky things, I can't
keep track."

"I'm just going skiing, Mom. If you didn't want me to ski
you never should have taught me how."

"You're not just skiing. You're also arriving in a helicopter,
travelling in grizzly bear country, and you'll be at the mercy of
the snow, avalanches, and weather." She ticked off the dangers
on her fingers. "Just promise me you'll be careful."

"Promise."

"No heroics."

"None."

"You won't go out alone? Not even to the outhouse at
night? You did say there was an outhouse there, right?"

"Mom, don't worry. It's not like I'm going to strap a t-bone to my face and stumble around in the dark."

The fact was, though, Mom was right. This place did have its dangers. A guest book in the cabin revealed the latest tragedy in vivid detail. Less than two months earlier, a skier had died in an avalanche at the base of the Kokanee Glacier. The first entry from that week's visitors listed the beauty of the snowfall. The drifts piling up around the cabin made them giddy. I imagined their eyeballs circling like cartoon characters. They had spent a day or two in the cabin, waiting for the slopes to stabilize. They knew the hazard was still high, so they stayed in the trees near the cabin when they ventured out. The next entry explained what happened. One member of the group died in an avalanche. It started above him, sweeping him through the trees, and he never had a chance. Risk takers often say that realizing the consequences of their potential mistakes make them feel closer to life. But I'm not so sure. I've seen people die doing what they love, and it's just as ugly as death can be. Death is death. There's nothing glorious about it.

The clouds above us darkened and it started to sleet—tiny frozen strips like splinters. I put my hood up and repositioned my feet, which had fallen asleep. I raised my hips slightly to sweet-talk a little blood through my limbs.

"Stay down," Anne called from nearby.

I crouched again. I knew why she was nervous. It was either now or never. The thundercloud hovered directly over us, obscuring our view. Those negative ions singed just above our heads, scanning the surface below for fresh meat. I could no longer see the col we needed to pass over, nor could I see Susanne or Martha. Anne's dark figure nearly blended in with the blackened sky, like someone had turned out the lights. I don't remember how long we sat like this. Long enough to think about my mom, plenty long to second guess our hasty decision to stash our skis, and certainly adequate time to wonder if I

should just quit my teaching job and turn my volunteer ski
patrolling weekend gig into a permanent post.

This last revelation came as a surprise. Susanne was my
teaching partner, and we worked together at Mercer Island High
School. It was a good job at one of the best high schools in the
state. But it wasn't like this. I might spend an entire year trying
to get through to a kid—to get him to appreciate Shakespeare or
Mark Twain, write for ten minutes each day in his journal, and
maybe even spin out a few well-written essays. I might have
gotten through to some of them (in the end they wrote beautiful
letters asking me to stay). But I wasn't saving anyone. I wasn't
making a real difference. Besides, there was something attractive
about the urgency here—I had to admit that I liked emergency
situations that forced me to focus and exploit my skills for
postponing emotion, while still capturing me in the moment.

The dark sky buzzed. Loose strands of hair, which had
fallen out of my braids, lifted against my cheek. I didn't brush
them away, afraid that any movement would attract the negative
ions. I hummed a little, matching the tone of the air around me,
as if in sync with it. It might have lasted fifteen minutes or it
could have been an hour. I will never know. Embedded deep in
the power of the moment, time passed differently, whirring and
ticking at erratic intervals. This is why I came here—to notice the
mutability of time, to notice how, when an intense moment sunk
its teeth into me, I wouldn't wriggle out. I stayed right there and
waited. My legs fell asleep.

When it was all over and we finally stretched our limbs into
a lightening, less target-rich sky, I had to admit that I had loved
the severity of it. I liked knowing that it was now or never, do or
die, black or white.

Perhaps, looking back on it years later, it was a naïve
outlook. It's easy to thumb your nose at death when you don't
have to look at its ugly face head on. Risk-taking for its own sake
wasn't it. Instead, certainty drew me to the mountains, to all

these adventures, to John. In the midst of a physical and mental challenge, my brain stopped agitating. Crouching in the snow, waiting for the singe of electricity, tamped my erratic thoughts — and I liked it. Like Ritalin for teenagers, outdoor pursuits had a calming effect on me. Ambiguity was for philosophers. Give me certainty, even if the outcome was dire, any day.

As I watched John lose weight, fighting the grueling pain of pancreatitis, I tried to remember these lessons. This would be worth it one day. We'd get through this. Someday, hopefully, John would be healthy again. Maybe, by concentrating only on each moment, we'd finally reach the col. Then we'd retrace our steps, hiking up the places where we'd descended and sliding down the stretches where we strained upward.

8

Thin As Glass

"Popsicles," John said.

"Okay. What else?"

"Ice cream." He moved his tongue around in his mouth. "Something with flavor." He'd tasted only ice chips these past nine days, which he chewed and spit back into a cup.

"Is this making it worse?" I asked. The doctors had just been in, and mentioned that soon he would be able to eat. If that went well, they would release him. Things were looking up.

"No. It's better. I like thinking about it." He closed his eyes, and then opened them. "Grape popsicle."

"Just one?"

"Yup," he said. "When they finally let me eat, I want a grape popsicle."

I glanced at my watch; I had thirty minutes before I should get back to the hospital. John's family members were leaving soon, and the doctors agreed to release John the next day, even though he said he wasn't ready. I swung my arms more briskly as my shoes hit the paved trail, hoping a good, hard walk would clear my head.

The day was already warm. The leaves on the trees swayed on their stems, alternately showing their shiny tops and pale undersides—a ridiculously bucolic scene. I tried to stay in the moment—to notice the freshly mowed pattern in the grass, the kids shrieking on the playground, the mosquitoes hovering. Instead, my mind raced ahead of me.

A man walked slowly in front of me. His pants hung low on his waist revealing a donut shaped abdomen covered by a snug sweatshirt. He shuffled his feet on the path and the hem of his jeans drug beneath his heels. Obviously, his mother hadn't taught him how to dress, and yet there was something about him. Maybe it was his slow gait or the way he looked deliberately at me as I passed. Why was I in such a hurry anyway? Still, I gave him plenty of room as I passed, my arms swinging precisely.

"Are you looking for a little good news?" His voice was startlingly kind. A small pamphlet waved in his hand.

"No," I shook my head quickly and continued, leaving him strolling behind me. *What was my problem?* I stretched my arms in front of me like a Gestapo soldier and marched on. This guy, let's call him Luke because I never did get his name, spread a goofy contentment with just his smile. Maybe everything would be okay if I could just mellow out. Maybe I didn't have to be in control every second.

I fought the urge to look back at him over my shoulder. I imagined him smiling beatifically at my stiff walk. He obviously knew something I didn't. I couldn't understand it, but as I walked away from him, I clearly wanted to hear his good news. Was his wife having a baby? Did a psychic tell him that Obama would be elected President? Could he confirm my secret hope, that John's cancer diagnosis was just a farce, and that the doctors were joking? *Just kidding, a little medical humor thing we like to do up here on the ninth floor. Isn't it a hoot?*

The bike path rolled along Cascade Creek, which ran through the center of Rochester. It would eventually meet up with the South Fork of the Zumbro River, where I planned to turn around. Almost there now, I considered the slow moving man behind me.

Usually when confronted with a stranger's request, I reacted with a quick shake of my head and moved on. Alone out here on a Monday afternoon, a timid voice in my head suggested I cross over the next bridge and take 2nd street back to the hospital. But something about him seemed so disarming. I wondered if God had sent me an angel and I'd just snubbed him. I had been pleading with God lately, begging him for some good news. Didn't that guy just ask me if I needed some good news?

I came to a small rise in the path and turned around. At first I didn't see my angel and I was a little disappointed. I imagined God pulling his hair out up in heaven. What did a Guy have to do to help around here? I shouldn't have snubbed him so quickly; now I'd lost my chance. Maybe he walked this path looking for distraught individuals whose loved ones had just been diagnosed with cancer and other horrible diseases.

I noticed Luke up ahead as if he had just appeared out of nowhere. *That's weird.* As I sped up my pace I started to think he really was an angel sent to me straight from God. I was almost convinced of it.

"Maybe I do need some good news," I said when I approached.

"Are you okay?" Luke's eyes were full of honest concern as if looking into the window of a car wreck.

"My husband was just diagnosed with cancer," I said. Suddenly I wanted this stranger's pity. I needed to hear some good news. Any good news.

"God loves you," he said and handed me the pamphlet. "Your pain and suffering will soon end."

My heart warmed a little. "Thank you." I looked into his kind eyes, ignoring his unshaven face and matted hair. I didn't look down at the pamphlet yet. I nurtured my secret hope that this was a big joke. Come on now, John isn't sick. *Can't you see we were just kidding?*

He smiled and walked on, his job complete.

I held the pamphlet in my hand and continued walking. It was like a lottery ticket, and I wanted to savor the fantasy of winning. What would I do with a million dollars? With a healthy husband? Several yards away I finally looked down at it. "Are you in pain?" The cover asked next to a picture of a bearded Jesus smiling into a glowing light. *Well, yeah.*

Inside, the first line explained the good news: the world would end in just twelve days. It wasn't what I had in mind. Where was the good news in that? Apparently, it was time for all God's creatures to return to Paradise. Soon we would all be in heaven, flapping our little angel wings through acres of butterflies and rainbows. No need to worry, the pamphlet prophesied.

No wonder my "angel" was moving so slowly. He wanted to take in the contents of this summer day, since it was going to be one of his last. Either this guy really was an angel sent from God to remind me to lighten up, or he was simply a misguided fruitcake. I folded the small pamphlet and slipped it into my back pocket. Maybe someone else would need it.

Back at the hospital, John still looked peaked and green. The doctors had given him the okay to eat popsicles, but he had overdone it. His mouth puckered against the sweetness, having had nothing to eat for so long. The doctors had been there while I was at the park. A surprise afternoon visit.

"They are going to release him tomorrow," John's sister, Amy, said when I walked in.

"Good." I looked at John. "Is that good?"

"I'm not so sure," John said.

I looked at him and sighed. "No more midnight visits by night janitors, honey. In the hotel, we can turn all the lights off. You can get a good night's sleep." I was speaking more for myself than for John. I hadn't slept more than a few hours at a time with the uncomfortable cot and all the interruptions.

He glanced at the IV pole where the medicine pumped into his arm. "No more Dilaudid."

"They'll give you something for the pain."

"Maybe Percocet," Amy said. "That stuff's good."

"If Percocet was so good, they would have been giving it to me already."

I stroked John's head and smiled. This was the John I knew and loved. "We'll see what the doctors say."

One day later, I lay there on the gurney in the dark and waited for the doctor. I wondered what John was doing, if he was waiting for me back on the ninth floor at St. Mary's. My left breast felt cold from the ultrasound liquid and still tender from the mammogram. I had noticed a lump a few days earlier and told Mom over breakfast this morning.

"You're here at the Mayo Clinic," she had reminded me. "Just go get it checked out."

This morning the doctors had said John could leave this afternoon, and of course the only mammogram time slot was 2 p.m. I worried that he would be released before I got back, but his nurse had assured me I had time.

This wasn't my first lump, and no matter how many mammograms I had, it didn't get any easier. Before, they had always been benign pockets of fluid, little reminders to stay vigilant. The blue light from the ultrasound machine illuminated the room in a strange, nightclub sort of way. I studied the ceiling and noticed how one of the puckered tiles had been moved slightly to reveal a sliver of darker black in the crack.

Sometimes it felt like one careless move could strip away the veneer and reveal an inky blackness behind a false ceiling. A small part of me wanted to stand up on that gurney and press my fingers into the darkness and feel the change in temperature, to wiggle my hand in there up to my wrist and see what grabbed it. Always the one to check under my bed, or peer in the dark closet, or kayak into the unknown, I'd spent my life looking for what lurked in the dark. I didn't want to; everyone knew that only led to trouble. But I had to press back against my fears. I explored boundaries—running my eyes, my fingers, my skis to the edge of the known world and pushing beyond it. Not knowing what prowling darkness lay in front of John and me made the task more difficult. And yet, that desire had lifted me before. And I could begin to feel its buoyancy now.

"Hi there," the doctor entered the room and turned on the light. He held a sheath of papers in his hand that I figured were the results of the mammogram. At home I would have wondered about the mammogram for several days, worried over it, fingering the lump until it ached. Here, the results and the doctor were before me in a matter of minutes. "You have a benign cyst in your left breast."

I left out a puff of air.

"Some women are more prone to them," he put his hand on my arm gently, his fingers barely resting on my elbow. "But they aren't a threat. Just keep up with regular checks. When you turn forty, you should start getting regular mammograms. But until then, only if you find something." He removed his arm and wrote in my chart.

Back in the changing room, I heard another woman in the room beside me. If I closed my eyes, I could be at a department store, checking out new clothes in a three-way mirror. She sighed out a long groan that wavered a little at the end. Her chair creaked as she sat in it. I unlocked the door and kept my hand on the knob for a moment, listening to her sob. The skulking darkness almost stopped my heart.

~~~

I curled my ski boot around the trunk of the tree and steadied myself. With one hand grasping the broken branch I'd often used as a handle, I used the other to extract the party pack from my parka. I had stashed it in there when I climbed the tree. It was early season and the snowpack hadn't filled in the space around the tree yet, and now I stood on the platform of the bomb tram ten feet off the ground.

We used bomb trams to deliver explosives in avalanche paths that were too dangerous or precarious for a patroller to approach. This path, Reynolds' Chute, was named for the young skier killed in this curving, avalanche-prone couloir. From my position, perched in a tree ten feet above the curling cornice at the top of the chute, I could not see the bottom.

He wouldn't have been able to see the bottom, even thirty years ago when the trees blocking the view would have been much smaller. Perhaps he didn't even know that it ended in a cliff, or that an avalanche would sweep him right off and cartwheel him mercilessly. He could not have known how the ski patrol would be called in their ski lodges that night, pulling them back into service to search the wreckage. He couldn't have seen from the top cornice how others would have come to the scene that night; friends and ski instructors forming probe lines, meticulously searching the debris. Nor could he have anticipated how it would be both a relief and a tragedy when they found him. They'd found the body. They could put down their search engines now, they could stop imagining what it would be like to be down there, still alive.

So the patrol had closed Reynolds' Chute and built bomb trams to mitigate the danger. Now I could hang an explosive on a metal hanger attached to a cable that spanned the top of the avalanche path. The same protocol ruled: attach the iggie to the fuse, light the iggie, check to make sure it was lit, and deploy the bomb. Trams were a little more difficult to use, but the results were far more effective.

From up in the tree, balancing on the narrow platform, I could feel the wind whip through the branches, making the tree sway back and forth. Trees fell on the mountain all the time, and it wouldn't be outrageous to worry about this one dropping too. My arms ached as I did my work. I first hooked the party pack onto the hanger, then positioned it around a branch so it would swing free. Then I pulled the igniter from my goggle strap, where I had stashed it earlier so I wouldn't have to unzip any pockets while suspended in the tree. I clipped the end of the fuse with my crimper tool to expose a dry powder train. Next I placed the igniter on the fuse and pulled the string. The fuse sputtered and smoked, and I unhooked the bomb and let it run.

But it didn't run. It stopped on the line. I shook the retrieval rope, creating little spasms of energy in hopes of freeing the snag. I could see the problem. The bomb had caught on a branch, which kept it from running freely down the cable into place above the slope. More importantly, it needed to run away from the platform I was standing on. I could either free the bomb and risk being unsuccessful, or climb down the tree and run away. I couldn't do both.

I hesitated. I'd hate to destroy this bomb tram. Blowing it up meant that another tree would have to be found, and I would have to climb it, attach steps without harming the tree, and build a platform in a crook between branches. Not all trams had platforms, but the ones this high up did.

On the other hand, I didn't want to get blown up trying to release the lit explosive.

I had to decide quickly. My boot slipped a little and I wrapped it around the trunk more tightly. It was now or never.

I reached out towards the offending branch and yanked it. Smoke from the fuse wafted up my nose. I could see where the red and white striped fuse had burned down a few inches already. The bomb didn't budge. I figured I needed to get down now. I'd tried. The thing was stuck.

Looking back one last time before I climbed down, I noticed something. A branch poked through the handle of the milk jug that held the explosive material. Breaking the branch off at the tree freed the jug, and it ran quickly down the slope. I let out a breath and looked at my route partner, who had backed up a few steps.

The bomb exploded and the chute broke apart in an impressive avalanche, grabbing the snow well down the ridge below my perch. It slid around the corner, towards the cliff and disappeared. When my bomb got snagged, I probably should have jumped out of the tree and hid. I wasn't following procedure, and I wondered how all of this was actually making the ski slopes safer. Bomb trams didn't make explosives control safe, nor did bombs make a slope avalanche free. But they mitigated the hazard. That was what I was trying to do. I hadn't wanted to run away and just give up, letting the tree explode because I was too afraid. And I believed in the efficacy of the bombs. Yet sometimes these measures felt as thin as glass.

~~~

"He looks so thin," Carol, John's mom, said as John walked back to the hotel room. She had been here for nearly a week.

"They didn't let him eat anything for nine days." I looked at his plate; he hadn't touched the mashed potatoes and turkey.

"I can't stand seeing my son like this."

"I know." I felt defeated. "We just have to get through it one day at a time. He'll gain the weight back, eventually." I wanted to tell her that, like when my bomb got snagged in the tree, I wasn't going to jump and let it blow up all our hard work.

"Do you think he will?'

"Of course." I pieced together the doctor's comments and my own research. "I have to believe that."

"Thank you for being here for him, dear."

I reached my hand across the table and held hers, which was folded into a loose fist beside her plate. "He's going to be fine." I looked at her face and down at the table in front of her, my eyes losing focus momentarily. "We're going to get through this." Even though I could almost smell the explosive fuse burning as the smoke snaked between us, making sinister curlicues, I had to believe what I told her.

"It's not supposed to be like this you know," she said looking in the direction that John just walked. He had excused himself to go back up to the hotel room and lie down. "Parents aren't supposed to watch their children," she paused for a moment, "get like this." She pursed her lips together, wrinkling the skin around her mouth into itself.

I wished that my own mom were still here. I had a sense of fragility within me, as if my skin was made of thin glass the width of a light bulb. Too much intensity could make me shatter. But it was that intense focus that I needed right now. Next week we had tests, but at least John was out of the hospital. We were moving forward. We would be fine, I had told my mom, convincing her it was okay to leave. Carol was departing the next morning and we had celebrated John's release from the hospital. We'd be on our own.

I had started looking for an apartment, in case it became necessary. I hoped it wouldn't. I was holding out for now, preferring to believe that we would be going home soon. My biggest fears were John's frailty, and I worried that the doctors had released him from the hospital too soon.

"Are you guys going to be okay?" Carol asked.

I smiled at her. "We're going to be fine." I wanted her to trust me. I didn't want her to think I'd jump and run, even if I was going against procedure. The trick now was to remain calm, untangle the difficult diagnosis from the tree and let it explode at a safe distance. What I'd learned in the tree above Reynolds Chute held true in this vinyl diner near the Mayo Clinic. "I'm glad you were here. So's John."

She nodded and looked at the napkin refolded beside her plate. She tugged at a loose thread. "Just keep an eye on him okay?"

"Of course," I said. "Of course."

9

The First Rule in an Emergency

"I'll sweep Powder Bowl." The chair creaked to a stop, and I clicked into my bindings outside the lift shack. Aluminum clouds stretched across the sky beyond Mt. Rainier to the West, cutting off the sun's trajectory. At the end of each day, ski patrollers "swept" the mountain, making sure not to leave any injured skiers behind. It had snowed a few inches in the past few hours, and the wind out of the south was reloading the avalanche start zones in Powder Bowl. I would need to be careful, maybe even ski-cut across the top of the slope before dropping in.

I followed a fresh track around the backside of the peak, where I peered over the edge and saw a dark figure pressed up against a small tree. "Hello?"

Emergency caregivers maintain specific protocols, often using pneumonics to help remember important procedures. The ABC's for an EMT refer to Airway, Breathing, and Circulation. First check for an airway, then breathing, and then move on to the pulse. These practices assist us during emergencies in remembering our roles, and most of all, prevent us from panicking. Giving us a set pattern to follow when crisis strikes, these methods help us stay focused and not forget any vital steps. Even before we apply our first pneumonic, we must enact the most important rule of all: first take care of yourself.

I thought I heard a small voice, but the wind was too strong, blowing light snow around my body and depositing it on the lee slope in front of me. I called Dispatch on my radio and alerted the patrol of a possible injury. It was only 3:45, but on one of the shortest days of the year, the light was already setting behind the thick clouds. The High Campbell Chair closed at 3:30, bringing the last chair to the top ten minutes later. At the time I didn't think too much about the impending darkness. I carried my headlamp in the top of my pack, other patrollers were on the way, and a patient obviously needed our help. However, over the next hour, time would slip through my fingers.

When I reached the tree and first saw the patient I used my radio again. "Crystal Base, I have an injured skier near the top of Powder Bowl, and I'm going to need a toboggan and additional patrollers." The others had already left for their sweeps and would have to hike back up to the top.

A middle-aged woman with a possible femur fracture lay pressed up against a tiny tree at the top of a rocky spine. When I examined her, she told me she'd been caught in an avalanche and the tree had stopped her. The windblown snow refilling the starting zone had already buried the crown—the topmost flank of the avalanche. Powder Bowl is a steep open bowl punctuated by flutes and couloirs. Cornices hanging over the top lip illustrate the common wind direction.

However, that day the steep top section of the bowl was filling in fast just below the cornices. In a maritime snowpack, most of the avalanche action happens at the top. Without the extreme temperatures of the Rockies, in the Northwest the deeper layers tend to sinter and bond over time, making the snowpack more stable. Alternatively, the Northwest gets more snow and it can be much heavier, causing stress on the snowpack, particularly in the top layers. When the stress on a snowpack exceeds its strength, something has to give.

In spite of her injuries, the patient was lucky. It could have been much worse. Had she been swept through the trees and over the rocky ridge to the slope below, she most likely would have been buried, and all traces of her would have vanished in the fading light.

In a precarious location above a steep chute, I stood up into the inky sky and waited for reinforcements. Mason, another patroller, appeared above me, where he would build the anchor we'd need to belay the toboggan several hundred feet down the long slope.

By the time the toboggan arrived, the patient shook from hypothermia and shock. I covered her with my parka and monitored her vitals. There wasn't much else I could do until the equipment arrived so we could stabilize the fracture in her leg with a traction splint. With one eye on the darkening gray sky, we decided to use a basic splint instead and get her to the first aid station as quickly as possible. Belaying a toboggan down a steep, avalanche prone area was bad enough. Doing it in the dark was downright dangerous. I checked my watch. Fifteen minutes had already gone by and we hadn't moved.

I called Dispatch with an update. "The toboggan has arrived. We're making this a rapid transport. It's getting dark. Do you have an ambulance on the way?"

"Yes and I'm also getting some snowcats heading your way. Hopefully they can shine their lights into Powder Bowl to give you some definition." I glanced over my shoulder down the bowl. The ridge just below me had faded into a graphite dullness, and I could no longer see the slope. Far beyond that, two sets of snowcat lights snaked their way up the cat track to the base of Powder Bowl.

Two other patrollers arrived; one manned the belay, while Mason and the other joined me with the patient. We loaded the shaking patient into the toboggan and strapped her in, hoping the splint would keep the jagged edges of her femur from severing her femoral artery. The biggest threat in a femur fracture was bleeding out internally, which could kill a patient in minutes. By now, the sky had turned a deep black, and the lights of the snowcats barely illuminated the contours of the chute below us.

Mason took the handles of the toboggan, while I carried the remainder of the gear—a heavy backpack full of oxygen, the traction splint we didn't use, and the patient's skis and poles.

Thinking I would traverse to the right, avoiding the toboggan as well as the steeper terrain, I ventured away from the small group while watching their headlamps darting across the snow. I could feel time sliding away from me, and I stopped to calm my breathing, reminding myself this was not my emergency. In a few more minutes the slope would be entirely black, and I still felt compelled to get down in the last remaining sliver of light.

Perhaps the twilight's shimmery metallic sheen lured me away from the group, blurring the shapes of the snow-filled bowl into a smooth patina. I should have turned around and stayed with the others. I could have taken a moment to load some of the extra gear into the toboggan to make my descent a little safer. I could have at least shared the burden with them. But I was in a hurry, letting time dictate the rules.

I made a few tentative turns, feeling my way down in the dark. Narrowly avoiding a rocky outcrop, I picked up a little too much speed and zoomed across the slope, hitting a pocket of fresh snow, which broke apart in an avalanche.

When caught in an avalanche, the first thing to do is jettison your heavy gear, including skis, poles, anything that weighs you down and prevents you from swimming to the surface, which will reduce your chances of survival. That dark evening in Powder Bowl, I carried not only my personal backpack but also the oxygen pack slung over one shoulder, the splint hung over the other and the patient's skis and poles under my arm.

The slide gathered momentum as the snow collapsed around me, tumbling me once, then twice as I gained speed. My first reaction was disbelief. *This thing was going to kill me.*

That wasn't supposed to happen. I'm the caregiver, not the victim. No one would even see me. They'd wait for a moment at the bottom of the bowl while untying the belay rope from the toboggan, and move on. The patient's life depended on it. They would assume I'd catch up, if they thought of me at all. Even if someone did wait for me, they'd never find me in this massive bowl in the dark.

Worse, with the exception of the patient's skis, I couldn't let go of my burden. The straps across my shoulders prevented me from releasing any of the weight, which would make swimming in the avalanche impossible. While churning down the slope, the snow maintained an almost swimmable liquidity that changed as the slide slowed down. Once over, an avalanche becomes like a tomb because the debris turns hard as rock. If a victim can keep her head on the surface while the snow still moved, she might survive.

As I somersaulted a third time, I reached out towards the base of the snow and dug in with the tip of my ski pole. When a skier first feels the shudder of snow beneath her skis, she can sometimes avoid burial with preparation. Ski patrollers train for this risk by knowing how to fight: First try to get off the moving slab before it breaks up. If that doesn't work try to self-arrest by using the sliding surface below the churning debris as a brake. The victim burrows a tool—a ski pole or an ice axe—into the surface to slow herself down. The worst of the sliding debris will quickly move past her. If that doesn't work, then she must swim like hell.

Luckily, I'd held onto one pole and now I used it to self-arrest, digging in with all my strength. It slowed me just enough to let the bulk of the avalanche slide past me, and I came to a rest against the hardened slope. The entire thing took less than a minute, but it felt like an hour.

I turned my head to see the light from the snowcat scan the slide path. Perhaps they had been keeping an eye on me. In the midst of helping the patient, I almost had my own emergency. I checked myself for injuries. Besides the sore muscles under my arms from self-arresting, I seemed to be okay. It would take me a while to gather my gear. I'd lost one ski and all of the patient's equipment.

To my left, I heard Mason calling to the others at the top that he was off belay. He had reached the gentler terrain at the bottom and would need another patroller to take the back handles. But before I traversed towards him, I checked myself. I needed to stay in the path of the avalanche that had already slid. I stood in the dark bowl and regained my breath. The first rule in handling emergencies was not to become one yourself.

In Powder Bowl, I took a deep breath and made a call on the radio, informing the others of the avalanche hazard. I told them I'd been caught in a "slough", minimizing the situation in order to maintain my calm. Instead, I concentrated on rejoining the rescue effort and focusing on the emergency.

As I stood up and gathered my gear, I watched splinters of light from the snowcats dance on the snow's surface. Night had come on completely now, carrying with it the dampened sounds of the windy ridge above and the snow falling in crisp stellars onto the slope at my feet. I slid towards the light of the snowcats, letting the glow from their spotlights guide me through the chunks of debris and refrozen snow that so easily could have been my demise.

What had become a hard-fought lesson on the mountain, I had to harvest the message again with John in the hospital. Don't become part of the emergency. First ensure my own health. I needed help with John.

We planned to go to Michigan to visit his sister for the weekend, and I looked forward to letting this burden down for a few days. His family would fill in for me, supporting him while I refilled my own dry well. I didn't want the weight of this disaster to pull me under the debris. I had to lighten my load. I had to let others take some of the heaviness.

10

Catastrophe

Dr. Malhi, a resident at Mayo, crossed her hands in her lap and looked at John. "We want to readmit you." Up on the top floor of the Clinic, the dark sky turned almost green in the window behind her. The view extended out across the streets of Rochester and to the darkening corn fields beyond. "You'll stay through the weekend until we get the infection under control."

I considered our plans to fly to Michigan. "Are you sure?" We were going to stay with John's sister, Kathryn; his family was going to help, and I needed a break. "We had planned to get out of Rochester for the weekend." I was whining. "Our flight leaves in a few hours."

The doctor's mouth formed a thin line as she turned to John. "Your temperature is quite high." She had just measured his temperature at 103.6 F. "You probably have an infection. I've arranged for a blood draw." She took a pad of paper from her breast pocket and wrote on it. A flash of lightning briefly lit the sky behind her, and I waited for the following boom of thunder. "I know it's late in the day, but they're waiting for you. We want to start the cultures soon—before the weekend—so we know how to fight this."

I glanced at my watch. It was 4:30 Friday afternoon. We were supposed to leave in less than two hours. We were supposed to have been finished with his appointments several hours ago. We should have been packed by now. All week his doctors had noted his high temperature. They'd blamed the pancreatitis and I'd believed them. Perhaps that's all this was. "Can't we just stay in the hotel tonight and if it gets any worse we can check him into the emergency room?" I crossed my legs and dropped my purse in my lap. I hadn't realized it was still around my shoulder.

Dr. Malhi looked at me for a moment as if considering the idea. Looking down at her paper, she tapped the end of her pencil on the pad, and then shook her head. "Your husband is a very strong man. I'm not sure how he made it this far."

I could feel John relax next to me. I wondered if he was deflating like a balloon or resting against the comfort of her sympathy. "It's okay," he said, turning to me. "I would rather be in the hospital where they can look after me."

My throat burned. Had I not taken good enough care of him? I wasn't sure I could spend another night on the cot beside his bed. I needed sleep. I was counting on the rest and help awaiting us in Michigan. I was back in Powder Bowl and the weight of John's illness was pulling me down into the debris, depriving me of my ability to fight. He had a high temperature, certainly, but he didn't seem sick. He was walking around, talking, and best of all the pain had leveled off.

I had to tell myself a different story. I knew that, and yet I couldn't. Returning to the hospital felt like a defeat. I didn't want to think there was something else—besides the pancreatitis—causing the fever.

"So it's all settled then," Dr. Malhi rose and smoothed her skirt. John stood up, too. I sat for a moment longer on the vinyl couch, unable to process. John held his hand out to me.

I'd rented an apartment that morning. We hadn't moved in yet, but the rental furniture had arrived. I'd planned on moving in on Monday, after we returned from Michigan.

"Kim? Let's go," John said. He stood next to the doctor, as if they were a team.

My hands shook as I gathered my purse to stand. I knew John would mirror my reaction, if not now, then later when he lay in the hospital bed. I had to go along, to fake it. I smiled towards Dr. Malhi, but I couldn't look her in the eye. As John and I walked down the long corridor toward the blood draw unit, the lights flickered and went out, the lightning storm having increased. In the dim glow of the emergency lighting, the nurses took John's blood. It felt almost intimate, like candlelight. The nurses spoke softly to John, and he said afterwards that it was the easiest stick he'd had yet.

To me, it felt like a betrayal.

~~~

"There's an infection," Dr. Williams said on Monday. John lay in a hospital bed again on the ninth floor. He hadn't seen any specialists over the weekend. I wondered if it had been worth it to stay in the hospital, where they had just monitored his temperature and given him medication through his IV.

"It's a form of staph, and we believe it's sensitive to antibiotics. Which is good."

I swallowed hard. Staph infection. *No wonder.* "How did he get it?"

The doctor shrugged, rubbing his starched collar against his neck. "It's always around. On our skin, on the surfaces we touch. He most likely got it during the first procedure. And the inflamed pancreatic fluid gave it a place to settle."

John bit the skin on the inside of his cheek and tried to smooth the sheets down on the bed. He glanced at his IV tubing. "So this is the antibiotic?"

"Yes," Dr. Williams nodded. "We've started you on one that we hope will attack the staph infection. But it's never..." he paused, "cut and dry."

I tensed. "When will he be able to continue with the transplant protocol?" I saw the deliveries all the time. A guy in a blue t-shirt with a little six-pack sized cooler got out of the elevator every other day. I knew he wasn't carrying beer in there. He had an organ. It was someone's lucky day. "We're anxious to get back to that." I did the math in my head. They hadn't yet told us how long he would have to wait for an organ. It all depended on the results of the work-up, which had just been postponed. This delayed the liver transplant—John's only hope for survival.

"It'll be a while," he said. "Probably six weeks of IV antibiotics and even then we will probably have to go in and drain the fluid."

John's eyes widened.

"But don't worry. You can do the infusions as an out-patient in the clinic, or even at home if you feel comfortable," he glanced at me with raised eyebrows. They would explain this to me later. Some of the doctors wanted to skip the six-week course of antibiotics and drain the fluid now. The draining procedure had its own dangers, however. The team ultimately decided to start with antibiotics and see what happened.

"So what will he be doing during that six weeks?" I asked. "Will he be able to continue with the tests?"

Dr. Williams looked at me and tried to smile, rubbing his finger across his forehead. "We just need you to get better from this, and then we can worry about the rest."

He put his hand on John's shoulder, which seemed to relieve John. I, on the other hand, wondered if he understood what the doctor was saying. *If you live through this.* If the infection was in his bloodstream, he could easily die, yet John seemed complacent. I wanted to blurt this out as the doctor stood up to leave. He and John exchanged pleasantries. I was too stunned to speak.

The IV stand swished melodically, pushing the medicine into my husband's veins. The sheets were crumpled on the bed, and John's face was rough with two days of growth that seemed to have suddenly turned gray. "At least we know what it is."

I crossed my legs and buried my hands under my thighs. The air conditioning blasting from the vents in the ceiling made the room feel like a snow cave. John's arms were covered in bandages from previous needle sticks and his bony shoulders poked through his thin hospital gown. He clutched his pain button. It was still set to fifteen-minute intervals. I inhaled deeply, taking additional sips of air until my sternum hurt, holding it in until I couldn't any longer. The air pressed against the inside of my ribs and I held it there for as long as I could as if caught in the heavy debris of an avalanche. Yesterday I had worried that he might be alive in a year's time. Today I wondered if he would live through the next week.

He pressed the button in his hand; it beeped softly indicating he'd gotten more Dilaudid. "That's it," I said, trying to be positive. "Just get through this, fifteen minutes at a time."

~~~

The air is dream-thick and I propel myself forward with great effort. I am on a steep sidewalk and I know the witch is nearby. She is dressed as a nurse to fit in, but I'm not fooled. I wheel John on a gurney against a pressing crowd. Hands grope at his sheets and travel along the folds like fingers on piano keys. I swat them away. *He's mine.* I press my body into the gurney to continue uphill, against the current of people.

John does not complain, and this worries me. I glance at this face. He's smiling innocently at a child who stares at him, her mouth open, her hand caught in her face as if stifling a yawn or suddenly surprised.

At the top of the hill, the crowd streams out of the hospital entrance. I push against them. As we enter, the crowd disappears and the metal doors hiss closed behind us. John is not on the gurney but swimming beside me, which makes me sad. I try to pull him back down but he floats above me. On his back is a green oxygen tank attached like a scuba diver's and it is attached to his arm like an IV. His hair floats above him.

It's fine in here, he says. *It's much better than I thought.*

I tell him to come back to me—that we have to check in.

They know I'm coming, he says. *I can just go straight up.* He's still smiling that ridiculous grin, and I feel very tired.

I can't go with you, I remind him.

He frowns and looks down at me. *I have to go without you then*. He floats away into dark blue water and I strain to see his figure—just a flash of silver, then he's gone.

I realize if I stay I will have to breathe water into my lungs, and I know it will hurt. I force myself to do it thinking that perhaps I can go with him, but my feet are hard on the linoleum floor. I open my mouth, but nothing happens. My lungs burn as I gasp. Choking, I realize that I have made a terrible mistake, and I begin to cry.

I woke up and reached over for John, but he wasn't next to me. I sat up gasping. It took me a few minutes to realize where I was. The hospital bed glowed its eerie light, and I looked over at John, his sleeping face awash in the blue glow. I watched him breathe, the steady rise of his chest for a few minutes before I rested my head again on the pillow. He wasn't leaving me, not yet. I wouldn't let him die on me like that. I just wouldn't.

~~~

My third year on the ski patrol saw five fatalities at the ski area, and I was on-scene for every one. The first was the boyfriend of a girl I knew from school. When I arrived at the accident, the victim lay in a toboggan, while another patroller continued CPR. As EMTs we weren't able to call off resuscitation efforts. We would continue CPR until a medic or doctor told us to stop. I looked briefly at the man's face, it was ashen and lifeless, and I thought: so this is what death looks like.

Then Rebecca, the man's girlfriend, recognized me. "Kim? I'm Rebecca. Remember me?"

Of course I did.

"This is Brian." She motioned towards the dead man in the toboggan. I had met Brian before and looking at him now, his skin turned waxy and thick, I could almost imagine the man alive. In fact, it was a strange trick of the mind. I stood for a moment and watched Brian's face, as it transformed in front of me between the young man I'd met and this dead body. I turned towards Rebecca to block her view. The toboggan headed down the hill, a patroller straddling the victim and continuing chest compressions. I slowed down and engaged Rebecca in conversation. I didn't want her to see what I knew waited at the bottom. We skied next to each other, our skis forming wedges like beginners, putting some distance between us and the toboggan.

"I didn't know what to do."

I shook my head. "There's nothing you could have done, or should have done, differently. Just tell me what happened."

Rebecca described how Brian skied the glade and hit the small jump at the bottom. It was merely a mogul, or perhaps a snow-covered stump. But Brian missed the landing and hit a nearby tree. At first, he was able to speak, telling Rebecca he needed help. She stood beside him and held his hand as he drifted away, his body still pressed up against the tree. She wanted to know if he would live, and I told her I didn't know.

"But this looks very serious." I didn't want to give her false hope.

Rebecca nodded and held her breath.

A week later a snowboarder died by falling into a creek, his head submerged in the icy water for several minutes. Another month later a man would have a heart attack and die on the slope, and I would continue CPR until a doctor intervened.

The following week something strange happened. Riding on a six-place chairlift, I looked across at four young men. Their voices were full of bravado and the lingo of locals. Each one wore a dark jacket and baggy pants—each one certain he would never die. They talked about how "sick" the lines were up in the Bowl, how they planned on "going bigger" this time. They laughed and offered high-fives all around. But when I looked across at them, I saw dead bodies. I didn't even have to close my eyes to imagine it. Their very faces turned gray and waxy, their lips bulged out, and their eyes turned dark and blank. I tried to shake the image loose, but I couldn't.

We arrived at the top of the lift and the four guys got off the chair, joking about their next run. I walked inside to the patrol station, wondering what was wrong with me.

Survivor trauma can make you cross a line. Firefighters and medics deal with this kind of thing all the time. Some feel tremendous guilt for living. Life's joys become mundane. In the face of death, what about life could hold that much power anymore? If it could all just fly away in an instant, why aren't we holding it close to us? Why am I not making it count? Death has a way of permeating the living, ripping loose our hope.

Because so many of the deaths I have witnessed were young men, even now my mind can play the same trick on me. In the midst of a brimming life, a man can transform into death. I know what it would look like. I want to shake these men, break them loose of their routines, reach up their sleeves and feel for a pulse. I want to remind them to be careful, that life is precious, even though it's full of stress and obligation. But human beings don't work that way. To talk of death is to invite pity, and it makes people uncomfortable.

Sudden death was one thing. John's illness was different. Rebecca never had a chance to say goodbye. While she held Brian's hand, his body losing its litheness and grace, she never thought death was so close. She knew he was injured, sure, but about to die? How could someone so young, such a good skier, such a wonderful man, die just like that?

At least I could hold John's hand, knowing that soon it may lose its warmth. I could mourn each passing heartbeat right alongside him, worrying over the countdown. At least I could fight with him, helping him gather strength, and if the end came, I would face it with him. I would, at least, have a chance to say goodbye.

This latest news wasn't catastrophic, not yet. Dr. Williams

wanted to let the antibiotics work on the staph infection before further intervention. Death's images taunted me, and when I looked at John I pressed them away. I knew death was fickle. It could choose John just as easily as anyone else.

But neither one of us was finished fighting yet.

~~~

John was stuck five times before they got a good vein. Later he would grit his teeth at the retelling, but now he was a gentleman.

"How is your weekend going?" He asked the second nurse. Each one only got three chances to get in a line, and then he or she had to pass it off to someone else. John had become a difficult case, his blood vessels shrinking back the moment the steel cart squeaked into his room. It was always early in the morning, or late at night, whichever way you looked at it: still dark outside.

"Alright." The nurse answered. "You?"

"Fine." He looked over at me and laughed a little.

I had sat up at least, the sheets from the cot pulled tight across my chest. *Why did he have to be so pleasant?* Every morning a different nurse came in to take blood. This morning it had already been a young woman, orange curls framing her face and now a middle-aged woman, her hair pulled back in a severe bun. When she missed the first vein, I wanted to scream at her.

"It's okay," John said just to me, holding his other arm out for her.

"Are you from Rochester?" She asked him, tapping her index finger against the soft skin in the crook of his arm.

"Seattle."

"Long way from home. What do you do out there?"

"Ski," he said. "We own and operate ski areas."

"Oh, my."

"Do you ski?" He always came around to that question.

"Used to. Not anymore. Not in years."

I laid my head back down on the pillow and waited for her to leave. I listened as she scraped the stiff paper sheet she'd draped below John's arm into the garbage. I heard the sound of rubber snapping against skin.

"Want me to turn out the lights?" She asked as she wheeled out the cart.

"Sure, okay." John said.

"You okay?" I asked.

"Did she wake you?"

"I was asleep. How about you?"

"I was awake. Just thinking."

"Doesn't it bother you how they come in here at all hours of the night like you aren't a real person?"

"She's just doing her job."

Why did he have to be so understanding? Why didn't I have this same strength?

"Go back to sleep," he said.

Something had changed in John. His patience with little annoyances made me wary. "You sure you're okay?" I asked, expecting him to sigh with frustration, swear, anything to tell me that things were getting back to normal. "Did that nurse hurt you?"

"Not the second time. The other nurse, she hurt me. But this time it was better." He reached across the space between my cot and his bed and held my hand. The light from the window lightened just slightly, and I knew we had only a few more minutes before the next shift arrived. "It's going to be okay, Kim."

The shadows in the room shifted from the headlights of a passing car as if the beam of a lighthouse shone across the seascape. I wondered if something else had shifted, too. Little pieces of metal lit up in the shaft of light: the knob on his IV pole, the oxygen valves behind his bed, the doorknob the nurse had just turned to leave. "I hope so," I said, almost whispering, and squeezed his hand. His breathing changed and I realized he'd fallen asleep. Where was his righteous indignation? Where was John's desire to catch every last stellar-filled moment before it was too late? He'd drifted into complacency, and that worried me. I returned his hand to his bed, turned on my side and watched him sleep until the sun rose, its amber swords, like an insistent warrior, all clanging bravado, thrust across the ceiling.

11
Turning Towards Fear

Planting ourselves in Rochester, like digging a snow cave in the midst of a fierce storm, forced me to face my biggest fears head on. I couldn't hide away and imagine the worst. We were here, and John was fighting for his life. I'd even signed a lease for an apartment in Rochester, though it felt I'd drawn it in my own blood. When John was finally released from the hospital for the second time, I realized we had to hunker down and embed ourselves near the epicenter of the disaster. Life in the mountains had taught me how to do this and not give in to anxiety. In fact, intensity was the perfect antidote to fear. One night a few years earlier, alone with my phobias at the top of Crystal Mountain, I learned the power of turning towards fear.

Even though the forecast had called for wind that night, I fell asleep to a clear sky and calm winds. Every night one ski patroller spent the night at Crystal Mountain's Summit House, watching the weather and keeping an eye on the building to make sure the pipes didn't freeze. Every Saturday and Sunday, my night at the summit, I huddled in my sleeping bag and watched the snow pile up outside the window as the long night stretched out in front of me.

Earlier in the evening, I had even skied off the backside in the moonlight and skinned back up, laughing at the weather forecasters and wondering about the warm front they'd predicted. Eating a bowl of soup and letting my gear hang to dry, I lit a few candles and watched the snowcat lights twinkle in the valley below.

Now, the wind howled around the corner of the building, rattling against the window, sending splinters of snow like sand against the glass. The clock beside the bed read 1 a.m. The forecast was spot on. I shifted in bed and heard Rocket sigh. The dog was awake too. Mice scratched in the wall next to my head, and I covered my ears.

On snowy nights the summit sleeper's job (we called the duty "Jack's" named for the late patroller that slept here every night of his ski patrol career) was to report fresh snow to the Snow Safety Director. If enough snow had fallen and we needed to do avalanche control, Jack called in the teams, waking each patroller at 4:30 a.m. to come in early. Soon I would don my boots and walk the ridge, checking for snow accumulation and deciding whether or not to report my findings to Doug.

The Summit House had an old desktop computer where I could check the telemetry—the automated recording of ridge top winds, temperatures and precipitation amounts. If it snowed at least six inches with winds averaging in the 30s, I would call everyone in. Less than that, and Doug would have to decide. It all depended on the snowpack. Even without much snowfall, wind could transport the snow, depositing it into dangerous slabs.

A strong gust of wind rattled the window beside my head, and I sat straight up in bed. My sleeping bag wrapped around me like a cocoon, and I searched for the zipper and tugged at it futilely. I hated wind. I imagined the roof of the Summit House pealing back like a tin can, while the wind lifted the eaves in violent blasts. I called to the dog and let him jump on the bed with me. He curled up quickly and fell back asleep. Considering my wind phobia, it was a wonder why I volunteered for this duty. I could have been down below, sleeping soundly in my cabin. But it was also a form of shock therapy—bringing myself closer to the source of my fear as a way of cauterizing the raw wound.

The squall continued, whistling through the chinks in the walls. Just when I thought the wind would die down, it picked up again, increasing its screeching hiss. I wanted the next few hours to fly by and wished I could go back to sleep. But fear slowed time.

Jack's apartment was an add-on to the Summit House, so it sat above the ground without a foundation. When the wind swirled around the building, it reached under the floor of the apartment and pressed against the boards. It was easy to imagine the entire corner apartment torn from the building and strewn down the slope below. Ragged bits of plastic and drywall would litter the ski area, along with my sleeping bag as it went cartwheeling through the air. I would land with a frightening thud against the snow, my slippery bag quickly gathering speed. I'd be trapped, unable to get to my zipper, the wind and snow pushing me towards my death.

The wind increased. A dial on the wall flickered, measuring gusts to 60 mph. I paced the cold floor for a few moments while Rocket looked at me with his big eyes. He whined; I got back in bed and curled up in a ball, pulled my sleeping bag to my chin and listened to the increased movements of the mice. Perhaps the wind bothered them too, forcing their little bodies to shake and dance, making them search vigilantly for a way through the walls of the apartment where a roll of Ritz crackers and a half bag of ground coffee were about the only rewards.

When the real Jack lived here he had a cat—a mouser that kept the place clean. Every day Stalker would bring him a black mouse, its neck neatly broken, and deposit it on the worn carpet. In exchange, Jack gave Stalk a piece of cheese or a pat on the neck. They had an understanding. When Jack retired, he took the cat with him. Like me, most of the replacement Jacks kept avalanche rescue dogs. But dogs weren't as keen to catch mice as cats. And I suspected that Rocket was as afraid of them as I was. I stroked his head and tried to calm the jitters rising in my body. I looked at the clock. Another fifteen minutes had gone by.

An hour later, I couldn't stand it any longer. The winds were averaging in the 30s, with gusts into the 50s. Judging by the amount of snow that was falling, I suspected we'd need to do avalanche control, and I had to go outside to check it out.

A sputtering motor ran through my body, shaking my fingers and flickering in my chest like an unshielded flame. This was real fear, and it was ridiculous. I had to get a grip. Like a call-and-response musical pattern, the wind rose in collaboration with my fear. It whistled through the windows and shook the walls. I reached out to touch the windowsill and felt the cold draft taunting me. The wind screamed, and my imagination reeled.

Sitting on the bed, the air around me seemed electrified. I was sure my hair stood on end. The room felt alive and whirling. Even the mice busied themselves behind the walls as if sensing the impending disaster. I reminded myself that this building had seen worse. Made of stone and heavy timbers, the Summit House had withstood years of windstorms. I rose reluctantly, pushing Rocket's sleeping paw to wake him. If I had to go out in this, he was coming with me. By now the wind blew a constant shriek through the boards of the apartment, clattering the windows against their casings. I imagined that once I walked outside, the wind would lift me up like Dorothy in the *Wizard of Oz*, swirling me around in the snowy gusts.

Outside, the snowdrifts covered my earlier boot prints, and the stairs had filled in with snow. Rocket paused at the front door, his dark body backlit against the swirling snow. He looked almost angelic. "Come on. You might as well come with me." I patted my pant leg, which the wind pasted against my thigh, and he obediently followed in my footsteps.

I lifted my hood to protect my face against the wind howling over the ridge. I hadn't planned on using my poles to steady myself, but the wind's constant pressure made it necessary. Against the wind, the pole's flimsy metal veered out at odd angles. Rocket walked at my side, hoping my legs would shield him from the worst gusts.

The beeping sounds of the snowcats drifted up the slope, but I could no longer see their lights illuminating the hills like giant flashlights. Wind-driven snow surrounded me like a halo, obscuring my view into the valley.

After a few steps, I realized I wasn't scared. Inside, I'd imagined the wind pulling off the roof, destroying the forty-year-old stone building like a trailer caught in a twister. But once outside, when it was just me with the wind, I calmed down. If a strong gust blew me off the ridge, I would need to stay focused. I'd calmly gather myself and crawl back up. I wouldn't snivel or whine; that doesn't help in an emergency. I realized that by increasing the intensity, my own nerves calmed down.

I planted each foot carefully, focusing all my energy on my route. Once across the flat ridge, I hiked to Grubstake. With each footstep I searched for the previous day's boot pack, sometimes sliding my boot into the well-worn steps, and at others breaking a new trail. Deeply focusing, I almost forgot about the wind. I knew I could turn around and call Doug now. He'd ask me about the snow accumulation, and I already had enough information. There was a solid six inches of wind-drifted snow. In a few hours, Jack's apartment would fill with avalanche teams, an assembly line for lacing the explosives forming in the hallway. But I knew Doug would ask me if I hiked to Grubstake. He'd want specifics, in order to know how much firepower to pull out of the explosives cache. Besides, I wanted to hike to the top. It felt a necessary act against the wind.

I glanced behind me looking for Rocket. A black dog against the dark sky was nearly impossible to see, but against the white snow I could just make him out. I reached back to pat his head and told him he was a good boy.

At the top, fresh cornices hung over the steep slopes. One jutted out in front of me and I called Rocket, knowing that even the weight of a dog could break it loose. Instead of turning back to the comfort of Jack's, I stomped a platform into the snow and turned to face the wind. Rocket stood in the space at my feet, scratching at the snow, a distant instinct telling him to hunker down. I held my arms out, working harder than I thought necessary to keep them in place with the full force of the wind screaming across the top of the peak.

I knew I should follow Rocket's example, but I didn't want to return to my bed, that cocoon of baseless fears. I'd rather stand out here, my face pressed into the oncoming wind and open my arms to it. Let it do its worst. I'd rather face the immediate threat than my imagination. Keeping my face into the wind tethered me to the moment. Extreme situations didn't allow me to wander into my past or worry about what might come next. I could only deal with the situation at hand and nothing else.

A strong gust came and for a moment, I thought it might pick me up and deposit me in the steep chutes below me. It could happen in an instant, and I didn't discount the hazard. A friend told me once about how the wind picked him up and threw him into the air. He'd been climbing down from the top of Mt. Hood, hoping to beat the incoming storm. Luckily, he'd landed only a few feet away and been able to self-arrest quickly. It had to have been a pretty strong gust to pick up a 210-pound man. Here, my position was a bit more precarious. I stood a few feet from the tender cornice that hung above steep chutes and realized that a strong gust could send me sprawling several hundred feet below.

As I leaned forward a little more, I felt calmer. I even smiled a little, careful not to open my mouth lest the wind reach in there. I wasn't afraid. Standing in the midst of the very object of my fear, pressing back against it, I gathered my strength. I checked my watch. It was 4:15. I needed to return and call Doug. He'd tell me to call in the teams, and I had only fifteen minutes to get back and start calling. Soon I would line my pack with explosives and throw them onto the slope. I'd hike in the wind again, attaching myself to the task at hand. While out in the storm I wouldn't think of anything else—not my fear or my regrets or my worries about my diabetes. For now, I just closed my eyes and lifted my chin into the full force of the wind, tilting forward into it until I reached equilibrium.

With John, I would learn to do the same thing. Each visit to the clinic, every time a nurse drew blood in search of infection, every time Dr. Gores entered the room with a dour look on his face as if to share some dire bit of news, I would turn towards the terrible thing and face it. I wouldn't shrink away, listening to the wind jangle my nerves like a set of keys. I would no longer weep in the shower or slink around the hospital, afraid of the diagnosis. I would turn towards the doctor's words, square my shoulders up to the onslaught and raise my arms. Bring it on. It couldn't be any worse than my imagination.

12

The Most Therapeutic Part

"Tomorrow morning we have to be there at nine a.m.," I said. John went into the Clinic, even on Sundays, for blood tests and his morning infusion. I administered his evening one at the apartment. I pulled the trash bin out from under the kitchen sink and brought it to the table so I could slide all of the remnants of his IV injection into the bin. It was nearly filled with plastic tubing and gauze bandages. Once a day we went through this routine at the kitchen table. I would take out the box they gave us at the hospital and drape the table in a special paper covering, then set out all of the needles, tubing and medicine. I mixed the antibiotics into the bag of saline and then hooked that up to the PICC line in his arm. Together we watched for air bubbles in the tubing.

John watched me work. "How do they know if this stuff is really working?"

"That's what the blood test is for. Afterwards you can eat whatever you want."

"How about nothing? Can I just eat nothing?"

"You have to eat something, but it can be whatever you want."

In the hospital John had shown a brave front for the nurses and doctors. I wanted to believe in his strength too. His façade of courage surrounded me like a sheath, giving me something to rest against. On our own now, I saw that layer crumble around him, and there were times when I longed for the pretense. I continued cleaning up in the kitchen, wiping the counters with disinfectant spray and scrubbing carefully around the edges of the sink.

"Food is exhausting." He slumped in his chair and rested his forehead on his arm. "If only I didn't have to eat, I'd be fine."

These infusions made me feel useful. In the hospital John wanted answers. He relied on my careful note taking, expecting an interpretation. Most times I just repeated what the doctors had said and wished I could offer more. It wasn't like ski patrolling, where I was an expert in immediate life threatening emergencies. I'd stopped major bleeding, affixed defibrillator pads, and taken blood pressures, but administering his medicine through the IV PICC line felt more like what I'd been trained to do. Even when he didn't want to eat anything, I could always nourish him with medicine.

Earlier at the dinner table, I pulled the needle cap off with my teeth and plunged it into the top of the vial like I'd done it a million times before, which, as a diabetic, I had. The small acts of attaching the plastic tubing to the catheter and checking for air bubbles gave me something to concentrate on, and it made me wonder if that's why hospitals used so many different instruments and types of tubing—it gave the nurses a sense that they were actually helping.

I switched the lights off in the kitchen, leaving the single bulb above the stove burning which cast a yellow spot onto the range and the empty countertops beside it. Only the clock on the coffee pot illuminated the corner. Everything was in its place.

John and I got into bed, and I pressed my leg against his. A triangle of light from the street lamp pointed across the ceiling like a shard of glass, and I wondered if John's lifestyle had been a way of cramming it all in before he died. "Did you always know this was coming?" I asked.

"I knew I'd have a liver transplant some day, if that's what you mean."

A breeze fluttered through the sliver of open window and rattled the curtains. "I guess I just didn't believe it."

"But I told you," he said. "You were warned, weren't you?"

"I just didn't believe that you could be this sick."

After a minute, he said, "I know. I guess I didn't either."

But I knew that's why he'd lived that way—why he'd collected stories like a memoirist to be told later, after the worst was over. Always willing to try anything, he'd accumulated experiences like an art collector.

Another gust of air slipped through the window, and I could hear crickets and other night sounds seeping into the room. The fragment of glass on the ceiling changed shape as the curtains trembled, undulating like a snowy slope. If I closed my eyes just right and looked at it through the shade of my eyelashes, cloud shadows danced across the slope, illuminating two sets of ski tracks. Narrowing my eyes a little further, I could almost see John arcing across the bottom of the bowl, the line of his tracks extending uphill behind him.

"Today is a great leap forward," John said at breakfast the next morning.

"Really?" It had been nearly a month since the pancreatitis started. Maybe things were looking up.

"I feel good," he said moving his body in jerky motions as if testing out his new theory. "Now I just want to start the transplant process."

I sat down beside him, quietly pulling my chair in.

"What are you thinking about?" he asked, pushing a spoonful of instant oatmeal around in his bowl.

"You haven't asked me that for a while."

"I know," he said, sounding so much like the old John that it broke my heart. "I'm sorry. It's just that I can't think about anything right now. When you're in so much pain, all you can do is breathe and count down the hours until the next pain pill," he said, slipping into the indefinite pronoun. He'd always done that—referring to himself in second person, as if stepping outside himself for a minute.

John relied on the future to illuminate the space in front of his feet. An upcoming trip or holiday season drew him like metal shavings to a magnet. He could get through almost anything as long as he had something to look forward to. I had other strategies. For me, the future was vaguely planned and set aside. Only in the present moment could I ever find refuge. Perhaps that's what made this so hard.

John pushed himself up from the table and placed his bowl in the kitchen sink. Sliding open the glass door to the deck, he stepped out and rested his hands on the banister. He inhaled deeply as if trying to extract a promise from the morning breeze.

I wanted to write an email telling everyone that we would be fine. Turning on my laptop, I gazed at John through the open door. His eyes, now closed, tilted towards the sun. These updates had been forwarded to prayer groups and circles of friends beyond our own, like a subterranean river of support I could tap into and would wash me clean. I looked forward to reading the responses, especially by survivors—the ones who'd also stood at this high altitude, the air as thin as glass. Some asked how I was doing. One friend, a cancer survivor, wrote that she wondered if it hadn't been hardest on her husband—the one who stood by and watched his wife as her body and spirit shriveled. For the patient, the certainty of pain filled the room like smoke, leaving a residue even when it subsided. The faithful onlooker lacked certainty, as if the very air had been sucked from the room, leaving her unable to even scream.

I wrote that it was okay to spread the awful news about John's diagnosis. As hard as it might be to say, I knew that it wasn't as hard as uttering the words "my husband has cancer." I also wrote *John will get through this*. I had even said these words aloud with conviction. As if I had faith. I left the email unsent and stood beside the open door, my bare foot resting on the threshold.

The slanted light cut like a blade across the deck, making John's skin look gray. His eyes were open now, and he looked down at the lawn, already tinged yellow at the edges from the advancing summer. In places, scattered tokens of darker green bloomed hopefully, unaware that the meager sprinkling system couldn't hold against the August heat that lay just around the corner.

~~~

My dreams were becoming almost prophetic, and I knew I was probably giving them more credit than I should. Last night I dreamt that John and I were outside in a tunnel with no roof, like a large shiny culvert cut open to the sky. We stood there within the bright light reflecting off the corrugated metal. I held him close to me, feeling his chest conform to the shape of my body, and he said, "I have to leave."

I held him tighter. "I won't let you. I won't."

"But I have to," he countered, the refracted light shining in streaks around us. Grooved rays fell across our bodies. "I can't explain, but we can't stay together."

I knew I had no choice, yet I couldn't let go. My mind softened to the fact, but I couldn't make my arms release him.

Then we were in a room inside a labyrinthine house with a party clamoring outside the door. I watched as John got a massage. The practitioner rubbed his entire body with iodine, staining it dark orange. She kept rubbing it in all over his legs. She announced that she was running late and he would have to finish the job. She didn't leave, however, and watched as he splashed it in his hands and rubbed it hastily over his face and arms. He kept his white t-shirt on, tingeing the edges of the sleeves with rust.

"Now," she said over her shoulder as she finally walked out the door. "You must get in the shower and wash it off." She looked at me when she said this. "You can help him. It's the most therapeutic part." As she opened the door to leave I saw my mom in the kitchen, taking a foil wrapped dish out of the oven.

She looked up at me, her eyebrows raised in a June Cleaver sort of way. "Dinner's ready." I looked back in at John, who stood in the shower, all the iodine stain dripping off of him. I walked over and adjusted the showerhead, rubbing it off his back. The orange stain swirled around his feet and down the drain.

He held his arms out in front of him and turned his hands over as if reading his own palm. "It's gone," he said. "It's just my own skin."

I wanted to believe that it was that easy. Could John's illness be something we could just wash off, like skin tinted by iodine could be scrubbed until it returns to normal? Of course not. Of course it couldn't. And yet the urge to believe it, especially in the blurry moments after waking buoyed me just enough to face another day.

~~~

"I guess this is it," John said.

I parked the Beetle at a yellow gate and we got out. We had just arrived at the closest ski area to Rochester, and it was for sale. On either side of the road, cornfields rose up over our heads, the long leaves like grass were just beginning to turn brown.

"So this is the top?"

"It's a top-down configuration," John said, looking around. "Which makes sense."

We walked over towards a tall white building that looked like a church. We had read about it in the local newspaper. The ski area owners dragged this old church up from the town a few miles away and turned it into the lodge. "Hence the name, Steeple Chase." I nodded my head towards the building.

We walked over towards the top of the chair lifts. The ski area had operated last year, but had announced it would close unless they found a buyer. Seat pads from the chair lift flapped in the warm air. "Doesn't look like lift maintenance is a top priority."

Gravel crunched behind us and a man stepped out of his truck. He introduced himself as Kevin, the owner and General

Manager. His father had always wanted to turn this part of his land into a ski area, but hadn't lived to see it open.

John explained why we were here. "I've been getting treated at the Mayo Clinic. Thought we'd check this place out."

Maybe John felt good today. Maybe he was right and this was a great leap forward. Standing here below these chairlifts, John's mind working through the operation, he seemed alive again.

Kevin explained how they had survived on a tight budget from the start and couldn't afford the expensive pumps for making snow that would have guaranteed operations. Last season had put them too far into the red. "Couldn't open for Christmas. Real cold, but no snow." Cold temperatures, common in Minnesota winters, practically ensured good conditions for snowmaking.

John's father had invented one of the earliest snow making machines. A high-powered hose fit around a strong fan and spread water high into the cold air. Once the water hit the air, provided it had just the right calibrations, it would turn into snow by the time it hit the ground.

Wheels turned in John's head. The last thing he needed to do was buy a ski area right now. But still, he must have said to himself: *it would be so easy.*

We toured the lodge and the top lift stations. Kevin gave us a trail map and we traced our fingers along the runs, imagining their potential. For John, running a profitable ski area was a formula. I couldn't quite understand it myself, but for him it was second nature. I tried to guess how he'd make decisions—which new project to start next, where to trim during lean years. Sometimes I guessed right, but most often I was way off. Instead of prioritizing a practical drain field, I'd opt for a sexy new tram. Or I'd increase the ski patrol staff and ignore the need to control payroll when the snow didn't fall.

In the rental shop of the now-closed ski area, John stood beside a pile of dusty green tower pads. These were used to pad the towers of the chair lifts, in the event of a skier collision. Tower pads were in the realm of ski patrollers, and if I closed my eyes I could conjure up whole weeks of my life spent affixing, raising and thawing the frozen buckles of these unwieldy beasts. "This ski area needs two things."

Kevin leaned in, his mouth parted. He must have heard of John. Or at least he knew about his father and the company, the largest private ski company in the country. While John had been sick in the hospital, Boyne Resorts had grown. They now managed several ski areas back east, including Sugarloaf, Sunday River, and Loon Mountain. Surely Kevin had heard of these, and he must have been flattered that John would take the time to tell him how to make this ski area profitable. He couldn't know, however, how good this was for John.

"Snow making, for one. That's obvious," John said. "But also, you need to do some marketing. You have a lot of people in Rochester who need something to do on the weekends." John spoke calmly. This was easy for him. He explained how, if Kevin could just find the capital to open back up this season with a few improvements, this place could make money. "The ski industry needs areas like this. This is where Mom, Dad, and the kids learn to ski."

When we finally left, John handed Kevin his card.

"I'll drive," he said to me.

"You sure?"

He backed the car up slowly, hunching forward and peering through the windshield at the top chairlift station a few feet away. The black circular bullwheel that turned the chair lift cable had begun to rust. "This place really needs to open again. The ski industry can't afford to lose these small operations. Without these, people just stop learning how to ski."

John drove all the way back to Rochester through rolling hills and river valleys. Everything was the dark, nearly black

Pine Green found in a Crayola box, acres of short alfalfa and corn stalks laden with ears ready to fall over. There was wheat too; shimmering Goldenrod stalks like princess hair. The soil on the side of the road was impossibly dark.

That night I took a walk near the pond while John slept. Darkness had descended already, and the dew had collected on the grass. Two months since the solstice and the days were getting shorter. At first I thought it was the headlamp of a distant nightwalker, or perhaps a family, each of them swinging their flashlights in and out of view. As I moved toward them I saw they weren't remote beams, they were right here. Fireflies.

I stopped in the long grass to watch them, the blades tickling my ankles. One flew erratically a few feet away, and then blinked off. I imagined where it might go and searched the darkness for its reappearance. Sure enough it, or perhaps another, twinkled back on and kept at its haphazard flight. More lights flickered on and off. There must have been a dozen or more, once I really looked.

I stood there for a long time, wishing I had a jar to catch them in. I could take them back to the apartment and wake John. *Here*, I would say. *Look at what I brought you.* He would smile, his eyes growing large like a child's.

Fireflies, he would whisper and, for a minute, everything would be okay.

I wanted John to get back to collecting transcendent moments. A jar of fireflies might open that door again. Contemplating saving Steeplechase might do it too. But before I had a chance to run inside to find a jar (did I even have a jar in the apartment, would a Ziploc baggie to the trick?) they were gone, becoming distant constellations over the black pond.

I shivered, rubbing my wet ankles on the backs of my shins. It was getting late. John would be asleep by now; perhaps dreaming of fire fly-lit nights back home.

13

Whiteout

I pressed my nose up to the Plexiglas window of the helicopter and searched the ridges and spines for avalanches. I spotted one and motioned to Paul, the patrol director and leader of this avalanche course, who asked the pilot to circle. A cornice breaking loose high up in the chute could have caused it, but it was impossible to tell. The crown of the avalanche spread across the couloir mid-slope, then downward along either spine. The pile of jagged debris at the bottom gave me a chill.

I had enrolled in an advanced avalanche class designed for ski patrollers and mountain guides, which had me flying in a helicopter bound for a remote peak in Washington's North Cascades backcountry. We were spotting recent avalanche activity, a clue as to what we would find at our destination. The day's objective would show how heli-ski guides evaluated terrain and safely moved their clients through dangerous topography. Two of our guides worked with me on the patrol at Crystal, and I looked forward to the day ahead, hoping for a little education and even more powder skiing. This was my first trip in a helicopter for the purpose of skiing, and I had grand visions.

Sean, our pilot, landed the helicopter on a tiny summit. We crawled out of the doors, keeping our heads down as he hovered. Anne, another instructor and former ski patroller, knelt beside the cockpit and raised her thumb, the universal sign for "all-clear." We watched him take off, knowing he'd meet us at the bottom of the first large slope.

The North Cascades were in a remote region of the state. With few roads and miles of steep, rugged terrain, it's a backcountry skier's dream. One of the few roads that ran through the range, Highway 20, was closed in the winter. As we stood under the remains of the helicopter wash, I looked out at endless, untouched peaks, most of them inaccessible by car and too far to traverse in a single day.

"Did you guys see that avalanche from the helicopter?" Anne gathered the group in a tight circle away from the landing zone. We told her we had seen it, knowing where there was one, others would follow.

We skied to a safe hillside separated from the larger bowl and dug a snow profile pit. These pits allowed avalanche professionals to test the stability and layers in the snowpack. By examining the snowpack with thermometers and microscopes, these examinations allowed us to predict avalanches.

I struck at the snow with my shovel, creating two smooth walls on which to conduct our tests. Once excavated, I ran my finger down the even wall, feeling for the weak layers. I found a distinct stratum, perhaps buried surface hoar—the frozen equivalent of dew, with its feathery crystals that, when buried, lie flat and make a perfect sliding layer. Each time I pounded on the shaft of snow with my shovel, the top two feet slid cleanly. When I turned the slab upside down I thought I saw the feathery crystals shimmer in the gray light.

The top of a cloud lifted like a finger over the ridge above us, a much lighter gray contrasted against the dark sky. It hovered there for a moment before it descended around us, wrapping our group in a thick cloak. "I don't like the results of the rutschblock," I told Anne. "The top two feet pulled out when I jumped on it."

A rutschblock is the last test in a snow pit. Once an avalanche forecaster has measured the layers and run her fingers along the interstices, isolated columns of snow and tested the bonds, she cuts the sidewalls of the pit away from the snowpack and jumps on the isolated table-sized column. If a slab sheers off right away, it's a sign of extreme avalanche hazard. On the other hand if the column remains intact no matter how many times a skier jumps on it, the hazard is low. It's the middle ground in between those two extremes that makes predicting avalanches so difficult.

"How many times did you jump on it?"

"Two," I said, glancing across the slope at a disappearing vertical wall of granite a few hundred yards away. What had only moments before been clear, now dimmed in the whiteout.

Instead of skiing the tempting powder straight down, the group decided to ski across the slope one at a time. I held my poles across my body in self-arrest position, ready to slow myself if the snow began to slide. I followed directly in Anne's tracks, trying not to put too much pressure on the precarious slab I had found in the snow pit.

The slab broke so slowly that at first I wasn't even alarmed. Below my tracks the snow slipped away like a paper towel being ripped from a large roll. I stayed in the track; my skis acted like pre-cut perforations, cutting away the huge block of snow beneath me.

Just below our tracks, the slope rolled over into a steep gully. When the avalanche hit the more vertical section, it gathered speed, broke into a million smaller chunks and disappeared into the murky whiteout. I heard it crash onto the slope below.

For a while the intensity of the moment overtook me. I followed the guide, my mind completely focused on getting to safety. We weren't out of the danger zone yet, and I strained to open my eyes to let in all available light. The sky melted into the snow, turning the world to a white sheet. John would call it skiing inside a golf ball. It was impossible to see the slope, or to know if what I saw was slope or sky. Only the occasional rock and the granite wall on our left, which came in and out of view, defined the mountainside. At first I was consumed by the task.

Breaking it down into smaller chunks, I concentrated solely on finding the next safe zone or rock that would illuminate the route.

It became a game. *Who can spot safety first?* Like a child's game of "hot lava rocks" in which you jumped from one safe zone to the next, this time we skied from one visible rock to the next, never quite sure that another safe zone would become evident. It was a conscious act of diminishing the daunting task by breaking it down into manageable chunks. Without visibility the group could easily pitch over a cliff or venture into an avalanche slope and be swept away. Reaching each safe zone was a small triumph.

After about a half an hour, the light changed. The murk lifted just slightly, allowing the smallest of difference between the white of the fog and the white of the snow. At first it was relief, followed by something else, anger. In a skiing hierarchy of needs, first comes visibility. You must see it to ski it. Goggle manufacturers and night-ski venues have made millions by offering a way to see when the light goes flat. And since mountains are often shrouded in snow and fog, flat light plagues skiers. Once visibility improved, my mind lost the zen koan-like quest keeping me focused on the task, and I thought about all that wasted snow. Back then my heart was lighter; I didn't yet have anything to lose.

We made it safely to the far rocky wall, and inched the group through the dangerous terrain, keeping ourselves away from the starting zones and skirting the steepest sections. What should have been just a few minutes to ski took over an hour. The flat light caused our biggest problem, and each one of us scanned the whiteness for a dark rock or discernible feature to guide us toward flatter, safer terrain.

The terrain flattened out and I relaxed. Still using the rocky wall on our left as a "handrail," we crept towards safety. Not until I noticed the look exchanged between Anne and Paul did my heart knock against my sternum. A brief moment — perhaps just a mere suggestion of uncertainty — passed between them. I could almost see Paul's lids rise and his chin tilt sideways as if to say "What now?" The helicopter pick-up zone, where we now stood, was encased in clouds. We were several days walk from the nearest road, and we only had a few hours of daylight left.

Paul and Anne weighed our options. The third guide led the remaining group to the edge of yet another steep face. Below us, the tops of trees poked through the clouds like ghosts. Two obvious drainages splintered in either direction. One would take us closer to the highway, but the terrain dropped more steeply. The other, while longer, would take us through mellower slopes.

Paul talked to Sean on the radio, explaining our predicament. He wanted to know which drainage we should head down, hoping the pilot could pick us up in either one or the other.

The pilot's response sobered me. "Neither one looks good."

I watched Paul's face, searching for a crack in his calm façade. "I think we should head east." Of the two drainages, the east was the longer one. While not as steep, it put the group much further away from the nearest road in case we had to walk out. I mentally scanned my backpack for supplies. I'd brought along a lunch, and kept my insulin warm in my chest pocket. But I didn't have enough food for a multi-day epic adventure. And a diabetic without food was an emergency. Add in a long physical push and it could become a crisis.

When a physical limitation such as diabetes or bile duct cancer enters the picture, there's not much one can do to combat it. No amount of bravery or sheer physical strength, or even making the right choice between two potentially dangerous descent routes, can overcome a body's lack of insulin or a liver's inability to process toxins. Even though I fought back with exercise and the right food, trying to keep my body as healthy as possible, I couldn't go hours, let alone days, without food and medicine.

Just then a member of the other group called out. The guide had fallen off a small cornice and been caught in an avalanche. While standing above the west drainage he'd misjudged the edge. It didn't take long for the guide to extricate himself from the debris—he'd self-arrested near the top—and climb back up to the failed landing zone. There was no other choice. We had to go east.

Paul radioed Sean that we planned on descending into the east drainage, and I strained to hear his response. His only words were a scratchy "Copy that," and I thought I sensed a dread in his voice.

I wondered which drainage I would choose if I were the guide. As much as I wanted to trust Paul and Anne, I, too, had experience in the mountains, and I didn't want to be lead to my death. I looked at Paul. "Do you think that's the best choice?"

He looked down at the snow, his skis moving slightly back and forth. When he glanced back up at me, he shrugged his shoulders. "I'm not sure. The weather is bad either way, but we can't stay here."

I nodded my head. Sometimes we have to act, even when we don't like our choices. How could I argue with that? "You do know that I'm diabetic."

Paul sucked in a sharp breath. "I know. Don't worry. We aren't going to spend the night out here. Not if I can help it."

If I were out here with my own group, I'd probably choose the same descent. I'd hope for some miracle from Sean, that his extensive military experience could somehow part the thick muck that had descended on our group and he could pick us up. But we couldn't stay where we were; it wasn't safe from avalanches above, nor could the pilot land there. We had to make a choice and stick with it. We descended into the new drainage, traversing across steep terrain, now covered in thick trees. Weaving through the thickest timber, away from the worst avalanche terrain, we tried to stay together. It had begun to

snow, and I wondered how far down the flakes turned to rain. I
didn't relish the idea of hiking down a steep river drainage in
the rain.

I thought I heard the distinctive thwap of helicopter blades
chopping the air, but Paul's radio remained silent. I skied right
behind him, hoping to pick up any word from Sean. I was
beginning to worry about my food supply, but I knew that
panicking wouldn't help. I had to stay calm.

We finally emerged at an open gully. The slope continued
above us, but by the looks of it, it had already slid. The safest
place in avalanche country is the slide path that already went.
Once a path has slid, the energy is removed from it and has to
reload with new snow before ready to avalanche again.

We skied down the avalanche path to a flat, broad river
bottom. From here I could see the drainage snake around to the
north, back towards civilization. I still didn't know how long it
would take to walk out. The sky had turned a milky gray; it
would be dark in less than an hour. We needed to take a
compass bearing now, while we still had light, and follow the
river as far as we could before we got exhausted. I looked over at
Paul, still exhibiting his mask of calm.

He spoke into the radio, describing our location. The radio
was silent for a long time.

The entire group had assembled, the guides huddled
around Paul and the radio. Paul checked his watch. "We'll give
him fifteen minutes." We looked directly at me when he spoke.
"If we haven't heard from him by then, we'll start walking out."

My heart fluttered in my chest, and I held my breath.
Sometimes that familiar flurry foretold a low blood sugar, and a
wave of adrenaline swept through me. I couldn't help it.
Adrenaline only made it worse, gobbling up all the available
sugar in my bloodstream, readying the body for fight or flight.
Instead, I needed my body to remain calm, saving that sugar for
my brain in case I really went low. It was a long fifteen minutes,

and I agonized over the wait, wondering about my blood sugar. Knowing that it rarely worked in the cold, I hadn't brought my glucometer. I reached in my pack and ate a few sugar tablets, enough to tide me over just in case, and focused on the scenery. I'd come to realize that when things got really tough, life broke down into smaller increments. Again, I waited the necessary fifteen-minute ration, wondering what wisdom I could gain.

Sean obviously wasn't coming, and we were burning the last of our daylight. But I also knew that once we entered the thick riverside, Sean would never see us, let alone find a flat spot to land. I reached into the hood of my backpack and grabbed my headlamp. I turned it on to check the light. It was adequate, but not brilliant, like my blood sugars, I figured. I cursed myself for not getting fresh batteries before the trip. But we had a helicopter. Who needed a headlamp when we had a helicopter?

Just then, I heard it. Rhythmic chops cut the silence, and I looked up. The helicopter appeared in the midst, lowering onto the flat zone a few yards from where we waited. Paul explained the situation. Sean might make only one hop, so leave all the food and supplies with the groups that were staying. No one moved.

Paul looked at me. "Anne's group goes first."

I knew he chose our group for me. The last thing he needed on an all-night bivouac was a diabetic. But still I felt guilty climbing into the heli. As we pulled away from the group, their downward glances were a little forlorn. Paul looked up with a smile and waved. In the backcountry or in the hospital, it doesn't help to panic when our options narrow down.

When Sean landed back at the heli-pad, I reached forward and spoke in his ear. "Will you be able to get everyone out tonight?"

He looked back at me and smiled. Then he raised his thumb high in the air and donned his earphones. I had begun to rely on the doctors at Mayo in much the same way. I imagined them giving me the pilot's thumbs-up, telling me they could save John's life. My experiences in the mountains told me how to act. Number one, don't panic. Number two, don't let the shimmery powder keep you from making the safe choice, and number three, trust the experts.

14

What I Like About You

Our first day back home in Seattle, I sat on the deck overlooking Lake Washington. We flew home the previous night, and security had been a nightmare. While John took a nap, Evelyn, John's five-year-old daughter, played inside. It had been five weeks since she'd seen him, and her insistent begging him to tickle her had quickly tired him out.

Ski boats were gathering on the lake. In just a few hours the water would froth with fathers pulling screaming girls in inner tubes and college kids thumping bass riffs from the speakers of their father's ski boats. Soon laughter would dance joyously across the bay towards our frightened little house. Happy people could be so irritating.

For now, the lake was quiet with only one skier carving the glassy water and cutting across his own wake. The solitude was interrupted when something crashed on the deck. A tiny black-capped chickadee lay on its side beside me. It must have hit the glass panels on the deck. I crouched down and picked it up gingerly in my palm.

"Evelyn?" I carried the bird in my hands and walked inside. "Look."

She peered closely into my hands. "Is it alive?"

"I don't know. Bring a basket or something to put it in." It wasn't breathing and its neck hung at an odd angle. But it was still warm. Evelyn retrieved the basket lined with cloth that she used for her stuffed animals when they had a broken leg.

I placed the bird in the small basket, and Evelyn carried it to the deck and set it on the table. The soft breast moved slightly, but maybe it was the breeze. We watched it carefully, wanting it to live. Its head no longer hung quite so precariously, which gave me some hope. A moment ago it had flown for its nest, and the now it rested in an unfamiliar basket that smelled like a little girl.

"Can I touch it?"

"Let me see first." I pressed my finger against its soft side, which gave a little. The downy feathers were lightweight, and I barely felt them brush against my finger. I breathed on it again, making the wing flutter.

She stroked the tiny bird. "Do you think it's going to live?"

"I hope so."

"Why did it fly into the window?" She put her head close to the bird and narrowed her eyes. "Do you think it was sick?"

"No, it's just injured."

"I mean maybe it was sick before," she said her eyes peering up at me.

"I don't think so, honey." I tucked a curl behind her ear.

"But maybe it was too sick to fly. Maybe it hit the window because it didn't feel good. Maybe it needs some medicine." She looked back at the basket.

"Birds hit windows all the time." I motioned to the sky. "They're always criss-crossing in front of the deck. This one just zigged when it should have zagged. That's all."

Evelyn was quiet for a moment. "Do you think Daddy's going to get better?"

"Yes. Daddy's getting better."

"When?"

"He needs a liver transplant. That's a big surgery. But after that, he'll be better." I glanced at the bird. "Maybe you should breathe on it."

I wished I could breathe life back into John. Evelyn pursed her lips and leaned towards the bird. It sounded like whispering, as if she was giving instructions.

The bird looked straight ahead, its eyes open now. I stroked it lightly, my finger next to Evelyn's. It was breathing. "It's going to be okay."

"Do you think I saved it?"

"Let's see if it flies away."

"Can't we keep it? This could be its nest." She touched the basket.

A few more boats entered the bay, and song lyrics floated on the water. I thought I heard "What I Like About You," by The Romantics. The swirling saxophone floated on the ripples and I made out a few of the words. "When we go up, down, turn around, think about true romance."

I closed my eyes, the sun warming my eyelids.

"Look."

I opened my eyes and saw Evelyn pointing. The basket was empty and I followed her finger. The small chickadee flapped twice and was gone.

I smiled in spite of her disappointment. A little girl could hone her nurturing skills against the misfortune of a small animal. Evelyn wanted to keep loving it, keep stroking its fur, keep taming it. Perhaps she imagined the bird a new pet, one wholly her own. But I took comfort in the chickadee's flight. If it, after appearing lifeless in my hands, could recover so undoubtedly, it gave me hope. I closed my eyes again and let the warm sanguine feeling fill the creases of my eyelids. I whispered a quiet prayer, like Evelyn's instructions for the bird, that John, too, would fly again.

~~~

In certain, life-threatening situations, opposing instincts fight for top billing. Not always does the will to live—to survive against all odds—necessarily win. An instinctual drive to just give up, to see what happens when we die, to simply cease the grueling struggle, often presses just as hard against our psyche.

Several years ago, alone one evening after work, I had a close call. At the tail end of a storm system that had deposited thirty inches of new snow, I was exhausted. All week I had climbed through waist deep snow with a heavy pack of explosives on my back, the wind drifts on the ridge rising like waves. At times I had to crawl through the snow on my hands and knees, spreading out my weight to keep myself from sinking deeper with each step.

I stripped off my clothes the minute I got home—shedding layers of fleece shirts, long underwear, and wool socks—and left them in a pile on the floor.

Stepping outside onto the porch to the hot tub, I hung my robe on the hook and removed the cover. Then I fell to my knees. The rough decking planks scratched my bare skin and shards of wood stuck under my fingernails as I grasped at the boards, trying to stop myself from shaking. My breath came in sharp gasps. Focusing my gaze on my hands and the ice patches on the deck, I slipped into an altered level of consciousness.

So this is diabetic shock. I was naked and cold and lying on the deck in the dark, my brain cut off. My thoughts were oddly clear. *This must be what an acid trip feels like.* Like a piece of thread hanging from a sweater, the ripe truth hung limply, ready to be teased out. I saw the world. The earth spun on its axis, and I saw the Northern Hemisphere tilt away from the sun. Winter storms rotated across the ocean and hit land, their dark clouds pressing against the mountains like a curved finger. Looking more closely, I zoomed in on Washington, easily picking out Crystal Mountain, just northeast of Mount Rainier. *And there's my house just a little way down the valley.* I panned closer and saw my body convulsing on the back deck. I hovered and watched like a spectator, with the narrator's voice dubbed in.

Sure enough. There she is naked and prone, the warm spa gurgling noisily beside her. It would be a shame if she freezes to death right beside such salvation. Can you see her there, too? Do you shudder as she convulses, her body wrapping in on itself like an Origami swan? If only she could wake up, just long enough to drink some orange juice. But if she knew what lay ahead, would she ever have the strength to get up?

Lying there, I could not make myself react to my predicament. The will to survive simply could not shine through the fog in my brain. I flopped on the deck, rubbing my knuckles, kneecaps and hips against the wooden timbers until they were raw, burning my chin.

Frost blossomed on the deck with each exhalation, and the temperature outside my little cabin dropped. Beside my ear, the hot tub jets hummed. If I could get into it, I would be okay. My body should tell me to get up, to go in the hot tub, to warm up. But I wasn't cold. Instead I sweated, hot from adrenaline—my brain's little army.

During diabetic shock, the brain senses a lack of blood sugar, which it relies on for normal functioning. Panicking, it sends out soldiers to fight for more food as if on the savannah chasing a woolly mammoth. My hands shake, my speech slurs, and I get confused. I hadn't noticed those early signs, attributing it to feeling cold and tired from the hard day of ski patrolling. My plan to soothe my muscles in the hot tub had proven disastrous.

The situation became dire. In the deepest part of my brain, the hypothalamus, a battle raged. One part of me wanted to ignore the problem, just ride the wave, and listen to the hot tub and my breath against the frozen wood. It was so peaceful, really. Seeing myself from above, I felt my body growing colder, the light in my mind dimming.

The other part of myself, and this part seemed even farther away, knew I had to do something. First, I needed to stand up. Then I would have to find some sugar. Anything. Orange juice, maybe. Meanwhile, as my face pressed into the deck, I wondered what kind of animal would find me later.

Cougars lived nearby. The neighborhood bisected the wilderness. Herds of elk walked through the streets, poking their big heads into the garbage cans, leaving tracks in the fresh snow.

I lay on the cold deck, my own body exposed to the elements; I'm not sure what made me get up. Perhaps the thought of wild animals scored a point for the survival instinct. I will never know. I only knew that I had to get up and go inside. Just one step at a time.

Sometimes that's all it takes — just one step in the right direction. This time it was towards the house, away from the cold, and closer to the sugar my body needed. Freed from the mental monologue pervasive in lucid moments, I was able to see, with single-minded clarity, the power of one step. And I saw something else, too. Our most vulnerable moments have the power to make us strong.

Raising myself just enough to get my feet beneath me, I realized my hands were frozen, their shapes like claws. On all fours, I found the door handle and twisted the knob, pressing it open with my shoulder. I slumped on the threshold and passed out for a minute. Or perhaps ten, I never knew. The phone rang. Getting up, I pinballed down the hall towards the kitchen. There was a bowl of oranges, nine of them stacked like a pyramid, their flesh pocked with pores. The phone still rang, but I didn't answer. I grabbed an orange and tore it open, juice collecting in the crook of my elbow. I didn't peel it, I just ripped it in half and sucked the juice, grateful somewhere in the back of my mind that I'd chosen ripe, juicy oranges. I slurped the juice until I became aware of my naked stickiness and how close I had come. I was cold and sweaty. Sitting down on the floor, I curled into a ball around the hum of the refrigerator and cried.

Diabetes has been a strange gift of weakness. True strength arises in our darkest moments. Just like when I forced myself up from the deck, making one step towards safety and then the next, I slipped on the toughness of Marty Pavelich and put on a mask of sturdiness and courage that saved my life. I could do the same with John. Diabetics won't tell you this, but low blood sugars are euphoric. They strip your mind of all clutter, forcing you into single thoughts and single actions. They are a terrible contribution to one's psyche. And while I fear others will see this weakness for a character flaw, I know I can use it to my advantage. I can cope with John's ordeal in the same way, by taking small steps toward safety.

15
It Must Be Hard

After two attempts, we finally made it to John's childhood home in Boyne Falls, Michigan to await the results of the ultrasound. John should have had this test back in July, before the pancreatitis, before the infection had a chance to grab hold. The two months waiting for it and uncertainty of what they'd find had shaken me. If the cancer had spread, the transplant was off. We were expecting a call from the Mayo Clinic any day now, and I was trying to occupy myself.

The past two months had vibrated my psyche, shaking loose old phobias and bringing forth new ones. John's doctor couldn't believe he'd beat the infection. His reaction when we'd arrived for the ultrasound last week vindicated my fears. *See, it was serious. Even the doctor never thought you'd live.*

In the living room of his childhood home, there was a post that held John's growth chart in slashes drawn in pen across the grain, each with a date and his initials. I ran my finger across the coarse wood.

Newer marks covered over some of these old ones with the initials of John's children, Evelyn and Andrew, a tapestry of faded and indelible lines, alternating initials JK, EK and AK. Each year John called his sister, Kathryn, to report his children's measurements, and she added the new lines to his post. Andrew was almost as tall as his father now. I touched the pocket of my pants, resisting the urge to pull out my cell phone and check for coverage. They would call when they called.

Instead, I decided to take a walk to clear my head and perhaps find John. I headed out in a well-worn jeep road and made a labyrinthine loop through the woods, where I came to a small building straight ahead of me. Slowing down, I saw John sitting on a bench, hunched over. This was the family mausoleum, where his father was buried.

I whispered his name. There were tears in his eyes when he looked up at me. The crypt's polished marble shone in the light rain. "I'm asking him for help."

I sat beside him and squeezed his hand. My breath steamed out in front of me, and I slowed it down as if I had just run headlong into a quiet church, wanting to match the silence.

"Dad," he said, praying. "I need some help here." His eyes pressed shut in concentration. "Today we find out if the cancer has spread. Maybe you could talk to God about it." He clamped my hand between his two, making it a part of his plea. "I just want to live."

He stood up and walked to the square building and pressed his palms against the smooth wet surface, rubbing them up and down. Dropping his head onto the marble, he let out a nearly inaudible sob.

I put my hand to his back, feeling relieved. He wanted to live. He wasn't giving up. Nor was he ignoring the enormity of the results. Like me, he stood naked and present in the midst of the moment. We could have stayed that way for hours, his forehead pressed against the mausoleum's marble, my palm stroking his back, but I glanced at my watch. It was 4:45. The doctor said she'd call by 5:00. I patted my pocket to make sure my cell phone was still there. It broke the spell.

John seemed to read my mind, even though his back was still turned. "How much time?"

I looked at him and shrugged. "Fifteen minutes."

Dr. Malhi called while John was still outside. He said he wanted to look at the garden, but I knew he couldn't bear the anticipation. This way, I would hear the verdict first and translate it to him, acting as a barrier between the test results and our prayers.

"Mrs. Kircher?"

My hands were shaking. "Yes."

"The test results are in." She spoke in her maddeningly slow cadence.

I glanced up at Kathryn standing next to me in the kitchen. She leaned against the counter, her hands held in front of her face in prayer. I could hear her breathing into the space around her fingers. I sat down at the kitchen table, my knees suddenly warm and wobbly.

"And?"

After all this waiting I wanted everything to slow down. I imagined the clock ticking unhurriedly, water dripping in slow motion from the faucet. If she said the wrong thing, would I faint? I imagined the phone dropping from my hand, Kathryn reaching out for me as I slowly slumped to the tiled floor. The pause in her voice contained a whole lifetime of moments piled up on each other, each one slowly shaking loose from the heap. My mind's eye saw all these moments: John's hand on his father's mausoleum, the wet marble glistening with raindrops; Evelyn's curly hair bouncing down the hallway, her lips forming the word *Daddy*; Andrew carving his skis around a race gate as the snow caught briefly in the air behind him. These snapshots played like a highlight video in my head.

John's face is tilted up to catch snowflakes on his cheeks, glancing up just once before dropping over a lip while the snow flew up over his head. I see him turn towards me as I light my bomb in the back of the helicopter, his new wife, hoping he'd found the right one, a woman who could keep up with him on the slopes. Hell some days he couldn't keep up with me. I see John press against the wind, just like I had at the top of Grubstake Peak the night I faced my own fears. He leans forward, closes his eyes and smiles.

The accumulated momentum of all those moments stopped as I pressed the phone to my ear.

It all came down to this.

"The results of the endoscopic ultrasound," she enunciated each syllable carefully. "Do not show any cancerous cells."

"It hasn't spread?" I said, glancing at Kath.

"That's correct. Your husband is still a candidate for liver transplantation."

Warm blood rushed into my fingers and down my legs. I felt faint and weak.

John's raincoat flashed at the window. I ended the call and walked outside. My cheeks already hurt from smiling.

"I get to live?"

We stood there for a moment, halfway in and out of the house where John grew up, as if lingering in a hot shower because the air outside is too cold, our fragile bodies still longing for the warmth. Later we would walk around in silence, holding hands, tears of relief falling on our raincoats. But right then, we both stood there for a moment, several feet away from another, letting the news wash us clean.

16
Heli-Skiing

A sucker for seductive scenery, I stood in the helicopter prop wash inhaling the landscape. The slope undulated below us, like a white sheet billowing in the breeze. Shards of light illuminated the snow as the sun pricked the sky, reflecting the clouds' movement across the surface. With our backs to the landing zone, the helicopter took off behind us, leaving us alone on the mountain. Bending my knees and bouncing a little, I heard the cold snow squeak beneath my skis. John and I were at Mike Wiegele's, helicopter skiing for a week in the Canadian mountains.

John looked over his shoulder at me and smiled. We'd been dating only two months when he asked me if I wanted to join him heli-skiing. What could I say? Of course I did. Skiing pristine slopes, surrounded by solitude and the crisp beauty of the mountains, heli-skiing soared as the pinnacle of the sport. I'd been in helicopters plenty, and expect for that one trip to the North Cascades when we traversed through the fog, I'd never experienced anything comparable. Like falling in love, heli-skiing drew grandiose conclusions in one's mind, convincing one that life could always be as untouched and pure as a day in the mountains. This was heli-skiing, and life couldn't get any better than this.

I followed John's tracks, spooning his arcs and letting his rhythm dictate mine. It felt good to be here. After fourteen years at Crystal Mountain, one divorce, a few boyfriends, and two summers spent living in the back of my pickup truck, my life had finally fallen into place. In spite of diabetes, and the danger of a solo low blood sugar, I had enjoyed my independence. It was easier than aligning myself with another person, checking my own desires in order to benefit the partnership, or—God forbid—foregoing my life in the mountains to follow someone else's dreams. All a mountain girl really needed was a good dog, a solid truck, and a fat quiver of skis.

When I first met John, and he asked for my phone number, I told him I simply wouldn't date my boss. I tallied all the reasons why I shouldn't go out with him. I didn't want to lose my job or have to move to another ski town when our soiree ran its course. But most of all, I didn't really think he could keep up with me. Now, as I followed his ski tracks down this beautiful unnamed bowl in Canada's wilderness, I thanked the universe for his persistence. In the end, I gave him my number and never looked back.

On either side of our tracks, two rippling ridges rose and dipped offering miles of untracked skiing. We could spend the entire week here and never cross our tracks again. I came over a little rise and laughed at the freedom. John's tracks continued for what seemed like miles towards the bottom of the basin. Picking up speed I moved away from his turns, giving myself just a little more room. All week our guide had taught us to spoon our tracks, leaving room for the next team. But today, I decided to gather a little more joy for myself.

I cut deeper into the powder, the snow billowing over my head and up the bottom of my jacket. I'd forgotten to snap the powder skirt inside the zipper, which prevented snow from blowing up. But I didn't care. I wanted to feel the cold lightness and wrap myself in the snow's giddy embrace. This was true joy with the icy tongues of cold snow licking my primary core. We decided to call this bowl, España, after the two Spanish members of our group.

Earlier in the week we had driven up from Seattle through the Canadian interior to Mike Wiegele's heli-ski operation set deep in the mountains between the Cariboo and Monashee ranges. We'd watched the weather forecast in horror. It rained the previous week, flooding the North Thompson River and stripping the snow low down on the hills. Cows stood in mud to their armpits as we drove past with eyes wide. The bridge to our lodge had nearly been wiped out, and the fiber optic cable bringing Internet to the chalet was destroyed.

Luckily the weather and the snowpack had stabilized, allowing us to fly deep into the high mountains, far above the trees and rain crust. This was it. I couldn't imagine a better skiing experience. All day we lapped pristine bowls and arcing crisp turns against the blue sky. Afterwards, we'd meet in the hot tub with a beer to exchange stories.

Any day in the mountains was better than a day in town. Any day in the mountains, skiing powder with my husband, was better than a day with him in the hospital. It was precisely this memory, this fleeting moment when I'd followed his tracks down this virgin terrain, that I turned to for strength while we waited for the next phase: the organ waiting list and chemotherapy. I would often return here in the weeks and months to come.

In just four years, John, whose smile waited for me at the bottom of the bowl, would be too sick to ski; his liver would fail and his skin would turn yellow. Our years together had been too brief. I longed for time to stretch out like the bowl we called España, like a sheet or an undulating snow-covered slope. When not engaged in a life-threatening crisis, I had too much time for regret. I wanted to reduce the future into manageable chunks.

After John's diagnosis, I looked at a photo from that heli-ski trip, at how my outstretched hand touched the shimmering light illuminating the powder cloud caused by my turn. Snow sprayed onto my chest and tickled my face. Closing my eyes, I completed the scene from that photo. John stood at the bottom

17
Dirty Deeds

"The weather service is calling for a La Niña this winter." My heart lifted as I scanned the computer screen. We had returned from Michigan and were in Seattle, seated at our kitchen table overlooking the lake and waiting to return to Rochester for radiation in a few days. The smooth water rippled slightly under the high clouds.

John nodded. He bit the inside of his cheek.

"So that's good," I said, "I mean at least we'll get some snow." A La Niña weather pattern brought colder and wetter storms to the Northwest. Every year at the beginning of autumn, the weather service released a long-term forecast for the winter. The winter weather outlook had just come out that morning, and now it was one less thing to worry over.

"I guess." John gazed out the window at the lake. Leaden clouds the color of pencils were drawn across the sky and reflected in the placid water. "It can also mean floods and mayhem and more snow than we can handle."

I knew what he meant. Seven years earlier had been a strong La Niña pattern. We had record snowfall, record floods and, at one point, too much snow to run the lifts. High Campbell Chair, an old double that reaches our most expert terrain, couldn't run. Chairs drug on the snow drifts, piling thirty feet above the ground. We ski patrollers dug a trench to make way for the chairs. Too steep for a snowcat, the High Campbell terrain was managed solely by the sweat of employees. We shoveled and scraped the snow away from the lift line each morning, and every night the snow blew back into the trench.

Someone, I can't remember who, had the not-so-brilliant idea of using explosives. Just toss a few bombs in the trench, cratering the new snow, and the problem would be solved. We hoped the built up snow would slide since the slope was certainly steep enough to avalanche. Yet the logic was flawed, and we knew it. An avalanche along the lift line could damage the towers. We usually tossed shots a little lower and to either side of the lift. Never right in the middle.

When it falls out of the sky, snow is soft and pliable and easy to shovel. Over time, snow grains bond together, creating denser slabs that take more effort to move. Add in mechanical forms of work hardening, such as skiing, shoveling, or explosives, and what were once light crystals became a cohesive casing.

After work one particularly stormy day, I stood with Brent, another patroller, on either side of the trench ready with explosives. "Ready?" Brent asked as we fit our igniter onto the fuse. "Three, two, one, pull!"

I pulled the igniter and watched the fuse smoke. Then I tossed my shot into the trough and backed up. We were all a little frisky with this explosive form of problem solving. If only everything could be this easy, just toss a bomb in there and make it all go away. We had radioed the lift operator to stop the chairs a safe distance from our objective. They'd called last chair a few minutes earlier. I looked down the line at the empty chairs swinging slightly in the breeze.

Our shots exploded three in a row like rapid gunfire. The slope stayed put. In our avalanche recordings, this would be indicated by the words "no results" in block letters. It meant our shots didn't cause an avalanche. I inched closer to the lift line. The trough had turned black with soot, but I could see no other discernable change in the depth. "I don't think it worked."

"Sure it did," Brent said. "It's much deeper."

We decided to let it be for the day, saving our backs from the now-common ritual of shoveling after last chair. It wasn't until the next evening when we realized our folly. The bombs had heated the snow just briefly, forming a skein of ice along the surface of the channel. What would have been fairly easy digging now was unbearable. That ice crust became our nemesis. It was impossible to dig through. We would never excavate deeper all season, the sooty snow mocking us with each scoop. Skiers would eventually straighten their boards in that section, letting their bases run along the tall drifts.

Now I looked at John from my place at the computer and considered the winter outlook. For the next few months we would follow this prediction, fingering the details until the first snow fell. We would also wait for news about a liver donor. John's doctors had told him that living donor transplantation was his best chance; he wouldn't have the long wait for a deceased donor. They just had to find a match in time. I looked over at him. "It's going to be a good snow year. I can feel it."

"Ric wants to be the donor. He says it's something he just has to do." John had known Ric for thirty years. They'd met at Big Sky.

"Where has Ric been anyway?"

"Virginia I guess," John shrugged and smiled. Ric had disappeared for a while. That was just how he was, around for a while, then gone without a forwarding address.

We found out later that when he saw the news of Hurricane Katrina, he sold his horses, took all the money from his savings account and headed down there. He filled his horse trailer with a barbeque and plenty of food and other items he thought the victims might need.

Later when he told us about his experience there, he said in his Southern drawl, "Well I just drove on down to Mississippi until I found some people who needed my help. I saw a guy on the street with his head in his hands looking for something and I figured this was as good a place as any," he said. "There weren't any houses left in that area, it was all flat. So I set up my cooking supplies and just started making food for people. Anyone that was hungry could come on by. After a while we had quite a little group stopping by every morning and night." Ric had stayed there for six weeks cooking for the victims.

I held John's hand. "Did he give you his phone number?"

"No," John said. "But he's going to call again tomorrow."

"Does he have a phone number?"

"He has a new cell phone, but he didn't know the number for it."

"He's in Virginia?"

"Why the twenty questions?"

"We just haven't heard from him in so long."

"That's just how Ric is. He blows in and out of my life."

"Well, this is going to take some commitment. It's not like he has to do it."

"You're right," John said and looked outside. "It would be nice to have the chance to opt out." Then he said, "You could."

"In sickness and in health, remember."

John bit the inside of his bottom lip and looked outside. The clouds were thinning, and rapiers of sun cast faint shadows across the porch. He shook his head. "I'm not going to hold you to that."

For a moment we were both silent. The roof shingles ticked loudly through the ceiling as they warmed in the sun.

"Well," I said. "I *am* going to hold you to it." The rays of sun grew crisper, falling in streaks through the slats of the deck furniture. I wanted to believe that Ric would save John. I wanted faith in a ski season full of snow and promises and a way out of this predicament.

~~~

We were back in Rochester, sitting in the radiology waiting room, brushing raindrops from our sleeves. Radiation was a cruel taskmaster, each day growing increasingly more painful.

The beams were transecting John's other organs, including his stomach, which caused pain and nausea — all the symptoms the doctors had warned us about. I felt John slipping away while watching him hunched over and waiting for the next treatment. It scared me to see him this way, but I refused to look away. If he could withstand the treatments, I could, at least, stand beside him and not avert my eyes.

The radiology receptionists were overly kind, and volunteers staffed a refreshment station offering juice and cookies. It felt like a death row inmate's last meal. Many of the patients wore bandanas over their hair loss. John's hair was thinning, and he'd lost more weight.

I'd cut his hair short the night before, evenly shearing the sides and back while leaving the top just an inch longer than the rest. He'd called it "the chemo cut." A few months ago, his hair was still black, which made him look a decade younger. Now, seemingly overnight, thin silver hairs shone in the light.

It had been a week since John had the first appointment with the radiologist, where they had tattooed tiny pinpoints on his abdomen. These would be the bull's eye to guide the beam. "Look I'm tattooed," he'd bragged afterwards, lifting his shirt to show them off. He was still feeling strong then. They were easy to spot; three tiny greenish-blue specks ringed by an angry red.

A nurse called his name. While I waited, a mother arrived with her daughter, who wore a blue bandana around her head. She must have been close to Evelyn's age, all limbs and loose teeth. I wondered if she ever giggled anymore, if her father tickled her at night or if he was afraid he'd break her, or make the nausea return. Sitting down gingerly on the chair while her mother checked her in, the girl fixed her eyes on the bell. Its base was nailed to the wall, and the office made a big deal about ringing it after a patient's last treatment. John would ring it in two days. After his first few treatments, when he was still full of hope and vitality, he looked forward to it. Now he didn't care. Perhaps, even when she'd lost her hair and grown increasingly sick, the little girl still had hope like a pilot light during a power outage that hadn't yet gone out.

John was on the radiation table while the technicians worked behind a window. I'd seen the room during our tour of the facility, when John's hair was still thick. They turned off the fluorescent overhead lights, so the dark room glowed blue from the instrument panel lights and a small lamp from the technician's window. Sometimes, he'd told me, they played AC/DC through the speakers. The walls were insulated and you could hear yourself breathe, so the music offered a nice distraction. On the tour, I had touched the cold metal of the machine with my fingers. *This is the way to kill the cancer.* I wondered if he could smell the flesh burning.

"That one hurt," John said when we left. We walked slowly into the lobby towards the front door.

"One step at a time." I led him slowly across the tiled floor. Therapy had forced this process of reduction, taking it in small chunks.

I told him to wait in the lobby while I got the car. He sat down obediently, like a child or an old man. He glanced around at the others in the lobby and composed himself. "We are going to get through this," I said, leaning close to him.

He placed his palms on his knees, pressing his back against the chair, his motions a staccato rhythm.

Later, in the car he said, "You know who I was thinking about back there? Marty Pavelich. I was just asking myself 'What would Marty do?' And you know what?" He paused. "He'd toughen up. He played hockey with broken limbs, for chrissake. He skied Mad Wolf after his sternum had cracked open. Cracked open all the way." I smiled at the reference to Marty Pavelich, the hockey player who played with broken bones. I knew John was channeling him, and I couldn't think of a better talisman to get him through.

"You're pretty tough, honey."

"Not like Marty. From now on I'm channeling him. I mean, look at the guy. He wouldn't be moaning and griping. He wouldn't be telling anyone about his terrible pain. Probably wouldn't even feel it."

"Hard to say," I said. "I think everyone feels it differently. How do you know that when you feel pain it's the same for someone else?"

"You don't. All I know is that Marty's tough, and that's exactly how I want to be. When it starts to get really bad, I'll just think of him."

"Tell yourself you'll get through it just like he would?"

He nodded. "Just like Marty."

Like Marty. John needed a strategy—a way to get through the pain. Telling himself a story about Marty could relight his hope, and he needed that.

"I've only got two more days of this. They're killing it you know."

"After this, we'll have some time," I said. "It's setting it back. This is a necessary evil." We arrived at the apartment, and I turned off the ignition. "I'll come around."

"I got it. Marty wouldn't need help getting out of the car."

Once inside, I turned on the music; it was still Cat Stevens.

"Too depressing," John said. "Can't we hear something uplifting?"

I had listened to the same lyrics that morning, and it had felt cathartic. Searching for melancholy lyrics that matched my mood was like taking sand paper to my raw heart and building a scab over the most exposed pain. All I wanted was to build an armor of scar tissue. John needed to ignore the pain and I needed to conjure it—to show it I was boss.

"Tell me that poem again."

I sat beside him on the couch and read to him as he rested his head in my lap. I took a deep breath and began. "Do not go gentle into that good night/ Old age should burn and rave at close of day; Rage, rage against the dying of the light." I recited the entire poem, pausing just before the end. "And you, my father, there on the sad height/ Curse, bless me now with your fierce tears, I pray. Do not go gentle into that good night."

John closed his eyes. "That's good." His face was calm; he was gathering his strength around himself like a blanket pulled up to his chin. "Marty would like that."

~~~

John put his head back on the couch, his body sagging. "How do you thank someone for saving your life?" He had just gotten off the phone with Ric, who had left for Rochester to start testing just a few days after we returned home. John rubbed his hands together like he was making a fire.

The surgical team would remove one of the two lobes in the donor's liver and reattach it within John's body. In just a few weeks the liver would grow to its original size in both the donor and the recipient. To be a good match, the donor must be in perfect health, his or her anatomy and blood type must fit with the recipient's, and he or she must have a significant relationship with the recipient.

"He said the doctors made him feel nervous," John said.

"Nervous? Why? God, I hope he passes all his tests."

"Ric is an angel. He really thinks they are going to choose him. He isn't smoking or drinking, and he's lost twenty pounds. His blood type is O positive."

"If they choose Ric, how soon would it be?"

He shrugged. "Christmas, maybe. The kids could come out there. Or we could fly to Michigan for the weekend after the transplant and have Christmas with my family. That would be good."

~~~

My arms were full when my cell phone rang. I put down the grocery bags, opened my purse and found the phone in the bottom of the mess.

"Hi Ric."

"Hey Kim," he drawled. "I just got out of a meeting with the social worker."

"How did it go?" I imagined Ric in the hallways of the Mayo Clinic and how his large combat boots pounding on the tile floor must have raised a few eyebrows.

"They make me feel like I'm crazy."

"What do you mean *crazy*?"

"They just don't understand why I would want to give my liver to John. I told them that I love John. I would do anything for him, but they just nod and write something down on their pad of paper."

"You're not crazy, Ric." I sat down on the step leading to our front door. "Listen to me. They just want to know you're sincere. They don't want you to back out at the last minute."

"Hell no. What kind of a guy do they think I am?"

"They don't know you. They've probably never met anyone like you."

"What if they don't pick me?"

"Then that's just the way it is."

"But John can't wait," Ric said. "Don't they know that the cancer could come back? Don't they realize that this is life or death?"

Tiny pricks hit the back of my throat, and I swallowed them away. "I think they do, but your doctors are worried for your own safety regardless."

"To hell with that. This isn't about my health. I'm just fine. This is about saving John."

Warm tears gathered in my eyes and I leaned forward to let them fall to the ground. "Yes, it is. But let your doctors worry about you. That's what they're supposed to do." Ric did seem like an angel. If he didn't get chosen, he would probably disappear again for a while. I knew this. "Just be honest with the doctors," I said. "Call me later if you need to."

I hung up with Ric and picked up the groceries, trying to ignore the little beast on my shoulder telling me Ric was doomed.

~~~

Evelyn and I sat at the kitchen counter. Her homework was spread out in front of us. We still hadn't heard anything back from Ric, but I was having my doubts. "So how did you and Ashley become best friends?"

"Well," she said, twirling her pencil. "One day we were walking out the door to recess, and I just asked her, 'Do you want to be my best friend?' And she said yes."

"Just like that?"

"She thought about it for a second." Evelyn held her pencil in the air.

"She's a good friend, isn't she?"

"Sometimes we fight though, like sisters. She's sort of like a little sister to me. I'm seven months older than her, you know."

"And taller."

"I'm bigger and older, so I get to boss her around sometimes. But that's not really fair, is it? I mean, just because I'm bigger doesn't mean I should get my way. Actually, she bosses me around sometimes too. So I guess we're sort of even."

"It's nice to have a best friend." I looked at the pages in front of us, shuffled the worksheets and spread them back out on the counter.

"Who's your best friend?" She asked.

"When I was your age, it was Paige. She lived two doors down and I told her everything. She lives in Cincinnati. Then later, it was Alissa. Then Heather. But now," I paused. "Your dad's my best friend."

"Is Ric Daddy's best friend?" She asked. "I mean besides you."

"No. I'm not sure. You'd have to ask him. I guess grownups don't really have best friends. Not the same way kids too. Life gets too busy." I touched the edge of her spelling worksheet. "How do you spell 'once'?"

"O-N-C-E," she said. "Why not? Why don't grownups have best friends? If Ric isn't Daddy's best friend, than why is he giving his liver to him? And if it's not him, does Daddy have another best friend who could give him one?" We had told Evelyn about the living donor process, that several family members and close friends had lined up to donate a portion of their liver to her father. She wasn't stupid; she knew this was no trifle.

"Come here." I scooted her stool closer to mine. "Ric is a very good friend of Dad's. But if he can't donate his liver, someone else will." I looked into her eyes and smiled the tight smile of a preacher ministering to the bereaved. I needed for her, at least, to buy into my story of salvation. If she started poking holes into it, questioning why anyone would even want to risk their own lives to save her father, I didn't think I could bear it. "You know what?"

"What?"

"I like your best friend story. I mean the way you guys met. It's important to have a good story about the beginning of your friendship."

"But it's not really a story. We just sort of decided."

"That's why I like it. You didn't need to think about it. You just asked her and she said yes. And from then on, you guys were like sisters. I think that's great."

"Why's it important to have a good story?"

"Your whole life, people will ask you guys how you met. 'When did you become best friends,' they'll ask. And you can say you've known each other since kindergarten. That one day on the playground you asked her to be your best friend and she said yes. From then on, you were like sisters. It has a nice ring to it, don't you think?" I didn't tell her that, like her best friend story, I, too, had a story keeping me afloat. We were too far into this now to start questioning the efficacy of the doctor's plan. John's only chance of seeing his daughter's next birthday was if a donor came forward to save his life. I couldn't consider the alternative.

"She's my BFF, my best friend forever."

I smiled, relieved she'd let it drop. "I know," I said. "I'm glad."

~~~

"Why don't the doctors tell you about this?" I said. "It's been almost three weeks and you're worse off than you were during the radiation."

"I don't think I can make it," John said as he slowed down, putting his hand out on the wall to steady himself.

I checked my watch. The plane boarded in ten minutes.

"Do you have that baggie?"

I nodded and pointed down the hallway. "There's a men's room just up ahead."

"I can't make it." Tiny beads of sweat had formed on John's upper lip.

I handed him the Ziploc bag, and he crouched beside a garbage can and vomited. The radiation beams had damaged his stomach. This was not the laser beam incision of fantasy novels, where the wound was cut away precisely and the blood vessels neatly cauterized. Instead, his nurse had explained, the interior of his abdomen probably looked more like charred flesh, much like the black pieces of steak stuck to the barbeque grill.

Now John was stooped over halfway down the terminal in the Seattle-Tacoma International Airport on our way back to Rochester for more radiation, and he was vomiting into a plastic baggie.

"Okay," he said standing up. "Got it." He tossed the baggie into the garbage and we continued walking.

"Do you want anything before we get on the plane?" I asked as we walked by an ice cream shop.

I wanted him to at least try. As of that morning, I officially outweighed him. I could have picked him up and carried him the length of the terminal, and for a moment I thought about it—my six-foot tall body cradling him like a child, his head slumping against my arm. Since the radiation, the weight had fallen off of him like a duffel bag slipping from his shoulder. He'd refused the wheelchair, so I knew he'd never let me carry him. But I entertained the thought.

"Do we have time for an ice cream cone?"

I was elated.

He ordered a vanilla cone and sat down on a bench to eat it, while I snuck a glance at my watch.

"You can look at your watch all you want," he said, his mouth slowed by the cold. "This is as fast as I can go. I am getting to that friggin' gate just as fast as I possibly can." He took another bite and looked at me. "This is definitely the hardest thing I've ever done." John was a master with hyperbole.

"I know, honey, just do your best." I thought about asking him what Marty would do, but thought better of it.

"This *is* my best. My friggin' best." He ate one more bite of the ice cream and tossed it into the garbage can. He seemed disgusted. "Let's just do this." His lips disappeared inside his mouth and his nostrils flared.

These waterspouts of anger had grown more frequent. I couldn't blame him, really. Maybe it was a better strategy than the lingering sadness and tears I used as my anger management method. I felt him soften next to me, his short burst of fury already deflating.

"Come on," he touched my hand, and I opened my eyes. "Fifteen minutes right?"

~~~

The next morning the doctors inserted a string of radioactive "pearls" into his nose, through his stomach and up into his bile ducts, where they would stay against the tumor for 24 hours. Afterwards I sat in his hospital room where a protective lead screen separated us. I was not really supposed to be there at all, but the nurse allowed me to stand in the doorway provided I kept the shield between us to protect against the radioactivity.

The surgeons arrived with John, and I asked how the tumor looked. "Hard to say," one said. "I could see where the external beam radiation had been in there. It was pretty—" He made a motion with his hand like opening a jar. "Damaged."

I explained about John's nausea.

"To be expected. The stomach is right there in the same area." He placed his palm on his right side. "He probably has some damage there too."

"Will it get better?"

"Oh sure," he said with a wave of his hand. "Tomorrow morning we will come in and remove it. Let us know if there's anything else he needs."

I wondered if they'd just pull the pellets out right there and if I'd get to watch.

Brachytherapy was an important step in treating bile duct cancer. The Mayo Clinic had transplanted ninety patients with cholangiocarcinoma, thanks to the amazing work of Dr. Gregory Gores. One doctor changed the treatment of this disease and saved lives. If it weren't for him, John would surely die.

"Are you there?" John asked.

I walked over to him. "I'm here."

"Don't get too close." He pushed my hand away. "The radiation." He pressed his hand against his side as if shielding me from it.

"I can be in here for one hour. The rest of the time I'm right in the hallway. I called the living donor people today."

"Oh?"

"I just did an initial interview and someone is going to call me later for a longer one."

"What did they ask you?"

"My blood type, my height and weight, stuff like that." After Ric had been rejected as a potential donor, I'd called, even though Dr. Malhi had said they wouldn't choose a diabetic. It took a few tries before they found the right match, the nurse on the phone had explained, and she'd said not to be discouraged. Watching Ric's experience from afar had been frustrating and cryptic, since they had to protect his privacy. If I was the donor, at least we'd be that much closer to ground zero.

Ric had seemed more devastated than John. After a full week of tests, they had sent him home inconclusively. They had told him he needed to return for three months of "counseling" so they could determine his motivation for donating. It didn't make any sense.

The surgeons said John couldn't wait for a deceased donor, which could be one or two years. The cancer would spread by then. So if he didn't have twelve months, we wondered, did he have three? Each passing day we knew the cancer could start growing again, or perhaps they hadn't gotten it all out. They wouldn't know until the transplant, when they opened him up and looked around with their bright lights pointing right at the wreckage.

Besides having diabetes, my blood type and liver size matched perfectly, and the more I thought about it, the better it seemed. My first interview that morning was encouraging, and I could feel a bulge of hope beginning to build.

I didn't want to get ahead of myself. They told me my chances were slim. Still as I sat in the doorway, watching my husband drift into sleep, I imagined myself as his savior. I traced my finger down my sternum and below my ribs on the right side, where the surgeons would cut me open to take out half of my liver. Then they would sew it into my husband's abdomen. It would start working immediately, ushering the bile out of his system. He could carry a piece of me around with him—not as a burden but as a part of himself. Pressing my fingers down into the place where my liver sat below my ribs, I stroked the skin there, wondering if it could really be that simple.

18

K2 Face

Gary, a fellow ski patroller, and I stood at the top of Chair 5. The old, blue chairlift had stopped running, and the lift mechanics had called for ski patrol. We needed to evacuate the chair. The wind blew a sharp blast across the slope, and I looked up at the loaded chair. Two skiers crouched together in the seat above me, protecting their faces from the flying pellets of ice. It was a busy Saturday, and the line below them was completely full.

Below the off-load ramp to my left, inside a narrow, drafty, plywood-walled room, the ski patrol kept one ear on the radio, waiting for directions to the next big crisis.

On most days inside that tiny room, I looked around at the veteran patrollers, ones with years of skills and a certain grizzled charm, and felt inexperienced. Their inside jokes and war stories flew over my head. *Remember the time we dropped that snowcat down Powder Bowl and it rolled all the way to the bottom of the basin? What about the night we searched for Reynolds in the avalanche debris at the bottom of Rock Face? Or the time Niagra's slid to the ground?*

I was only nineteen years old, half their age, and fresh, and hopeful, and terrified. Looking back on it now, I wonder how I ever got involved with the ski patrol. Why hadn't I followed in my parents' ski boots and become a ski instructor, teaching young kids the thrill of the ride? What led me to think I could be calm in a crisis, offering some kind of solace to the injured, perhaps even save a life when it came right down to it?

Outside at the top of the chairlift, patrollers paired up and put on their harnesses. Gary grabbed an evacuation device and slung it over his shoulder. We were to head to tower 9 to evacuate the chairs hanging above K2 Face. A steep, cross-fall line run, K2 sliced through tall trees all the way to the bottom of the chairlift, where two snowmobiles blocked the entrance to the line. The mechanics had given it their best shot, but couldn't get the old chair started again. The ski patrol would have to evacuate the riders who'd already been hanging for nearly an hour.

We were in the middle of an "ice-age" — that terrible weather pattern after a rainstorm when the temperatures drop and the skies clear, leaving the slopes icy and slick. Off the groomed slopes, the chunks of snow that had rolled down during the previous rain had now turned to coral reef, and threatened to knock a ski off and send a skier flying. The slopes that were groomed or skied flat were equally treacherous. K2 was side-slipped smooth during the rain and was now a near-vertical ice rink. One mistake and a skier would slide all the way to the bottom.

Every year before the season started, ski patrollers practiced evacuating chairlifts. In the early years, I worried over the complex rope system, checking and rechecking my harness and belay device. I didn't quite trust myself. How could I, a college freshman, be trusted to lower another person out of the chair? What if I dropped him? We threw a rope over the cable, then pulled up a chair-like device, which the riders fit around themselves. Then we lowered them down to the ground. We had always practiced on the beginner chair, on a gentle slope. Now Gary and I stopped at the top of K2 and assessed our assignment.

A college student during the week, I had chosen ski patrolling for the free skiing. Now, in the middle of my second year on the patrol, I was charged with safely evacuating a line of stranded riders. I'd done it in practice, but this was for real. Furthermore, the slope below me glistened with ice. I wasn't even sure the riders could ski it once lowered down. I looked up at two riders who shivered in the cold. "We're going to get you guys down, okay?"

The man nodded. Or perhaps it was merely an exaggerated shiver. A gust of ice-laden wind skimmed the top of the slope.

I looked at Gary. "Can you throw the rope over while I get the device ready?" I knew my limitations, and one was my aim. We needed to throw a heavy ball with a piece of long string attached to it over the cable. Connected to that piece of string was the end of the heavy evacuation rope. Knowing my aim, the ball would most likely end up in the rider's lap, so I offered to ready the device while he did the precision work. I loved ropes and harnesses and the thrill of high-angle rescue. I imagined belaying toboggans, building anchors around stout trees and using ropes and pulleys to safely reach the bottom. But the life-saving stuff made me nervous.

Years later, holding vigil over my husband as we waited for a liver, I could use the skills I'd acquired in the mountains. I knew now how to stop major bleeding and take vitals. I was no longer afraid of sickness or injury, these fears rubbed away by the repeated washings of fragile bodies on the brink of death. Watching the nurses in his room as they took his temperature and blood pressure, I understood their movements, as their fingers glided over the gauges, registering a high temperature in the sharp intake of breath. Most importantly, I'd learned how to keep myself from flying into a panic when crisis struck.

Gary tried to toss the ball over the cable, but the wind caught it and blew it off course. Opening the evacuation device bag, I quickly realized that anything I set down on the icy slope would take off towards the trees below. I used my shovel to chip a small ledge into the ice on which to rest the wooden seat we would use to lower the stranded riders. That's when I noticed Gary had taken off his skis.

Gary had been on the patrol for ten years, an old-timer in comparison to me. I'd seen him work first-aid scenes and admired his skills. In the face of pain and injury, he had a confidence that I envied. It would be years before I felt comfortable in the presence of other's pain, before I could rely on my practiced skills to get me through difficult situations. First-aid skills took training and exposure, and judgment was borrowed from peering into death's face and swallowing hard against the dark certainty of it. Only serious accidents could wear away at a new patroller's inexperience. Confidence came with looking the danger in the eye and still taking action.

Before I had a chance to warn Gary about the slick slope, he tossed the ball again. Surely he'd noticed the ice. I watched the edges of his boots as he raised his throwing arm. His orange Langes kicked up shards of frozen snow. The ball left his arm in a beautiful arc, rising higher and higher towards the cable, the trailing string like a comet against the metallic sky. I thought for sure it would make it. The trajectory, the aim, the trailing string, all pressed forward towards the cable in a graceful sweep. The ball was going over.

And it would have. But the end of the string, where I tied it to the thicker rope, wrapped around Gary's leg. He must have stepped into a loop when he threw the ball. The coils of rope I had carefully laid out now slipped down the slope in long loops. The thrown ball brought the closest loop up around his ankle and tugged. The ball fell short of the cable, and Gary went down.

A black diamond run, K2 is a formidable slope under the best of conditions. With the fall line angling towards the trees on the left, any uncontrolled slide would push a skier into them. When skiing K2, I usually started far to the right to avoid the threat of the thick timber in case I caught an edge and slid.

When Gary fell under the lift line, he was already well to the left, positioned above the thickest trees. In a second, Gary's left Lange lost contact with the snow and flew into the air. He landed on his back, his hands grasping at the air. He slid quickly by a loop of rope, and I yelled out for him to grab it, but it was no use. His hands splayed out on the ice and his body rotated until his head pointed downhill. Gary was out of control, sliding fast on a steep, icy slope towards the trees.

I raised my hands to my head and watched. I must have yelled at him to turn around and try to self-arrest. The spectators on the chairlift must have flinched, watching the flailing man spin helplessly towards his demise. Sucking in a deep breath, I held it until he hit the trees. His body thudded hideously, and he yelled out.

I skied down to the accident. Covered in fir needles, with thick branches hugging his body to the trees, Gary lay crumpled against the tree trunk. With skiers yelling from the chairlift and other patrollers arriving quickly, the scene was chaotic. I leaned over Gary and touched his shoulder. I would have to get in there and really assess his injuries, but first I had to get over the nausea. He winced and told me he'd broken his leg. First we had to get him away from the tree, and then we'd look at his leg. Still on the precarious slope, once again I pulled out my shovel to hack into the ice to form a platform. I needed another moment out in the fresh air before I committed myself to the gruesome task. Besides, we'd need a flat spot for the backboard and toboggan already on their way.

In tremendous pain, Gary yelped when he tried to help us. "Don't move." I touched his shoulder gently, and then put my hand on his head. I reached in further. With an obvious airway, he was breathing, so we decided to bring in the equipment before moving him again. Another patroller checked his spine and held his head while I moved around below the tree trunk to get a look at his face. Ashen and grimacing, his face told the best story, and I cringed.

A dark, oily feeling welled up from my stomach and I had to swallow to keep myself from crumpling. For a moment I

wondered if he would die right there. His impact with the tree
could have caused internal injuries. A ruptured spleen could kill
him in minutes. We would pull a dead body from the trees while
several hundred skiers looked on, my own mind losing control.
It would be so easy to let my mind flash forward into a worst-
case scenario, my arteries pounding against my skull, my breath
growing quick and shallow. I had been on scene of minor
injuries such as twisted knees and dislocated shoulders, but this
was my first major. And I didn't want to panic.

I thought of how Gary would respond if I were injured.
He'd breathe evenly and speak in calm tones, breaking the
rescue down into recognizable steps. First, he would call
Dispatch and report the situation, portraying a sense of control
and competence. Then, he would check my ABCs, fixing
immediate threats to life. Next, he'd work down my body to find
my injuries, splinting them to prevent further injury. Within
fifteen minutes, my "golden quarter" of rescue, Gary would
figure out the situation without a single thread of panic.

"Gary," I leaned closer to the trunk, allowing the stiff
branches to grab at my jacket. "Gary, look at me." Crouching
lower, I turned my head so he could see me without moving. I
thought of what he would do in this situation. A branch had
scratched his cheek, sending a trickle of blood onto the snow.
Tiny droplets glistened on the needles of the trees. "You're going
to be okay."

"It's my leg. It's broken."

"I know it is. That was quite a ride you took."

He asked me what happened.

"You got caught in the rope." I glanced around the corner
of the tree and saw the toboggan being lowered to us. His face
was so white, I told him to take a deep breath. He followed my
instructions. Realizing that he was listening, I repeated them,
leading him through several deep breaths until his color started
coming back. He looked up at me just as the toboggan arrived,

locking his gaze to mine for an instant. I calmed down and let my first-aid protocols flood my memory.

Carefully extricating him, we pulled Gary away from the tree's embrace so we could better tend to his injuries. Above his right knee, his leg bent at a sickening angle, his femur obviously broken. Figuring I owed it to him since he was my evacuation partner, I volunteered to stay at his head, keeping him from moving it until he was securely strapped to the backboard.

The group worked quickly. One patroller attached the splint to Gary's boot and fit the adjustable arm into his crotch. Kneeling behind Gary's head, I kept my hands in place and spoke calmly into his ear while keeping him from moving his neck. Not sure where my sudden comfort came from, I settled into it. "This is going to hurt for a minute, then it'll get better."

The longest bone in the body, the femur can withstand great force. But once broken, the strong quadriceps muscles pull the shattered ends back together, rubbing nerves and blood vessels against the saw-like bone. A patient with a femur fracture can bleed out internally in a matter of minutes. A traction splint pulls the bone fragments apart, saving the femoral artery and relieving much of the pain.

"Ready?" The patroller at the foot asked. He would pull traction from his end, while the others held Gary's arms to keep him from sliding.

Since I controlled his head, I nodded and told him to pull. I reminded Gary to relax. He opened his eyes and smiled slightly. I felt a surge of self-importance, thinking maybe I was gaining experience here.

Then Gary screamed, and his face strained against the anguish. With a loaded chair of stranded skiers above us and several patrollers working on the steep slope just uphill, I knew we needed to get out of there quickly. Another slider could smash into us, and Gary needed to get to a hospital. "Pull," I looked up at the patroller at his feet.

"I am!"

"Pull harder." I kept my voice calm and looked again at Gary. A sharp smell of wet wool and fear rose up from him. "Just relax and let us do the work. Don't try to resist. Just breathe."

Gary relaxed the muscles in his face and breathed out.

I coaxed him a little more. "Now take a deep breath in."

"That's it." Gary's voice had changed, the usual calm returned. "Much better."

"Okay lock it off there." I looked at the patroller at his feet, who strapped the splint in place. I stayed at his head while we fastened him to the backboard and put him in the toboggan, all the while reminding him to breathe and stay calm. Each time he listened, he loosened his grip a little more. Watching this transformation, I, too, stepped into a groove that propelled me towards my next right action. By treating a medical emergency in shorter strides, each one adding up to the whole, I could get through it. Place a strap here, check a pulse there, attach the oxygen mask and ask the patient to relax—I provided medical care in small, distinct moves.

The remainder of the rescue skidded by. We strapped Gary to a backboard and applied the oxygen mask. He groaned and flinched, and each time I leaned in close and spoke directly. It seemed to calm him.

Once his head was strapped down, I could finally stand up. He looked contained there on the backboard, his arms across his chest like a mummy, his eyes half closed. My skis were put together and stuck in the softer snow beside the tree. Someone had gathered them and put them out of the way. There was much I still needed to learn about scene management, little tricks to keep an accident from spiraling out of control. Loose skis and equipment could fly down the hill, injuring a caregiver or another skier below.

As I put my skis back on and sidestepped up to help with the chair evacuation, I realized I'd learned something. In the face of another's pain, I could offer comfort. I could slow down and quell my anxiety. By taking it in small steps, I could work through each one, focusing on only that task. My "golden quarter" was solidifying in my mind, reminding me that during a crisis I needn't get through the entire thing in one breath, instead work through incrementally — only what the mind could absorb. In that way, I had helped Gary and now I would do the same for John.

19

Stress vs. Strength

I looked out the window of our Crystal Mountain apartment at the snow falling in large flakes. Just a few weeks earlier, the slopes had been bare dirt. We had waited for snow as we waited for word on the donors. Everything hung in the air like dust suspended in a beam of sunlight. Another week would go by and still no change in the forecast, and still no word from Mayo about the donors. For them it was just another week at work. The receptionist would ask for John's Mayo Clinic number, which she would type into her computer before telling me there was nothing new. After I'd been rejected because of my diabetes, several others had called, and now we waited to hear who'd be tested next.

The forecast had not changed either. A storm brewing out in the northern Pacific approached tantalizingly close, but was pushed north by the stubborn high pressure system circling over our heads. For non-skiers, the winter delay must have been nice. Normally the lights dimmed on the city by November, bringing a gloom that remained until spring. But that year, winter sun slanted across the sky, brightening the evergreens and casting long shadows on the lake. The local weathermen smiled through their make-up at the five day forecast full of sunny icons like egg yolks while John and I had grumbled.

But all that had finally changed with the first promises of winter. Funny how snowfall creates amnesia. Watching the promised inches pile up, I found it hard to remember the earlier drought. The stubborn high pressure had finally moved on, and several storms lined up back-to-back waiting to slam into the

Cascades like ocean swells on a beach. Mother Nature dumped four feet of snow, which was enough to open up the lifts and fully occupy me for the first blessed five days. For hours at a time I didn't think at all about John's illness, or the wait for the donors, or my cell phone in my parka.

But then the forecast called for a "pineapple express" to bring rain from Hawaii. I refused to believe it. Maybe Mt. Rainier would block us, which it often did, and perhaps the moisture would go south or north, or miss us entirely. Maybe it wouldn't be as bad as they predicted. The meteorologists called for eight to ten inches of rain that would usher in floods and landslides and a total annihilation of the snow we had accumulated. John's prediction had been right; the La Niña wasn't bringing what we needed. Back to square one—an early season blessing turned into regret. That's what it felt like when Ric and I were rejected.

It rained hard. Every steep slope avalanched, leaving our snowpack in deep piles at the bottom. What didn't slide merely shrunk like Shrinky Dinks those plastic shapes that, when heated, lost over half their size. When the rains started we closed the ski area and waited.

A group of snowboarders hiked up the peak across from the ski area, intending to ride before the rain turned all the snow to mush. They planned on traversing to Chinook Pass, spending two nights in the snow along the route. But they never made it back, and after a few days, the rescuers called off the search.

That day when we returned to our Crystal apartment, having learned the fate of the snowboarders, John said, "Sometimes people don't make it out alive."

I had assured him that we'd find a donor. But he was right. Some people died from cancer. Some transplant hopefuls didn't make it long enough for a suitable organ. Sometimes skiers who set out to have a good time, ended up lost in the snow or buried in avalanches. Fickle and shifting, hope danced in and out of our lives. Mayo would call a new donor, and our faith would soar. A few days later, he or she would be rejected depositing us at the bottom of the slope like an avalanche.

Now, six inches of snow had fallen already and I watched it out the window as it dropped thickly on the driveway. I loved the first snowfall that covered over all the stumps and holes and fallen limbs, like icing a lumpy cake. It was easy to pretend this was a new start. There was always hope in the next snowstorm, always the chance for redemption. Storms brought danger too, and new snow could turn hazardous or mushy or get washed away entirely. But the embedded promise of each new storm gave me hope. Once again the forecast models showed storms with lines tightly squeezed together, carrying moisture on their path across the ocean. Within those lines lay salvation. They carried newly fallen snow, arranged flake by flake across the barren hillsides, rendering them smooth and skiable.

I walked outside and kicked my boots through the snow and imagined the slopes turning white again. This time it would stick around. These flakes would remain until spring, having morphed into rounded shapes, perhaps stuck together like peanut butter and compacted from all the weight of the future snowfalls riding on it. Depending on the weather the next few weeks, these crystals would either round out and become strong or degrade and become brittle. While they made up the surface in their stompable, packable form, their future depended entirely on the temperature of the next few days. If it was too cold and this snowfall was left alone on the hill, without further snow to insulate it, it would rot out and become something else entirely—tiny Styrofoam boxes that would not form a snowball no matter how hard you squeezed. If repeated layers of snow lay down on top of this, it would form the long forgotten base that behaved itself and thus never got noticed. It would be the foundation that the rest of the pack relied on, interfacing between the living world of dirt and grass and rocks beneath and the white, magical snow on top. Or it might just melt entirely.

Like the forecast models that promised snow and the radars that blinked bright greens and reds, I had to believe that a new donor would emerge soon, brought to us across this vast ocean of doubt. I would scan the forecasts and keep my eye to the sky. I'd wait and watch for the promise of snow.

On the chairlift I sat with two other skiers—guys wearing powder boards and talking about their run.

One leaned over and looked at me. "Is Campbell open yet?"

"Opened about thirty minutes ago."

"Sweet."

"Just finished a control route up there, and it's really good."

"Which way'd you come down? We were thinking either Powder Bowl or Bear Pits."

They'd probably spent the week checking the forecast and the website, and by the time the weekend came around, they were trembling with longing. Standing in line at the bottom before the lifts open, they had planned their day and wanted to be in line when the upper lifts opened so they could ski the best snow. It had just snowed eight inches on top of the seven inches we had yesterday. The skiing was good, but if you wanted untracked powder you had to get there first.

"I looked into Powder Bowl. It looked good. I couldn't even see any tracks from yesterday, I think it blew in there pretty smooth."

"Thanks." We got ready to unload as we approached the top.

"Also, Southback'll open in about forty five minutes."

"Dude."

We were three days into this storm cycle. In eighteen years patrolling it always went like this. When the snow finally came, it didn't stop, and an early storm could last for days and dump several feet of snow. Earlier that morning, I hiked the Throne, a peak overhanging a beginner run, and placed explosives in the chutes along the ridge. Thanks to the cold temperatures, the snowpack remained stable considering the amount of snow we'd had. Warming always weakened the snow. At the end of my route, the powder flew over my waist. As my skis brushed the snowpack, a blast of tiny snowflakes fluttered into my face, and filled my nose and mouth. It was more than just the bliss of powder skiing. While almost enough to forego a lifetime of other, more mundane, goals, the adrenaline rush of powder wasn't the only thing keeping me here. The mountains, with their changeable nature, could bring bountiful joy one minute and devastating terror the next. A slope, filled several feet high with glistening snow crystals, could avalanche, destroying trees and anything else in its way. The mountains taught me how to capture a fleeting, joyful moment and never let it go.

Snowfall could do the same thing. My husband loved snow, and his giddiness was contagious. Walking through a parking lot, he'd suddenly scrape the snow off a parked car, forming it into a snowball and make a game of it. "See how many times you can hit the letter S in that sign," he'd say. Or, "Try to hit the trunk of that tree; you have five tries." He had an entire lexicon dedicated to snow, different words that revealed not just its uses or its physical characteristics, but his attitude towards it. Really wet snow, he termed chunky rain. When it came down lightly he christened it spitting snow, a little more and he'd call it chicken dandruff. Orographic snow fell hard when the mountains rung out any moisture left in the clouds as they passed by, and often it dumped then but only for brief periods. Those he called stormlets. Then there was real snow, like this that fell now. It could snow dinner plates around here and when it really got going it snowed ten-year-olds.

I got off the chair at the top and wiped the snow that had accumulated in my lap. I knew where to find a stash of undisturbed snow — a place hidden by trees, a small opening barely wide enough for one skier. This time I would wiggle through the opening and float down, turning on the pillows of snow, and emerge into the brightness below feeling a little lighter. Powder skiing could so wholly consume me that, for just a moment, it crowded out everything else.

I found the pristine entrance through the branches and squirreled my way through. I tapped my ski pole on a tree with its limb pinned down by snow, and it sprang to life, shaking its heavy burden. The snow had momentarily stopped and light sabers of sun slanted across the slope, illuminating individual snowflakes resting on the slope like shards of glass. A small snowball had slid down the nearly smooth surface, like a finger running through condensation in the shower. Even the trees across the valley were covered in white as if an eraser had removed the top layer of each branch.

I pushed off in the powder. Like sinking straight down into cold cotton balls, I rose up on each turn just enough to see. It was wide open here now. Again I turned and the snow sprayed on my legs, my neck, my face, like a million tiny fairies beating their wings against me. It filled my mouth, and I had to chew to breathe. My neck tingled, and I burrowed my chin deeper into my wet collar to keep from inhaling snow through the gaps in my teeth. *This is good. If I could just stay here, right here, everything could be okay.* Turning deep inside the snowpack, I transformed the clean surface of the snow into a frozen wake. I heard only a soft rushing like water running in an insulated room and my breath in my ears. Cold sap from the alpine fir trees filled my nose, like I just opened a freezer full of Christmas boughs and inhaled the frozen mist.

Once you arced a few good turns in deep powder it became an addiction made more intense by its scarcity. If only this could go on forever. I wanted the slope to rotate like an escalator, to descend down into the cool, light snow on each turn. I wanted it to keep snowing and fill over my tracks behind me so I could come back here and do it again. One run like this could haunt a skier, all week checking the forecast for the next big storm and making her line up before the lifts open to be the first. But once tracked, snow changed forever, losing its soft fluffy nature and becoming work-hardened. Those turns stabilized the snowpack against avalanches. Working snow helped it withstand the harsh rigors of stress and weather. It strengthened under stress, much like the human intellect. Like tracks through a once-naïve enthusiasm, life had a way of hardening a person.

Once a run opened, the patrol depended on the skiing public to transform it from a powdery slope into moguls. Sitting around looking pretty only made snow more hazardous. Like a hothouse flower, frail and compromised, an untouched slope grew weaker over time. We needed people like the two I'd ridden with earlier—their enthusiasm making the slopes safe. Perhaps if I saw them again I could tell them about my secret spot, a little slot through the trees that most people never found. But then again, I thought as I poled down to the chairlift at the bottom, perhaps I'd keep it for myself. Holding onto my run, keeping those turns to myself, maybe I could deposit them in a box for safekeeping and take them out again when I needed them later.

20

Bystanders

"Are you sick Uncle John?" Jack asked after we gathered around the dinner table for Christmas. My brother JD and my sister BG (seems I was the only one without initials for a name) joined us with their children. We'd hoped to be in Rochester on Christmas—John recovering from surgery. The search for a donor was taking much longer than anticipated, so instead we celebrated at my parent's log cabin near the ski resort. Since our first Christmas dinner John had always carved the meat. Tonight, however, he couldn't do it, so my dad had filled in. I'd overheard my parents tsk tsking over his condition.

"Yeah buddy. I am." He pushed his green beans around on his plate and cut into his roast before leaning in closer to Jack. "But I'm going to get better."

I fingered a piece of silver ribbon that wound around the candlesticks on the table. Dark green garland and red berries highlighted the silver and china.

"Snow," Jack pointed out the window. The forecast had called for more snow that night. Tomorrow the kids would make snowmen and go skiing.

"Here's to Harold," John raised his wine glass. BG's husband, Harold, had called the Mayo Clinic and put himself on the donor list.

Harold smiled. "This is what family does." We all touched our glasses. Our family had grown since John's first Christmas with us, adding husbands and children. The threat of losing one of our own made our bond even stronger.

"And if, God forbid, Harold isn't a suitable donor," my brother, JD, said. "Then I'm next." He reached for his wife, Angie's, hand. "That is if you want my liver." He sipped from his wine glass and wiggled his eyebrows.

"Me too, man," Whitney, Angie's brother, said. "Count me in."

I held John's hand under the table, my heart brimming. It wasn't just me; my family loved him too. I glanced over at John's other hand, which rested on his water glass. Tiny beads of condensation glistened in the candlelight. I wanted to tell them all how proud I was. I knew my sister or brother would give me a kidney if my diabetes got bad enough. My mother would have laid down on a train track for me if she thought it would save my life. But my husband's life? They knew what I did: John was part of me now and their generosity validated it. I wanted to thank them, but the syrupy air put a stopper in my throat.

~~~

"I just wish we had a definitive answer one way or the other," I told my mother into the phone, as I stood on the side of Downhill, an intermediate groomer.

"What do they think the spot is?"

"They don't know. I talked to BG this morning and tried to tell her not to worry. But how can she not?" It was snowing again and the flakes dropped onto my bare hand.

"Oh," Mom said. "My baby girls are both so worried about their husbands," she said, falling into the third person as if discussing her life with someone who wasn't intimately connected with it. "My poor babies."

"Why can't the Mayo just choose someone?" I asked. "Don't they understand this is life and death?" I anchored the tail of my right ski into the snow and rested on it.

"I think they do, honey."

"And now Harold's in limbo. They say this is for his sake, but they just sent him home and now what is he supposed to do?" They'd found a spot on Harold's lung during his work-up. It wasn't cancer; we knew that. But they didn't know what it was.

"They gave him antibiotics."

"I wish they would start testing a new donor, just in case." I knew I was whining. "They're just wasting time. I called yesterday and spoke to John's coordinator. She says that they can work up only one donor at a time because that's all the staff they have. So it's a matter of money. But I'll tell you," I said, tugging at my soggy braids poking out beneath my hat. "You should see the expensive marble floors in the lobby at the Clinic. And the art on the wall." I sounded petty, and I knew it. Mom wouldn't judge my complaints. "Maybe they could spend some of that money on actual doctors and nurses. The people that are going to save my husband's life." I looked around to see if anyone heard me, the maniac crying into her cell phone on the side of a ski run. I must have looked pathetic.

"It must be so hard to be patient."

"It is." Someone skied by and I tucked myself behind a tree. "Course that's all I can do, isn't it? I mean, what choice do we have?"

"It's okay to get frustrated, Kimmy." Mom wanted to give me permission to be angry, but she didn't need to.

"John tells me that too. He thinks I should get angry more often. That it will help me get things out."

"Maybe you should go to a private place and just let it all out."

I could imagine finding a quiet group of trees on the ridge at the top of the ski area and having a good cry. Not screaming, just a gentle weep — more like bloodletting. I told her I had to go.

After the conversation with my mom, I felt a little better, almost lighter. Maybe releasing my frustration could be healthy. Another pair of skiers went by and I stood still — just a red and black blur in the corner of their eyes.

John would often ask me why I never got angry at anything. Always calm and patient, taking life's setbacks in stride. Maybe I'd been kidding myself. BG once asked me, "Why did you get all the patience and I got all the neuroses?" She was just more honest with her feelings, while I had learned to sweep things under the rug.

Like life on a moving sidewalk, conflict walked past me and I observed it, never getting too attached. I just set my eyes straight ahead, hardly ever pivoting around to watch these moments, content with whatever came my way. I would have made a fine Buddhist.

Then I met John. My inner peace, so carefully cultivated before, was set aside in favor of his enthusiastic embrace of life. John didn't stand by and watch life as it moved past. He reached out for it and grabbed large handfuls. Before I met him, I never yearned for anything— disappointment could lurk beneath every desire. But then again, before John, maybe I never had anything worth fighting for. It had started to snow, and I watched the small flecks drift slowly onto the shoulders of my jacket.

A call came over the radio. A skier below me was injured and I responded, saying that I was close by and would check it out. Two skiers collided and at least one of them was hurt with a possible leg injury. Skiing down the run, I scanned the slope for the accident, looking for a group of people huddled together in a mass, hunched over someone.

Arriving at an accident, a great deal can be determined in the first thirty seconds by looking at the bystanders—was the person seriously injured? Had he just twisted a knee or had his heart stopped beating? Was his wife checking her watch or timing his labored breaths? Other EMTs might go right to the injured skier, but I looked first at the witnesses. There could be a woman, mute and distraught, looking down at the snow. Her husband might be laying there, his leg twisted beneath him. He could be clutching his side in pain from internal injuries. After all, each patient belonged to someone, and his pain might draw out her own like a thread tying them together.

A woman in a light blue ski suit stood near the side of the trail and waved her arms. The chairlift rumbled overhead and I noticed riders leaning out, watching the clustered group. A man was on the ground, his hand on his head as if trying to keep his hat from falling off. The woman looked relieved when I arrived as if my presence somehow eased her responsibility. As if she could ever stop fighting for the man lying in the snow.

I nodded to her and asked if I could help. I stepped into my caregiver persona easily now, my years on the mountain a force of accumulation propelling me forward.

"My husband's hurt."

A younger man sat nearby clutching his leg. I quickly assessed the injuries and called for backup. The woman described the sound of the two skiers colliding, saying the loud noise made her sick. She knew her husband was terribly injured.

I understood her concern. A wife knows these things. When the equipment arrived, I affixed an oxygen mask to the man's face and let another patroller take over with the injured leg. "Your husband's going to be okay," I told the wife.

As my mouth formed the words, I tried to memorize the motion of my lips. I wanted to hear a doctor say these same words to me.

She clutched her hands in front of her and grasped at the fingers of her gloves. "Do you think so?"

We put the man on a backboard and loaded him into a toboggan. "Yes. I do." I looked at the patient's face; his color seemed fine and he responded to verbal commands. Instinct told me he'd be okay. But was that enough? Did I want John's doctors to claim victory based on a fleeting instinct?

I put my hand on her arm, close to her elbow. "We'll see when we get to the aid room. Sounds like he was hit pretty hard. We're doing everything we can for him."

She looked at the snow.

I knew these weren't the most comforting words from a caregiver, but it was all I could offer. The toboggan driver stood between the front handles and nodded towards me to release the anchors holding it in place on the slope. I watched the patient recede, as the wife in the blue jacket followed closely by, and tried to plug the fear—not for her, but for myself—rising out of my chest.

~~~

Outside our Crystal apartment, the streetlight illuminated the falling snow. It was dumping again. I gazed at our SUV through the dining room window and could see that at least two inches of snow had fallen on the hood since we got home. Snow sliding off the roof had covered nearly all the windows in our first floor apartment, obscuring our view and forming a protective cocoon.

"What's happening for the next two weeks?" John asked. He was watching the democratic debate. Wolf Blitzer's monotone covered the room like cream cheese.

"It's supposed to snow." I stood up from the forecast models on the computer. John lay on the couch a few yards away.

He sighed. "I mean at the Mayo Clinic."

"Oh." I walked into the kitchen. "Does spaghetti sound good tonight?"

"Not really."

"Well. What does?"

"Nothing," he turned down the volume of the debate. Hillary Clinton was talking about health care. "I can't stand her."

"Do you want me to make anything?"

"I should eat. But I'm just not hungry. You know I don't even know what it feels like to be well anymore."

"I could fix you a smoothie."

"Not another smoothie."

"Okay," I said taking a deep breath. "What then?"

John shifted on the couch. He seemed agitated. "What the hell are they doing for the next two weeks?" His eyes were glued to the TV. "Are they just going to let me rot here while Harold goes on antibiotics? Aren't they going to start working up another donor?"

Doctors at the Mayo Clinic had told Harold the spot on his lung wasn't cancer. They had given him antibiotics, but figured it was old scar tissue—nothing serious for Harold, but it could pose a problem for John.

"I don't know, honey. I wish I knew. They called Whitney." My brother's brother-in-law, Whitney, had stayed true to his word and put his name in the queue.

"And?"

"He got a blood test this week. So we'll see."

John turned the volume back up. Hillary smiled broadly at the camera.

"How about eggs?" I opened the cupboards and looked in. "Rice and beans? Cream of mushroom soup? Grits?"

I leaned my head on the cupboard door and willed myself to be patient. I wanted to hit the fast forward button and watch my image hurry through to the next scene where I'm frying eggs at breakneck speed and handing the plate off to John while he frowns. He would look briefly at it before putting it down. Faster than you can blink your eyes, I'd pick it up and scrape it into the garbage.

There is a moment of exhausted sagging in which I place the back of my hand on my brow. I am holding a spatula and it feels very Lillian Gish in a silent movie star sort of way. She's at the end of her rope. The bad guy has lashed her to the rail lines and she can feel the train coming. It's vibrating through her back. She panics for a moment, but it's useless. It's too late. He's not going to come and save her this time. The steam rises ominously from the train as it rounds the bend. It's all over for her. What's worse, the bad guys are getting away.

I craned my head around the corner and watched the television for a moment. Senator Obama spoke about how the close race between he and Hillary had galvanized the country. He seemed so poised and polished. I wouldn't have wanted to be Hillary up there sitting next to such unblemished perfection. The camera panned the audience where someone held a small sign that read "Yes, We Can."

"How about dinner? Any ideas?"

I think of the damsel on the tracks. It's all over. She's having a synching spell. The hero is nowhere to be seen. The music chimes the suspense chords. The bad guys are getting away with the loot. Suddenly the hero appears as if out of nowhere, swashbuckling in that irresistible Errol Flynn sort of way.

On the television the camera panned across the stage; Obama sat stick straight and Hillary seemed to hunch forward.

The hero unties the damsel just in time. Her large eyes bat at his handsome capability. The chord resolves to the tonic. The movie-going public is released once again into the predictability of the real world.

I walked back to the cupboard and waited for John's response.

"Grits?" He said.

I relaxed. "Grits it is." I opened the package and filled a saucepan with water. "JD called Mayo last week."

"There you go. Why haven't they called JD? What's wrong with him? Your brother is in perfect health. Why the Hell don't they ask him for a blood test?"

"I'm not sure. You're right, he is in perfect health. But maybe he's too tall." At 6'8", my brother was nearly five inches taller than John. I imagined him for a second, my tall, handsome, strong brother. Maybe he could be our savior. Perhaps he could swashbuckle his way onto the scene. "I'm making grits," I said, faking my enthusiasm, batting my eyes at his unseeing back. "A scrumptious plate of grits coming your way."

I looked out the window again. "It's dumping." I never knew what would make him happy anymore. The site of snow falling below the street lamp used to thrill him.

"Good," he said. He'd taken off his frustration like a pair of soiled jeans.

For me it could fester for days or even years if never fleshed out. John just let it out. I'd learned to postpone emotion until after the crisis. I had to admit that it was a great strategy in an emergency, but perhaps it wasn't the best in the long run. Maybe I didn't have all the answers. Maybe I didn't have any of them.

"How much has it snowed?"

"Probably four inches. It's really coming down. Like two inches an hour now," I said, looking out the window. "Huge flakes the size of dinner plates." We were snow farmers, relying on the weather for our livelihood, needing the snow to fall at just the right times. Not so much that it kept us from opening the ski area, but enough to cover over the turns and jibes of the previous days. Some people talk about the weather as a substitute for real dialogue. For us, the weather *was* real conversation. We cultivated the snow, sending our prayers and hopes to ward against the capriciousness of the climate — hoping that warm rain wouldn't show up and take it all away.

"Flakes the size of ten-year-olds?" he said.

This was the John I loved, sloughing off negativity like an avalanche and letting the new snow make him clean and pristine again. I could be so smug sometimes. I could hold my own avalanche back until the anxiety drifted so high and deep that the impending slide was too deadly to let loose. Maybe I had more to learn.

21
Reality TV

Reality TV isn't reality; it's anything but. When John told the ski patrol that he'd agreed to allow a team of cameramen to follow us around as we did our jobs for the season, the patrol groaned. TruTV, the cop show channel, wanted to bring their cameras to the mountains and record the "real lives" of the ski patrol.

Ski patrollers aren't publicity hounds. Most of us lean towards end-of-the-road escape artists, reticent to even "go to town" for groceries and gas. Ski patrollers, like most ski bums, are temporary, spending a few years in the mountains before moving on. But the experienced cadre of patrollers who had spent more than just a few seasons in the mountains had tasted the real world and found it lacking. Reality TV smacked far too loudly of the real world.

As I waited for news from the Mayo Clinic, I figured I could use a diversion. Every week my hopes rose, expecting to hear they had found a donor. Perhaps these cameramen could distract me just a little. At least that's what I hoped.

Alex—the snowboarding cameraman—smiled into the wind. "What you do up here is pretty awesome."

Mt. Rainier glistened across the valley, and I had stopped my rope line maintenance to take in the view. A thick layer of rime had built up on the rope overnight, making it sag. I tapped on the rope with my pole, shattering the mask of hard snow, which fell to the ground in ragged bits. Each morning we chose a ski run to maintain, and Alex had asked if he could join me. We checked rope lines, marked hazards, and drilled in the bamboo sticks that held up warning signs. I loved sign runs, especially ones that let me bask in a sunny view while I work my way down the ridge before the crowds uploaded the lifts.

Alex told me to explain my task to the camera. "I'm cleaning off this rope," I said, thinking it must be obvious. "So it's visible." It seemed pretty mundane once I said it out loud. "Look. This isn't very exciting. Maybe you can just follow me along and film if something comes up." The dark square of the camera lens reflected the blue sky. He hoped I'd get a call on my radio, alerting me to some disaster on the hill. He wanted to catch my expression, my look of measured calm. They called these scenes "in-the-moments" or ITMs, and they were the staple of reality television.

A call came in on the radio. Someone was injured at Powder Pass. I stopped to check it out while Alex stood at a distance with his camera pointed towards me. By now the crowds had arrived at the ski area. Skiers and boarders wove around the accident site, slaloming around us. Another patroller stood uphill and crossed his skis, the universal sign for an injury.

The patient, Becky, had a minor knee injury, so we strapped her into the toboggan and headed down the long run. I had almost forgotten about Alex and his figure shadowing us. He must have thought the scene a happy accident. As I maneuvered the toboggan around a curve on the cat track, another skier zipped around me, passing me like a car on the highway.

"Whoa. That was close." Alex sounded excited.

I glanced at the camera and shrugged. It wasn't that close. When running a patient, the front handles of a toboggan lock into place, allowing the patroller control to maneuver and turn at will. A chain brake drags underneath the toboggan when needed to slow down. While it may feel uncontrolled to a patient, toboggan handling is quite safe. And for a woman who'd been patrolling for nearly two decades, it was like riding a bike.

Once at the bottom, the patient hobbled into the aid room and sat down on a cot, while I filled out the paperwork. Alex introduced himself to the woman, who perked up. "Reality show?"

Alex smiled and handed her the release form he carried in his camera bag for just such an event. With other people's "reality" becoming entertainment, I could see the appeal for the patient. Becky would be a star, or at least she would have a great story to tell. Reality TV transformed the otherwise mundane events of our lives and weaved a new narrative, a new significance into them. The stories we told about our lives could transplant the actual events, our memories changed by the retelling. Humans have always told stories about their experiences, recreating the past to fit a storyline that made sense. Conceivably only the word "reality" made it seem false; otherwise the spin the show's producers put on the events of that season evoked distant memories of ancient scratches on cave walls. We humans have always enhanced our everyday lives through story.

Later, watching the "rough-cut" of that scene, I marveled at the camera angles. Alex really did have a way with the lens. From his viewpoint, the skier seemed to cut right in front of the toboggan, making me slow down or risk veering off the narrow cat track. The narration increased the drama. *The crowded slopes make it impossible to transport the patient. Will Kim be able to get Becky down before it's too late?* I had to shake my head. Even a routine toboggan ride could seem like life and death if viewed from the right direction.

~~~

I knew this was going to hurt. Affixing the climbing skins to the bottom of my skis, I looked up the steep face of Lower Ferk's Run. I was about to climb three thousand vertical feet with fifty other competitors. Alex, the cameraman, was nowhere in sight.

It was called a randonee rally, and last year John and I competed together. This year, John watched from the window of his office, and I suspected he swallowed back a little bit of envy—not that it was fun, but the sense of accomplishment afterwards made it almost worth it.

Oddly, I had looked forward to this, so I could translate my mental agony into something physical. I couldn't feel John's pain; that was his battle alone. I had worked it out in my mind that by racing until my lungs burned and quads melted I could know my fear. Just like Alex's camera angle, if I looked at it from just the right vista, maybe I could alter my torment into something else. See look, there it is, that searing pain in my chest and legs. That's what it feels like to watch your husband dying, like whipping myself with thorns. I wanted to cause the pain and then smother it. Behind the human drive to tell one's own story, even when it heightened and invigorated the pain, perhaps lay the need to somehow control it.

My sternum burned as I drove each knee forward with my arms piercing the air in front of me. My lungs felt like the first few days of John's illness when my chest shrank, unable to contain all the new anguish. Now I was the one in control, the one causing it. Each deep inhalation increased the pain, and I found it steadily and strangely comforting. Before, I'd lived with a dull ache that occasionally blossomed into a forceful sting, like after speaking to John's nurse several times since Ric's rejection. She still she didn't have any comforting answers and the unspoken dread gripped me. Flying down the mountain with my hair on fire was a pain of my choosing. Maybe, when this was over and the ache evaporated, so would the old twinge. Perhaps if I told myself this new story, I could disperse the agony through sheer will.

The most grueling incline, the first hill quickly separated the pros from the rest of us in the recreational division. The Lycra-clad leaders crested the hill before I even reached the steepest part. The ski crampons I had attached to my bindings kept me from losing my friction on the snow, and I stayed towards the front of the pack. Taking it one step at a time, I breathed in between strides and put my head down. Don't think too far ahead, I told myself. Stay focused on each step, just fifteen minutes at a time.

At the top of the pitch the slope eased a little and the course forced us through a gate. Snow fell in big flakes, wetting my ski pants and the sleeves of my jacket. I was working too hard to unzip my collar. Beads of sweat dripped down my spine, while my fingertips froze.

This was a familiar feeling. Hiking up the ridge to the King, where we did avalanche control, the wind could bite my hands while the rest of my body melted. Perhaps it was my poor circulation, brought on by diabetes. Once my hands did warm up, usually about halfway to the top, they would give me the "screaming barfies," a term used by ice climbers to describe the moment when their hands began to thaw and the warm blood rushed back into their frozen digits. An awful relief, it was a painful hurdle to get over before the body could be whole again.

At the bottom of K2 Face, clicking off my skis and hoisting them on my shoulder, I passed a few other racers and sprinted to the top. It felt good. By now, the boot pack was well established, but it must have slowed down the leaders, who hiked in fresh snow.

I remembered John's face during the pancreatitis as he watched the clock, waiting to hit his pain button again. His IV machine hissed and the sound of the clock's second hand echoed through the room. I had flailed then, my heart sinking through the tiers of torment. Like the first hikers setting the boot pack, I pressed down through the layers, trying to establish a solid route. Snowflakes were like anguish; at first you flail in the bottomless layers, unable to make progress. Then you toughen the things down to hard nubs that actually hold your weight. Now I had found a boot pack, and I would follow it along until I reached the summit, whatever that may offer.

Near the top of the peak, I began to flag. The last five hundred feet of elevation stretched out above me. The peak rolled away out of sight, and I pushed harder. I thought of John and the different pain we both felt this year. This was my chance to put that pain in a specific box. Here it was in my lungs and hip flexors as I slowly made each step. My triceps burned as I hoisted myself forward with my ski poles. This was where that pain belonged. It didn't fit in my heart or my sternum as a dull longing. It could be right here in this moment and maybe I could burn it all up. At the end of the race I wouldn't hurt anymore.

At the top I stripped off my skins, the hard part was behind me now. I pushed off on my skis and headed down, making fast turns down the familiar terrain. Race officials held other skiers back as I zoomed past them. The world stood perfectly still. I kept moving, but everyone else stepped out of the way. *Here she comes, let her go by, she's been through quite an ordeal.*

I crossed the finish line as the first woman in my division, and Alex congratulated me. He wanted an interview for the camera. Then he asked me if I'd go back up the next day so he could catch me on the racetrack. He needed more ITMs for the scene.

It struck me as funny. That was the thing about life. There was the hellish reality, and then there was the triumphant story we told later. He gave me my lines, wanting me to speak into the camera about how I chased down the other women in my division, picking them off one by one so I could be victorious. I knew that's not how I did it at all. But it would become the reality if only I told the story that way.

The next day, when I climbed up the top few steps of K2 Face for the fifth time, I would realize the pretense of it all. My reaction to John's illness was like a reality TV taping, where I presented the sanitized version. Even my reliance on the fifteen-minute strategy was merely a ruse to show how plucky I was.

"Why are you hiking so hard?" Alex stood at the top of the steep face, his camera pointed at me for the fifth time.

I wanted to stop now. He'd gotten his shot. I looked beyond the camera at Alex, his yellow jacket stark against the white snow. I no longer felt triumphant, now I just wanted to cry. I almost told the camera everything—that my husband was sick and I was afraid he'd die, that I couldn't save him, that I was afraid by mind would yank apart and all the pieces would shatter to the snow like the grip of rime on a rope line.

Then I smiled and looked straight at the camera and said the line we'd rehearsed. "Because I want to win." I faked it. Even if my strategies were false, it was my story and I was sticking with it. My game plan for getting through just fifteen minutes at a time might be bullshit, but I couldn't give up now.

When I skied back down to the bottom, Alex satisfied with the scene, I looked up at John's office. The window reflected back the beginner slope crowded with children and first-timers. I would go up to him, balancing the two versions of reality—the fear I had pressed into a hard boot pack, working it into a little conveyor belt, and the promise of a reward at the top. Regardless of the condition of the snow, we had to keep moving towards that reward.

22

Setbacks

I reached over to John's side of the bed, it was empty but warm. The sun hadn't fully risen yet and I saw only the dark shapes of trees and light patches of snow. If it kept snowing, it wouldn't take long before the windows were fully covered. The snow pressed against them in wet globs, encasing us.

I found John in the living room. He was sitting on the couch, hunched over in front of the TV. His chest heaved and his head rested in his hands.

I sat next to him, resting my hand on his shoulder. I scratched his back, and he leaned slightly toward me. "What is it? Are you in pain?

"No. I'm pissed."

I inhaled sharply. "Because of Harold's spot?"

"Why the hell did those bastards send him back there if they were just going to reject him again?"

"I don't get it." We'd heard the report the day before when Harold called from Rochester. They were sending him home again, this time for good. The news had flattened me.

He lifted his head and looked at me. "Do they think I have enough time? The doctor said I couldn't wait a year, well it's been seven months."

"Maybe they thought the spot would have gone away by now. Or that Harold was your best chance."

When Harold called, something inside me stopped feeling. Like how a trauma dressing will eventually stop bleeding if applied with enough pressure, Harold's news turned something off inside me. I'd been gushing, and maybe now I would just go numb. Maybe I needed to apply a tourniquet to my heart.

"Exactly." John stood up, letting the blanket that had been wrapped around him fall to the couch. "That's exactly the problem. If Harold, with this mysterious spot, is my best chance right now, then I'm screwed. I mean I can't even believe he wanted to donate, but they find this spot on his lung and say it's nothing. But they won't choose him. Plus they won't move on."

The morning news blared behind him, warning of more snow in the mountain passes.

I nodded toward the TV. "The ski report is coming up."

"Who cares? I want to know what the Mayo Clinic is going to do now."

"Do you want me to call your nurse coordinator today? Maybe she could tell me how many more donors they have in the works."

"None. I can tell you that right now. They have zero."

"That's funny. Because what about all those people who I've talked to that want to donate?"

"Like who?" John was suddenly serious and calm.

"My brother for one. And Whitney."

"Your brother's still an option." John looked away from me, his eyes narrowed down to slits. Whitney, Angie's brother, had already been rejected once; we knew how that went.

The alarm clock blared in the bedroom and I stood up to go turn it off. "I'll get it."

"No, I'll get it." He stayed seated on the couch and watched the TV.

I walked into the bedroom and turned off the alarm. I sat on the bed and put my hands to my head and cried. The Novocain feeling I'd had yesterday was wearing off. I just wanted this to be over. I didn't care how or by whom. I knew I had to do the next right thing, but other than crying into my hands I couldn't think of anything else to do. The Mayo Clinic had strict protocols to protect the donors. But it felt like an elaborate maze. The donor process grew more mysterious every day, and our lack of knowledge made it harder.

If we could just get to the surgeons waiting on the distant shore, then John would live. I could see them over there, smiling beatifically, their arms open. Meanwhile, we thrashed about in the water. Each new life raft that drifted by carried us for only a few minutes until it started to leak. Eventually we had to abandon it and swim alone again. It let us catch our breath and see how far yet we had to go. My mom would tell me that we were getting closer, and she believed each new hope carried us nearer to the other shore. But I wasn't so sure. Maybe the wind was driving us backward. Perhaps we'd do better just to stay in the water and tread our legs and arms in oblivion.

I had spoken to other survivors in the waiting rooms at the Mayo Clinic, where there was always someone with a story. For them it was easy, it seemed. His wife or her husband could donate, the couple a perfect match, the donor unmarred by diabetes. They didn't have to wait long at all.

I wiped my tears. John's work pants hung on a hook on the bedroom door. I stood up and touched them, their stiff nap softened with use. Pulling them on under my nightgown, the legs dragging on the floor, I wiggled the waist up and down, until it rested loosely on my hips.

"Kim?"

I looked up and dropped my nightgown over the pants.

John's face was pinched and quiet. "Maybe you could call the nurse coordinator today."

"Okay," I said, unbuttoning the pants. They dropped to the floor, and I quickly stepped out of them and gathered them in my arms before he could notice. "I will."

"Are those my pants? Here, give them to me."

I handed them over and walked towards the bathroom, already forming my request for his nurse in my mind.

After a few minutes John cleared his throat. "Sweetie do I feel hot to you?"

I turned around and felt his head—it was burning. In an instant our lives had shifted again.

~~~

"Do you want me to drop you off at the Emergency Room?"

"I can walk," John said. "If you can find a parking spot that isn't in Timbuktu."

"That's just the thing. I'm not sure I can."

He pointed at a parking garage. "Just park in here."

John hated parking garages. Just descending into a dark, concrete hole in the ground where the ceiling threatened to scrape the top of our SUV could throw him into a fit that lasted until we stood out in the open air again.

"Right there," he said.

"Honey, that's a handicapped spot."

"I feel handicapped."

"Well, you're not," I said and continued driving around a corner, ignoring his heavy sigh.

When I finally found an open spot and parked, John's body temperature seemed to have risen even higher.

We walked slowly towards Virginia Mason hospital and found the emergency room entrance. I had called his nurse coordinator at Mayo when I'd felt John's forehead. She had directed us to go straight to the ER. His temperature was 104, he was burning up. Probably, I should have just dropped him off at the front door.

~~~

"The ultrasound shows that the liver may be enlarged," the doctor said. "And the blood test reveals elevated liver functions." He looked at us solemnly and crossed his hands in front of him. "This blood test helps us determine how well his liver is actually functioning."

"What's his bilirubin level?" I asked. I wanted to cut to the chase.

"It's 14, which is quite high."

"Yeah, we know." John tugged at the edge of his gown.

"Since the initial ERCP when the stents were placed, how many times have they been blocked? How many ERCPs have you had?"

John looked at me. "Is this nine or ten?"

"I think it's ten." John had been back to the Mayo Clinic several times in the past few months for this procedure, but this time it had happened too suddenly.

"Do you think I need another one?"

"All of your symptoms point towards a blockage."

I sighed deeply. We'd just returned from his last stent change in Rochester. Each time, there was the threat of pancreatitis, not to mention the anesthesia, which John's liver struggled to clear out of his body. "Will you be able to do one this afternoon?"

"If not tonight, then first thing tomorrow morning."

When we'd left the ski area, eight inches of snow blanketed the driveway, and I had heard the distant rumble of explosives setting off avalanches. Someone was up on Brand X, causing avalanches, wiping the danger clean. It felt odd that our old lives were so tantalizingly close.

Winter storms had brought me in to work early during the previous weeks. Those first chair rides, my headlamp illuminating a circle of snowflakes at my ski tips and the cold wind clearing away my fears, it was easy to forget about our predicament. In the ninety seconds from lighting a fuse to hearing the explosion, my mind cleared. Handling explosives required mental focus. Once the slopes slid, I took credit for mitigation. Unlike with John's illness, I reduced danger on the slopes. I had been looking forward to working—the physical labor of it, the management of other people's emergencies, the chance to be the savior and not the victim.

"Well," John said once the doctor had left. "I'm glad."

I looked at him. *How could he be glad?*

"Something isn't right. I could tell last night when we went to bed, but tried to ignore it."

"I hope they can see you tonight." I sat on his bed.

"Actually I want to wait until the morning. The doctors will be fresh first thing in the morning." He had become an expert on these things.

"Do you think anyone else has ever had ten ERCPs in just eight months? How long are they supposed to last anyway?"

"Anywhere from six weeks to a few months."

"As if."

I looked wanly at the plastic chair in the corner. Emergency rooms weren't set up for long-term visitors, but it would have to do. It was going to be a long night.

23
Avalanche Control

I am dreaming. Standing at the top of a snowy slope with my pack of avalanche control explosives, I take one out of my pack and light it with the small brown paper-wrapped igniter.

The rest of the explosives are stashed in my pack, securely closed beside me. Holding up the two-pound charge, I try to throw it but can't let go. The explosive is duct taped to my glove. Looking down, I see that all the other explosives are also taped to my body. I can't take off my gloves because the clasps and snaps are frozen shut.

The smoke presses against my face, forcing my chin down into the collar of my parka. Nothing moves. Vapors waft in my nostrils like asps rising to the music of a flute. The snowy slope of my dream could be anywhere at Crystal—a white field lined by spectator-like trees. The smoke stings my nose, and I can't brush it away. I can't pull off the explosives and throw them each one by one onto the slope. I'm trapped, and I have less than ninety seconds.

I woke up struggling, a scream caught in my throat. I was in bed at Crystal with snow pressing up against the windows. After two days in the hospital, and another ERCP under our belts, we'd returned to the mountains. John woke up too, asking what was wrong.

"Another bad dream." I held his hand under the sheets and pressed my face into his shoulder. I wished I could hold him tighter, squeezing him until the nightmare vanished.

"Go back to sleep."

I closed my eyes and the dream returned.

The sinister smoke keeps rising into my nose. I try to re-dream the scene. Half asleep, I imagine myself peeling off the duct tape, my fingers working efficiently. I throw the shots onto the field below me. But I know I don't have enough time. There's too many.

I turned over again and stared at the ceiling.

It wasn't uncommon for the weather to rage during avalanche control. I'd huddle against dwarfed trees for protection while I waited for the explosion. Sometimes, though, the weather changed, and the snow would sparkle like jewels in the morning light.

My mind glided again towards my dream. Under the sheets I shook my hand like a cat that's stepped in water, trying to avoid it. Sometimes it was possible to go back to a dream and rewrite it, avoiding the terrible ending, rerouting the dream's path towards a better end. But it always felt false.

I snuggled closer to John and pressed my nose against his shoulder, pulling the comforter up to my neck. It was 4:00 a.m. I had either two more hours to sleep or fifteen minutes. If it had snowed enough overnight the phone would ring, the patroller on duty at the top of the mountain would call in the teams, and I would head up the chairlift in the dark to do more avalanche control. Unable to go back to sleep, I hoped for the phone call. I would rather feel a real explosive in my hand than return to my dream. I got out of bed.

The streetlamp outside the guestroom window shone a circle of yellow light into the large falling snowflakes. The power lines hung low, their expanses weighted down by the new snow. On the ground, the old tire tracks had nearly disappeared, blending together to form a mere suggestion. High on the mountain, the snow lay in deep drifts.

The week before, I controlled Brand X, a "face route." Instead of waiting on the safety of the ridge, this route required me to zig-zag across it, feeling exposed and vulnerable. The first big shot of the route must be placed by hand. I taped the large explosive to a stick of bamboo, which we called an "air shot" or a "party in the air," if using a party pack. Standing at the window now, not wanting to return to my dream, I remembered the scene.

My partner watched me traverse onto the middle of the slope, right about where I expected it would crack, set the bamboo in the snow and light the shot. My nerves clanged as I skied away, the hissing sound of the igniter receding behind me. I held my Avalung with my teeth. It was a new piece of avalanche safety equipment that I carried—a tube that I could breathe through in case I got buried in an avalanche. Watching the explosive detonate from the other side, I saw it crack the surface of the snow, sending it sliding down the slope, obliterating my ski tracks. Gathering momentum, the slab pulled at the sides of the run, peeling them away like shards of broken glass. The avalanche hit the narrow chute halfway down and exploded into the small trees below, clouding them over with the solidified debris. It was strangely satisfying, this work. Setting off a destructive avalanche felt powerful and important and yet, also quite humbling. It was dangerous. I could no longer deny that. No matter how many times I'd told my mother that ski patrolling was no more dangerous than, say, computer programming, I knew it was a lie.

I wondered about the patroller up in Jack's apartment. He would be checking the telemetry and maybe even walking the ridge towards Grubstake. He'd poke his ski pole into the snow and call the snow safety director with the report.

I hugged myself and leaned against the windowsill in the guest room. John slept in our bedroom just a few feet away as snow fell in big flakes outside the window. I wondered what it must be like for him every morning I left for avalanche duty.

A few years ago, when John was the GM at Big Sky, an explosive accident there rocked the ski industry. On a windy

Christmas Day on the top of Lone Peak, a patroller and her partner stood near the summit and saw her objective: destroy a large cornice overhanging the slope. She'd used an igniter to start the fuse burning, but didn't realize it was lit. This was the part that made me cringe—she actually placed the shot between her legs and tried to relight it. Somehow she missed the smoke and hissing sound in the wind. She'd tried to light it three times, each time re-trimming the fuse and starting again with another igniter.

Safety fuse burns at a rate of about 140 seconds per meter. As it burns, it smokes and deforms like a Black Snake firecracker. Under our current protocols, blasters have one chance to light the fuse. If you didn't see smoke or other evidence of burning, you must immediately disarm the shot and throw the cap and fuse assembly into the snow, and wait thirty minutes to retrieve it.

At the time of the accident, the industry standard still allowed one re-light attempt; the blaster could re-cut the fuse and place a second igniter on the end. But I heard she tried it twice. Either way, you have twenty seconds to get rid of the charge, even if you don't think it's lit. Once the igniter is placed on the fuse, the clock starts ticking. Somehow she monkeyed around with that shot between her legs for a full ninety seconds.

When it blew up, the explosion showered her partner in dark smoke and tiny, blood-rimmed snow pellets. At first the other patroller didn't know what happened, she thought it was her own blood. She eventually found what remained of her partner a hundred yards away. Thinking about it now, while watching the snow fall underneath the circle of light outside our apartment, I shivered. A hundred yards.

I wondered what it had been like for John. He would have heard about it on the radio and it must have made his bones sting. He still talked about eliminating hand routes entirely and using GazEx, a system that detonated explosives remotely from the warmth and safety of a computer.

When I told him that, for some patrollers, explosives control was the best part of the job, he scoffed. "Tell that to the ski patroller who died."

Sometimes, if I really let myself think about it, explosives gave me the creeps. That wasn't why I liked it so much. Standing out there first thing in the morning, the sun just rising and the wind howling, I felt like I was cheating death having a pack full of explosives strapped to my back. I liked looking at a snowy hillside, examining its contours and predicting avalanches. If I kicked this cornice right here, letting the full weight of the thing drop onto the slope below, maybe that would do it. Or how about a shot thrown right there over that lip, where the hillside steepens and the snow clings to itself—would that trigger a slide and make it happen right now and not later, when someone could get buried?

What I liked the best about avalanche control was the ability to knock all that energy out of the snowpack, making it bland and benign while taking one more chance away from death. It's an awesome thing to cause an avalanche, to watch it build until the flowing debris rises to a crescendo before slowing down until only snow dust settles back onto the slope. But knowing that it would bury no one was even better. Throwing bombs on a slope didn't make it safe, but causing the avalanche and watching it rip down the path all the way to the bottom meant that the slope wouldn't slide again, at least until the snow re-loaded. Right now, the slopes were filling up. I pressed my forehead against the window and waited for the phone to ring. I imagined the patroller on duty running through his list of phone numbers.

I returned to the bedroom and checked the clock. It was 4:15 a.m. It was now or never. I picked the phone up on the first ring.

A few hours later, I stood at the top of the King. The wind had averaged around 20 mph that night, but had picked up in the last hour. It deposited new snow in large drifts on the leeward side of the ridges. I looked out across Silver Basin and could see that the clouds were low enough to drift around us like the dry ice mist at Halloween parties. Some skiers would see a snowy, pristine slope, but I saw avalanche terrain by way of the contours of the snowpack and the way the wind blew the fresh snow into pillows and pockets that added weight to its already tenuous hold.

Certainly I noticed the beauty of the bowl and the jagged peaks just beyond like teeth biting into cotton balls. On a clear day Mount Rainier towered above my left shoulder, less than twenty miles away. But I was trained to look for the dangers. I anticipated hazards and tried to erase them. I was a fixer. If not in the hospital, at least I could do it out here.

I looked for weak spots in the snowpack, places where an explosive or even the weight of a single skier's body would trigger an avalanche. I aimed for the shallows, where the fluff of new snow couldn't cover over the scabs of old wounds like a hospital bed sheet. This was where avalanches started.

Standing on a windy ridge, just off the southeast side of the King, the tallest peak at Crystal, my fingers plugging my ears, I waited for the explosion. My partner, a new patroller named Shannon, stood beside me, another woman trying this mostly male line of work. While waiting, we avoided eye contact. Every time I threw a shot, I worried it could be a dud, and I didn't want to jinx it. These pauses punctuated the otherwise noisy, physical work.

This was her first time on an avalanche control route in the South Backcountry, and it had taken over an hour to hike out here. The new snow covered over the old tracks, and we shared the trail breaking with two other teams, post-holing in the deep snow. At the summit, we took small sips of water and broke off bits of a Clif Bar. She told me that she didn't know it would be this hard. I didn't tell her that if she wanted to keep doing it, she had to pretend like it was a piece of cake, that keeping up with

the guys—even breaking trail most of the way—was the only way
she'd get to come back out here.

I opened my mouth slightly, so the explosion wouldn't
rupture my eardrums and I pressed my gloved fingers more
deeply in my ears. It seemed to be taking too long. The ninety-
second fuse should have burned down by now. I prayed it wasn't
a dud, requiring me to gingerly ski out onto the slope and retrieve
the live hand charge.

Someone called me on the radio asking about my progress.
Dispatch had been getting calls. *When is the Southback going to
open?* It would be a refrain inbounds, where on this busy Saturday
the crowds had already carved up the fresh snow. Some would
hike out here and ski this too, jumping onto the steep faces, feeling
safe about the avalanche hazard. But they didn't know what I did.

My shot went off and left a hole in the snow. No results—
which didn't make me feel any better. The route adjacent to mine
had already called in a one-foot crown that ran full distance. The
new snow, having formed a weak bond to the snowpack, let go all
at once and slid to the bottom of the slope. Perhaps I just hadn't
found the weak spot. My route started off down a ridge, and then
double backed on itself. We would have to traverse across mid
slope a hundred feet below this shot hole, and that made me
nervous. I considered throwing another shot now. "How many
shots do you have left?" I asked Shannon.

"Five."

I did the math. Just below where I stood, the snow formed a
drift that I couldn't quite see over. But I knew that just beyond it,
the pack was weak. My first shot had been short. But if I threw
another one here, I might not have enough.

I had left John in bed that morning after the avalanche
control wakeup call. He said, *be extra careful today.* Death seemed
to be knocking at our door. I'd promised him I would.

I pictured the rest of the route, counting my shots. If I threw
one more here, I wouldn't have any extras in case I needed them

later. Yet perhaps my first shot hadn't penetrated the weak flesh of the slope. Maybe it hit a callous and would release only with the weight of a skier. There are all sorts of ways to bridge over pain and weakness. Trusting the bond, like trusting John's doctors, wasn't always the safest route. I wasn't even sure if I could trust his doctors anymore. They hadn't found a donor yet, and I wondered if I could rely on their promise to save his life. How could they know what lay ahead for him? I imagined looking uphill as I cut the slope, wondering if I would be the trigger that penetrated the weak spot, causing the whole slope to fail.

First I would hear a whoomfing sound as the air collapsed from the snowpack. If I paid close attention, I might see little puffs of snow escape from the crack as it formed in front of me. Then the slope would move beneath me like standing on a giant surfboard.

If I had all my body weight on my uphill ski and had plenty of speed and momentum to ski across the moving slab before it broke apart, I might just make it to the trees on the other side. If not, and the avalanche gained the upper hand, I would be caught. In an instant the huge slab would break into a million shards, trapping me inside. Like the time I got caught in the slide in Powder Bowl, I might get tumbled like a rag doll, becoming helpless in the churning debris. I might lose my skis. I might shake off my heavy backpack, still weighted down by explosive charges. I may or may not be able to swim to the surface once it swallowed me.

Dry slab avalanches can reach speeds of a hundred yards per second — the distance of a football field. The powder cloud itself, let alone the main debris of the slide, can blow down tall trees. A stand of trees split the run below the ridge, where I was currently standing, and below the lower line where I would traverse across the slope. I imagined hitting those trees at high speed — like a hundred baseball bats striking my skull. It would be ugly. If I survived that, or somehow missed the trees altogether, I could be buried in the debris as it slowed down, solidifying into a hard, chucky scar at the bottom of the slope.

Shannon would watch it all. It was her job to spot me, to keep "eyes on." She would call Dispatch. *Code Two*. She would blurt into her radio mic. *My partner's been caught in an avalanche. I'm starting a transceiver search.* She would try not to panic.

John would be in his office by now, his radio turned on and propped on his desk as he sorted through the pile of papers. He would hear the radio call, stopping his pen mid-air and turning up the volume. He'd press his ear closer to the radio, wondering if it was me. If I were still alive and conscious, I might even hear my cell phone ring as he tried to call.

Breaking out of my reverie, I held out my hand to Shannon. "Can I have one of your shots?"

"Do you want me to throw this one?"

"I'll do it. I know just the spot."

This time my shot hit its mark. The avalanche started slowly, just twin cracks like a finger pressed into hard frosting, and then the whole thing went. Even the pillow slid. A cloud built up and I knew the tumbling chaos inside. I could feel it.

From our vantage point, we saw the tops of the trees that split the slope near the bottom. They shook violently as the debris raked through them—bending, breaking, and tumbling about like driftwood.

Witnessing an avalanche was awesome. But starting one was another thing entirely. It began with an explosion that made the rest of the show seem gentle. When it did pull away, it obliterated all in its path, like cooled lava getting pulled back into the flow, splitting and cracking until it moved as one body.

"It was good you threw that extra shot."

I knew that I needed to call in my results to the other teams. This was a big one. I also knew we had to keep moving because Dispatch was getting calls. I wanted John to know I was being careful, that I had made the right choice. But I stood there for a few moments, listening to the wind, the noise of the avalanche gone now. For a minute, I just stood there and breathed.

~~~

"Listen," John said, raising his head slightly. We were back at the apartment, the snow gathering around us.

For a second I didn't hear anything, and then the roof slid. It started like wind blowing beneath a doorway—a high-pitched whistle. Then it deepened to a roar as we watched the chunks of snow fly past the windows. Looking into the backyard, the snow piled up quickly and then blocked the view. It had finally encased us. Against the windows, the snow pressed firmly like a layer of frosting had covered over the glass.

It reminded me of the time I found an avalanche victim, brutally killed while skiing off the backside of Crystal. Unlike the victim Rocket had found, this time I later came to know the friends and family. It would become my job to help the witness—the victim's best friend—immediately after the accident, and I would coax him along.

Out of bounds and caught in a slide, the victim was battered against the trees. His friend and skiing partner had called for help on his cell phone and stood beside me as we extricated the body. It was grim—by far the most gruesome violence I'd ever witnessed. So I turned my focus to the survivor. The victim could no longer be helped. For him, it must have seemed unreal. Just a few minutes earlier they had stood within the ski area boundary, deciding whether to venture under the boundary rope into the backcountry. They must have talked about the weather—all the new snow and wind that had kept the King closed that day, how the snow had sloughed around them when they'd skied Northway Bowl—and wondered about the avalanche hazard. A few hours before that, the two had made arrangements for someone to pick them up from the highway below. Maybe the two men felt obligated, as if something had been set in motion that couldn't be stopped. Perhaps the mere fact that shuttle arrangements had been made kept them from turning back. Without cell service at the bottom of the access road, where the two had planned to eventually arrive after an hour or so of walking on the closed highway, their shuttle driver would be unable to contact them. That might have lead to their decision to ski the heavily loaded slope anyway. It's easy to get caught up like that, especially when the snow is as light and deep as a promise.

To witness is to "have personal knowledge of something," and also to "be present at a transaction as to be able to testify to its having taken place." For the victim's wife and family, that would be the role of the survivor.

"You have an important job," I said as we picked our way through the deep forest to the road below. The bottom half of the backcountry run, nearly 1,500 vertical feet, was choked with downed trees and crisscrossed with creeks and waterfalls. The other rescuers followed behind us with the body. I wanted to keep the survivor from watching them slog through the woods, hoisting the toboggan over trees and scraping it across the creek, grunting and sweating.

He stopped and looked at me. "Really?"

I nodded, pressing forward, the others closing in behind us. "I know that right now this isn't real yet. It hasn't sunk in. But when you see his family you will have to be the witness for them. His children." The victim's wife and teenage daughter were to pick them up at the bottom. "They need to know how it happened. What he was saying right up 'til the end."

He breathed in sharply. "Okay."

"It's important because it will be so hard for them to understand it all. You have to tell them. They will need to know that he lived right up until the moment he died."

"He was my best friend. He was my skiing buddy." He paused and shook his head. "I can't believe it."

"I'm sorry." I really was. We continued on through the woods, over slick trees until we finally had to carry our skis. It was dark by the time we hit the road. Then we slowly piled into a van and arranged ourselves around the body, trying not to notice the stench of blood and iron rising up from the dark, wet mass at our feet.

The snow had already begun to melt against the glass, creating wet splotches that floated on the window towards each other. I knew that I would soon go out and shovel off the front steps.

Watching the snow encapsulate our windows, I thought of the wife of the avalanche victim. She still skied at Crystal, perhaps gaining strength from the remnants of the life they once shared. I had spoken with her, noticing her wedding band on a gold chain around her neck. She didn't have a chance to say goodbye to her husband. Her loss happened in an instant—their marriage vaporized by a split-second decision. I wondered which was worse, losing him instantly or slowly—knowing he died whole or only after a long, hard battle had exhausted his body and spirit?

24

Saving a Life

I rolled my body into a tight ball, rocking back and forth, not sure if I could do this anymore. The chair I'd just sat on lay beside me, and my shoulder brushed against it as I rocked. Crying hard now, I rubbed my palms against my scalp, holding my hair in chunky handfuls. Just a few minutes earlier I'd sat reading about cholangiocarcinoma on the computer. Sometimes while John slept I slipped into the office and did research—a strangely guilty query, like having a toothache that the tongue returned back to, jabbing into the pain. Each investigation brought renewed agony, but one couldn't resist the question: does it still hurt? Even with each fresh layer, with my heart already blazing in my chest, I returned here hoping to find something different.

I told myself there could be a breakthrough, some glimmer of hope in these postings. Yet I knew I wouldn't find it here. Wasn't that the definition of insanity—to keep playing out the same actions and hoping for a different result?

John looked peaceful with the blanket pulled up to his chin, and I didn't want to wake him with my crying. Instead I wanted to quit. Monday mornings brought hope that always compressed down to a hard nub by the end of the week. Another week had gone by and still no donor had been found. The words burned in my throat and I forced myself to smile when I told John to have hope, to trust the doctors. To the nurses at the Mayo who received my weekly progress calls, I felt like John was just another Mr. So-and-So with a clinic number and a dire diagnosis. I'd been on their side of the fence and understood the studied distance the job required.

Earlier that day, I'd spoken to a doctor in New Zealand. It took three tries and several disconnections while I stood inside the top lift shack at Crystal, pressing my index finger to my ear to hear. He was a friend of a friend who knew someone at the Mayo Clinic. As it turned out, his best friend and colleague used to be on the staff there. I asked if there was something else I could do. Crouched away from the single-pane window with ice crystals forming near the edge, I told him that, in the end, I wanted to know I had tried everything. He understood what I meant; that if John died before a donor could be found, I wanted to tell myself that I followed every unraveling string, hoping that one of them would finally hold.

He had given me a little hope, explaining that there were financial incentives even in big institutions such as Mayo. We could offer to pay extra for the donor screeners to work overtime. He wasn't sure if they did that sort of thing at the Mayo Clinic, but his acknowledgement of our dilemma felt strangely comforting. Even from a doctor I had never met.

Afterward, I called Mayo and asked immediately about getting more screeners on the job. "That's not how this works," the nurse had explained. *We are the Mayo Clinic,* she seemed to say. *You don't have to pay extra for our excellent care.* There was the unspoken admonishment. *What kind of place do you think this is?*

I couldn't conjure up the courage to explain to John why they hadn't found a donor yet. Every day I tried to make sense of it; to translate the slings and arrows of our path, to remind him of all the "good" that was coming out of this, even when I had stopped believing it myself.

I got up from the floor and went into the bathroom with a renewed sense of purpose. I could just quit, go down in glorious flames. Here were John's pills, I thought as I picked up his pain medication. If I took most of these and left him enough to get through the weekend, it would definitely kill me. It would be so easy to end it. I opened the pill bottle and peered inside. It was a new prescription and the chalky white pills lay on top of each other like jelly beans. I bounced the bottle up and down, watching the pills dance. It would be so easy. I imagined myself lying down next to John and never waking up.

Of course, he would have to find me. It would take him a minute of nudging before he saw how my mouth had sucked in on itself. He'd know something was wrong even before he turned on the light and touched my gray skin, his nose registering the smell of death.

"Kim?" John called me from the bedroom.

"Yeah," I said wiping my face and replacing the cap on the bottle.

"Are my pain pills in there?"

I looked down at my shaking hand. "Let me see."

"I think I need one."

I slowly poured water in the glass beside the sink, filling it halfway. Placing the glass on the counter, I looked into the mirror. "Okay. I got it." My hair fell haphazardly around my puffy eyes. I shook it loose to hide them. Brushing my fingertips through my tangled hair, I tried to smile. *See how silly you are?*

Taking the water and the pills I walked into the bedroom. John sat up, with his hands folded in his lap. "Does it hurt?"

"It always hurts."

I handed him the glass and shook a single pill out of the bottle and held it out in my hand. He swallowed it down with a sip of water. "Thanks," he said and lay down on his back. "Are you coming to bed?"

"In a minute." I made a decision right then and there. If I ever felt the urge to kill myself again, the least I could do was wait until we got to the Mayo Clinic. At least they could use my organs. I could make it look like a tragic accident, or else I could write a note beforehand that explained specifically what I wanted them to do with my liver. I could be like Juliet, dying senselessly for the love of her man. It would be so tragic and beautiful and strangely cathartic for the audience. I could always kill myself later. Right now my husband needed me.

~~~

"Is this Robert?" I asked. "My sister, BG, gave me your number."

"Oh yes. I remember BG."

"I called to see if you could help me."

"Hold on."

Shifting the phone to my other ear, I couldn't believe I actually called a psychic. A few days ago my sister gave me his number. I wondered where she found him. She wasn't necessarily the type to consult a psychic, but you never knew.

"Yes," he said, as if he'd had to decide. "I can help you. First of all, I need to know your name."

"Kim."

"Okay," he was quiet for a minute. "Okay. Yes."

I pressed the phone to my ear harder to make sure I didn't miss anything.

"I could clear your spirit easily if you like."

"Sure."

He was quiet again. "There."

I took a breath, wondering if I should feel anything.

"You should feel a weight off your chest." He read my mind. He asked me a few questions about John. I told him about the cancer and how we were waiting for a liver transplant. After a moment, he told me John would be fine. He said it so nonchalantly, as if reading a script. When he told me he would live, I felt ridiculous. *Had it really come to this? Had I really called a psychic on the phone? Was I really as bad as those desperate souls watching late-night television?* Robert sensed I had a disease.

"I'm diabetic."

"Yes. That's it."

I heard him breathing and wondered if I was supposed to say anything.

"Not anymore," he finally said. "You don't have diabetes anymore." He explained that he could see the diabetes on my life-force and had asked his spirit-partners to clear me of it.

"Great," I said, trying to sound enthusiastic.

Robert explained how he got in touch with the spirit world. There were angels all around us, he said. If you pay attention you could hear the angels speak to you. You could communicate with them. He was not a psychic, he explained. Instead, he was a voice for the angels.

"Okay."

Later, I laughed at myself for calling a psychic. Or whatever he was. He'd said diabetes was a blotch on my spirit that had to be erased like a smudge, and immediately I thought guiltily about peering into John's pill bottle. He had "cleared" John's spirit too; his had a few more burrs that needed to be sanded off. He called it something else, but that's how I visualized it. Even from a phone psychic that talked to angels, I liked to hear that my spirit was free of its smudges now.

~~~

My blood sugar was low again for the second time that day, and I wondered about the psychic's declarations. Earlier I had taken the dog for a hike in the snow and had to stop and eat something. Now I was in the kitchen, and with shaking hands I poured myself a glass of orange juice. I checked my blood sugar: fifty. Pressing my palms on the countertop, I leaned over and tried to breathe slowly, knowing I should lie down. This was the hardest part, eating something and waiting for it to take effect. At least I could stop panicking now. Pearls of sweat pricked my forehead and armpits. I breathed through my mouth, pressing the air against my teeth like I did when climbing. Maybe I should call John. He was at his office and could be home in just a few minutes. By the time he got here, I would probably be fine. I decided to wait it out.

Perhaps the psychic was right. Maybe I didn't have diabetes anymore. This would be the reaction if suddenly my body began producing its own insulin. My doctor told me I would always need to take insulin shots. Type 1 Diabetes never went away.

Low blood sugar reactions felt like a drug-induced high. The starving brain lost track of its logical synaptic connections. Muscles relaxed and contracted on their own. Certain truths, like doors falling off their hinges, hung loosely and unwanted. Maybe the doctors were wrong. Perhaps cancer was just a made up diagnosis to explain the psychological burrs that built up over time. If this was the end of my diabetes, then perhaps I could believe that John was cancer-free. All because of a phone call that cost $19.95 for the first five minutes and $10.99 for every minute after that. It was a bargain, really.

I seemed to be sinking further and my knees buckled. *I'll just lie down here on the kitchen floor.* The wood felt soft under my hips, and I curled into a ball. I shook, holding my hands close to my chest. *Had I really drunk some juice?* The panic rose bitterly as I ran my tongue around my mouth unable to detect the sweet leftovers.

I had heard about a diabetic who died while waiting for delivery pizza. He had accidentally administered two insulin shots instead of one. At the time, I hadn't understood how this could happen. How could you forget that you had just given yourself a shot? But I would come to have this same amnesia. After going through the motions of shots, finger pricks, and glasses of juice so many times, they lost their hold on your memory.

The floor tipped forward and I turned, pressing my back to the ground. I dug my heels in as if trying to stop a slide down an icy slope. I clawed the kitchen floor with my fingers and reached out for the small rug, clutching it tightly. *Maybe this was it.* Now that I didn't have diabetes anymore, the insulin from my pump would kill me, administering a steady drip of the liquid and starving my brain of vital blood sugar. I wanted to take it all back, to call the psychic and tell him to call it off. Put the burrs back on my psyche. At least I would live.

Convulsing, I grasped the rug tighter, imagining it was a rope keeping me from slipping on the ice. The back of my head hit the floor rhythmically, and I wondered if it was bleeding. If I reached deep down into my body I remembered where I was. This is the hard wood of the kitchen floor. I am having a seizure. I will be okay if I just hold on. The orange juice will take effect soon. That is, if I did drink some.

Then the convulsions returned, transporting me once again to a steep slope, sending me barreling towards the trees below. A dark, green mass between the jerky shapes of my feet, hard, jagged trees waited to batter me as I slid through. My body bounced higher as I picked up speed, my head hitting the kitchen floor with each jump. I wondered who would find me. *Would the ski patrollers have to extract me from the trees?* Would they shake their heads, wishing I had just listened to the psychic and turned off my insulin pump? Such a shame, they would say. So young. So full of life. So much ahead of her.

My hand ached where I grasped the rug. I released it and gingerly touched my mouth. It felt sticky and wet. I had bit my lip. My head throbbed and I lifted it slowly, touching my fingers to my scalp where I felt the beginnings of a lump. Carefully I sat up and took stock. I could see the remains of a glass of orange juice on the counter. So I had drunk it. It must have finally taken effect.

I pressed my hands to my face and sat there a minute. It was just a low blood sugar. Sometimes merely holding on was the best method. If I could only wait for the crisis to be over, quelling the panic as long as possible, I could get through anything. But who was I kidding? This was a close call. John's method of embracing his emotions, letting them roll out in peels of thunder might be better after all.

The air in the kitchen sparkled with electricity. The seizure had felt almost soothing, like releasing something wild and caged that I'd carefully kept hidden. Raw and loose, my joints felt unhinged. I waited for the solidity of my body to return to me. Soon my joints would tighten, bringing my muscles back into alignment. The pathways in my brain would smooth out, no longer calling attention to themselves and the alternative world they illuminated. For a moment, I wondered if I could just stay here.

~~~

"Hey Kim, it's Whitney." My cell had rung inside my ski parka and I'd take off my glove to answer it.

"Hi Whit." My sister in-law's brother, Whitney, had returned for his second work-up at Mayo, and I held my breath waiting for the report.

"My CT scan looks good. They say I am a good size and blood type and all that."

"Yeah?" Sitting on the chairlift, I maneuvered the phone away from the wind.

"So far they are pretty happy with me. But they say my ALT levels are still a little high. They are in the normal range, but at the high end of normal."

I pressed the phone into my ear. My hand was getting cold. "But didn't they know that already?"

"They did. Yeah they did. So I'm a little surprised that they are making such a big deal out of it now."

"What causes elevated ALT levels?"

"Well, the other thing is that I have high triglycerides."

"Oh." I approached the top of the chairlift.

"So they are sending me home." Whitney must have known how devastating those words were. He'd already been sent home once. This time it felt final. He was no longer a candidate.

"Well. Thanks for trying."

"I read about this diet. A diet high in sweets can elevate your triglycerides. I have been drinking a lot of those health drinks that are high in carbs. So I'm going on a low-carb diet and see how quickly I can get my triglycerides down."

I reached the top of the lift and skied over to a secluded tree. "Okay." I appreciated his effort and all, but I just wanted to end the conversation now and cry. "Are you still at the apartment?"

"I'm packing up now. Flying back tonight."

So that's it, I thought. A week ago, when Whitney had called to say the Mayo wanted him back out there, our hopes had flown. We'd had a few glorious days. "Well, let me know if there's anything else you need on your way home." I got off the phone and remembered the surgeon's words when he explained it all last summer. The wait for a deceased donor would be over a year. "And you don't have a year," he had said. It had been nine months now since John's diagnosis. The radiation slowed it down. But that was more than six months ago. We were officially running out of time.

The sharp north face of the King loomed above me. I needed to hike up there, I decided. I needed to hike and ski and be alone for a while.

What if John died and I took over managing this place like I had promised? Even after all the time I had known him, I had never tapped into the secret DNA encoding that allowed him to understand the ski industry. John was like a migrating whale whose brains were embedded with iron oxide that helped them navigate north towards their feeding grounds. John's brain contained an inner navigational aid that pointed him towards ski area management. Sniffing the air, he could smell a good idea just as easily as he could the next snowstorm. He knew when to spend money and how to save it. A great manager, John knew when to be the boss and when to listen as a friend.

John had woven himself into the fabric at Crystal. Here was the beautiful new restaurant he built at the top of this chair.

What if I walked in there on a busy Saturday? Would I remember the names of local skiers who wanted to shake my hand? I doubted I could manage his personal touch. He even created personalized ski-related fortune cookies doled out from the Asian food station. *You will have first tracks under the chairlift in the near future. I see you on a heli-ski trip. Soon, you will meet a hottie in the hot tub.* Would I know to check the number of pizzas in the cooler predicting within a single slice how many we would need to prep?

I looked back at the chair I'd just ridden — a six-place chair that he constructed, the first one in the state. At first it had seemed like a ridiculous contraption that would be too hard to load and unload with five over skiers or riders. Where would small children sit? How would beginner snowboarders exit without running over one another? Somehow it had worked. Of course John would have known that it would gobble up weekend lift lines like a Pacman game, handling crowds and shortening the wait.

I rode up the double chair to the top of the ridge. John had plans for this chair too. It was nearly forty years old and offered the only access to this expert terrain, including the King. He wanted to build a narrow road across the top of the ridge. Now only a trail of "whoopdy-dos" punctuated by tree stobs and rocks that led to the hike to the South Backcountry. Never satisfied with the status quo, John wanted to transform this traverse too.

I unloaded the chair and skied across the ridge, dodging branches and rocks. I had come to accept this obstacle course as a rite of passage. If you could make it across the ridge, you were good enough to hike the King. John, on the other hand, imagined it for the rest of the skiing public — the ones who didn't work up here and didn't know the hill so intimately. He wanted to make it easy to reach our prized terrain. He knew skiers wanted to stand at the top of a narrow chute and look through their ski tips at the bottom. They wanted to brag to their coworkers and classmates on Monday. *I hiked the King. I skied Brain Damage.* Modern ski movies had a nomenclature that had evolved over the decades for this type of off-piste skiing. In the seventies it was *hot dogging,* then *extreme skiing* in the late eighties and nineties, and most recently *big mountain riding.* Whatever they called it, regular skiers wanted access to it, even if it meant just sidling up next to it and feeling the wind in their faces as they peered over the edge.

To John, ski terrain came first. The infrastructure supported the terrain. Since Crystal operated on a Forest Service permit, the opportunity for hotels and a village at the base was limited. Instead, John improved access to the terrain with new lifts, on-mountain restaurants (so customers could eat close to the slopes) and careful tree trimming. "We are essentially a ski lift company," he would say. The rest was extra.

I shouldered my skis and started the hike, trying to remember what Whitney had said about his diet. How long did it take to lower your triglycerides? That left one other in the queue, my brother, JD.

I slid my ski boots into each frozen step and hiked quickly, wanting to burn out the pain rising in my sternum. I worried about my brother's height and the size of his liver would probably be too large.

That still left me. I had already tried to put myself back on the list several times. One of John's nurses explained to me that only if he had no other options, would they reconsider me. Well, we were almost there.

The wind died down as I approached the top, stepping carefully around the wind-scoured rock. I was alone at the summit. Mount Rainier's upper flanks disappeared into a gun metal gray cloud. Elsewhere, the rough peaks and glaciers poked up into the cloud like pencils in a ceiling. I peeked over the edge at Pinball, the slot off the summit and decided it was too narrow for turning and too steep for straightlining—at least for me, anyway. It still needed another few feet of snow before I would try it.

I leaned on my ski poles and slid my tips toward the edge and gazed at the run. A light breeze rose up the couloir and I pressed slightly against it, imagining dropping into Pinball. Once inside the steep chute, the rock walls narrowed down to a few feet, forcing you to point your skis straight down. From my vantage point on the summit, it seemed nearly vertical. What remained was a thousand foot free fall, your skis just barely staying in contact with the surface. After a few seconds the walls backed off enough for a large arcing left turn, slowing you down just a little.

Today frozen avalanche debris pocked that area and a skier would have to continue straight, keeping arms tucked in and head down just slightly to keep the wind from being knocked over until the slope at the bottom backed off into the basin. Too fast, and the compression at the bottom could throw a skier backwards. In fact at any point, one moment of inattention would end spectacularly, like the opening scene from Wide World of Sports, when ABC promised to showcase the "human drama" that was athletic competition.

As a kid, I'd watched that intro in awe. The announcer promised both the "thrill of victory… and the agony of defeat," demonstrated by the Yugoslavian ski jumper Vinko Bogataj at the 1970 World Ski Flying Championships. After gaining tremendous speed on the in-run to the jump, Bogataj slid off the side of the ramp, cart-wheeling uncontrollably into the audience and the slope below, becoming the embodiment for spectacular failure.

I winced and stepped back from the edge. I would ski something more forgiving today, a run that allowed for turns and controlling speed and one that I didn't have to mention to others or brag about. I dropped over the edge into Hourglass,

216 Kim Kircher

pressing my body forward into the turn. Whatever lay ahead, I had to keep my weight forward, keep the momentum going, lest I lose my balance like the infamous jumper. Maybe it would be JD. If not, once they got to the end of the list, maybe they would take another look at me, the student in the front of the room with all the answers whose wildly waving arms kept getting passed up by the teacher. Either way, I still had to negotiate the terrain that lay at my feet — whether on the slopes or at the hospital.

~~~

People have asked me if I have ever saved anyone's life. They imagine skiers colliding with trees or massive trauma that can be resolved simply by applying pressure in just the right spot. They get these images from reality shows and movies featuring emergency rooms. I want to tell them that I save lives by preventing accidents. But that isn't as newsworthy as stopping a hemorrhage or digging someone out of an avalanche. Nor is it as honorable as donating half your liver to your husband so the doctors can save his life.

So I tell them this story.

It was New Year's Day, and I was on Lower Exterminator cleaning up from the previous night's fireworks display and torchlight parade. Carrying a load of bamboo in my arms and sliding back and forth on my skis, I had gathered up most of the debris. A call came in for a Code 1, medical emergency, just up from the base lodge. I dropped my load and called in on the radio. I'd be right there. I was one of the first EMT's on scene. An older man, perhaps seventy, lay in the snow, his skin gray, his mouth hanging open. Feeling no pulse or breath sounds, I began CPR. By that point, a few others had joined me.

We tried to resuscitate him for a few minutes, all hands and knees bumping each other, attaching oxygen to the bag valve mask and defibrillator pads to his chest. I worked at the head, squeezing the bag as it inflated, filling his lungs with oxygen. Paul leaned over his chest, fixing the pads. It wasn't like it is in the movies, when time slows down a little and the background noise disappears. I'd been on other medical emergencies—too many to count. The only advantage here was our proximity to the first aid room, namely the defibrillator unit. It was there in two minutes.

"All clear?" Paul called out and I brought the mask away from the patient's mouth.

Looking behind me to keep anyone from touching him while we administered the charge, I saw two women standing there. One looked at me and said, "He's our father." The defibrillator unit sat beside my knee, charging.

When it was ready, I pressed the charge button and watched the father of the two women at my shoulder rise off the snow. He wasn't just a patient anymore, he was someone's dad.

"Continue CPR," I said, reading the screen. We'd have to wait another minute. I deflated the oxygen bag against my thigh and imagined his skin changing color. I thought I could see him pink up. "All clear?" I asked and waited for all the rescuers to step back. Again, he rose off the ground as if having a single convulsion. "Wait." I looked at the screen. "Check pulse." I could feel his daughters behind me like a tiny solar system, pulling me into their gravity. Perhaps they would become the new sun, the other planets of their family no longer orbiting around the father after his death. It was awful to watch that single focal point dim so dramatically.

I watched the patient's skin as Paul rested his fingers against the man's neck. His lips had changed; they weren't blue anymore.

"I feel a pulse," Paul finally said, looking up at me in surprise. "Continue breathing." The defibrillator confirmed it, the patient's heart had started pumping.

After that, rescue operations changed. This guy might live. We transferred him to a toboggan to take him the short way to the base lodge where an ambulance waited for him. On the slope, the detritus of the rescue fluttered in the breeze. I stood up as the toboggan rolled away and touched the hand of one of the daughters. "Are you okay?"

"Is he going to live?" She watched as the toboggan pulled away.

A year later, the patient returned to Crystal with his family to ski together and celebrate their luck. Only a few minutes after the massive heart attack that could have killed him, we had shocked his heart just in time. If he'd been anywhere else besides an emergency room, he might not have made it. I have a plaque on my wall—a purple star for saving a life. But it hadn't felt like anything I did consciously. I didn't set out that day to make any real difference, just to mop up from the previous night, maybe help with a hangover or two.

That was the thing about emergency work—often it happened so quickly, the actions are just rote training kicking in. But it took on a different significance when a father's life was saved while his children watched him return from the edge of death. Sometimes, I reminded myself, patients lived. Perhaps John's doctors worked the same way. Training, protocols, and treatments—every day Mayo clinic saved lives, and I just hoped John's would be one of them.

25

Let's Not Talk About Anything Serious

"I really think I could be the donor," JD said.

"What does Angie think?" I stood in our back yard looking out at the gray lake, talking to my brother on my cell phone. The winter had wound down and we had moved back to our lake house.

"She had to really think about it."

"I bet," I said, walking carefully down the slippery steps. I sat down on the stairs with my feet on the dock. The boards had turned algae-green, a common occurrence that permeated throughout Seattle at the end of a long winter.

"But we're ready. And if God chooses me, than it's part of His plan."

I wondered about God's so-called plan. Was this really what He had intended for John and me? Whenever anything bad happens, we called it God's Plan. But did we ever say that when things went right? We tended to take the bad news stoically and downplayed the good. Taught not to brag about our own situation, we avoided the sin of humility. Yet when faced with hardship, we easily played the role with an affected stoicism as God's little soldiers acting out His campaign.

"When you first offered, I didn't want you to." I slipped my feet back and forth along the grain of the dock boards. He had children, and I wasn't sure he was close enough to John to risk his life to help him. "But now I think you might be our only hope left."

"I want to do this. I'm ready," he said. "Besides, you deserve it."

"You think so?"

"Of course, Bimp." JD said, using my childhood nickname. "You've always set aside your own happiness, making sure everyone else was first. And I don't think you had much happiness before you met John."

"I don't know. I think I was pretty happy."

"But this is real. You guys. I want to do what I can to help him live."

I slid my feet along the boards, cleaning the green slime a little with my shoe. The calm lake lapped at the underside of the dock and slapped against the boards. "Thanks. It means a lot."

After hanging up, I sat on the steps a few minutes longer. Now that JD would go to Rochester, I felt relieved, like I'd stepped into a hot shower. His tests began the next day.

Earlier the nurses had explained the surgeon's schedule. If he were chosen this week, we would know by Friday. They would schedule the surgery by the end of May or early June. This whole thing could be over in a month. My heart opened like sunlight bursting into a dark room. It was easy to put hope in my brother. A former professional basketball player, JD was an Adonis. In addition to his stellar anatomy, his emotional savvy and mentally stability would catapult him through the tests. I just knew it.

A large wave splashed against the retaining wall beside me and up through the boards on the dock. I lifted my feet as the water spilled over and then sucked back. He would be the rock star of liver donors. They would want to make him their mascot. He was so good-looking and generous and wonderful and healthy. Everything was going to be okay now. I hugged my arms against my chest. We had slowly been undressed of our hope like a sick game of strip poker. But here was our salvation. JD called it God's plan.

I walked up toward the house, several rose bushes lined the walkway, and I stopped to look at them. John always smelled them. I pressed my nose to the purple ones with the sweetest smell. The soft folds tickled my nose and I thought of Evelyn's soft spot on her blanket. I inhaled quickly and sharply, letting the fragrance coat my nose. Standing up, the blossom fell off in my hand.

I carried it like a wounded bird up the steps to the deck and inside to the kitchen and gingerly placed it in a bowl of water. The leaves had already separated from the core, looking more like a lotus than a rose. It still smelled sweet, and I let that be enough.

~~~

Our dogs ran along in front of us, sniffing the ground. Mom and I pumped our arms as we walked the trail. The doctors had told us that if (they had started using the word *if*) John got a transplant, he shouldn't be around animals for at least six months. We would have to find another home for our one-year-old Chocolate Lab.

"You know, Mom," I said. "I don't want to talk about anything serious today."

"I know. That's why I asked you to join me. I thought you would need a distraction."

My brother was in Rochester. He had made it to Friday, the last day of the five-day workup, without being sent home. John was working at the ski area today. He needed to stay busy, too. When he left this morning, we acted like it was any other day. We pretended not to think about my brother, shuttling himself from one appointment to the next, hands folded as he waited to hear our fate on the lavender chairs of the waiting room. I promised I would call as soon as I heard from JD.

"Let's talk about Charlie," I proposed.

"Okay," she said, going along. "I think he is a sweet, but misguided dog." She had watched him tirelessly this past year.

"Yes, he is." I agreed. "John doesn't really like him, though."

"No?" Mom didn't sound surprised.

"He says he's like living with a horse. He's not very well behaved. He's not like Rocket, always quietly sleeping in the corner. Instead, Charlie thinks he's a lap dog. He wants to sleep with us and he's always sneaking onto the bed."

Rocket loved to search, to press his wet nose to cold snow and inhale. He sneezed when the fresh snow drifted into his nose like fine dust, and it pleased him. I had hoped that Charlie would learn to heel as we loaded the chairlift, folding his paws across my lap as the wind lifted the flaps of his ears. I had wanted to urge Charlie into a search, watching his tail wag within the piles of debris as if finding an avalanche victim was as much fun as a game of fetch. It had been three years since Rocket died and still I was comparing this new dog to him. Since John's illness, I had backed off on his training. I just didn't have enough time. And now, he eluded my grasp.

I thought about Charlie's latest escapade. Rushing into the house, knowing I had only a few minutes to change before picking up Evelyn at school, I planned on grabbing the dog (he was finally potty trained, but still just a few months old at the time) and heading out the door. I'd only left him for an hour, but apparently that had been enough for him to wreak havoc. At first, I had thought it was a joke—John sprinkling that store-bought snow made of chemical shavings all over the carpet. Then I realized it was down feathers. Charlie must have ripped apart an entire couch pillow—only the green shell remained like a folded leaf on the floor. A thick fluffy coating covered the entire floor. Charlie knew he was in trouble. He sat there, his tail thumping hopefully and regrettably on the floor, and a single feather stuck to his nose. Sucking in his breath, the feather fluttered against his snout, and when he exhaled the feather flew just a little bit like a piece of lint caught on a sweater.

"I see," Mom said. She always had big, lovable dogs that followed her around the house and slobbered on visitors.

"I'm afraid we are going to have to give him away."

"I thought you didn't want to talk about anything serious."

"I know. But this is okay. It's strange, before John got sick, losing the dog would have been devastating. But now it just seems automatic. He's just a dog after all." Charlie looked back at me just at that moment, his nose glistening.

"You sort of have to prioritize your grief, don't you?"

"I mean I love this dog. Call me crazy, but his sweetness and his unconditional love—"

She held my hand as we walked and squeezed it gently. I felt her looking at me, waiting for me to fall apart, ready to hold me or pick me up if I should fall. I said, "I just can't go there."

The dogs rushed back at us. Mom's Golden Retriever, Annie, wagged her tail and bobbed her head back and forth in unison. Charlie ran towards me; his was mouth wide open and his tongue hung out. While her dog walked beside us, Charlie ran past looking at me through sideways glancing eyes. "Charlie come," I said. He ran harder, bowing towards Annie to get her to chase him. He thought this was fun.

We walked in silence for a few minutes while I glanced at my watch and calculated the time difference in Rochester. I fingered my cell phone in the pocket of my sweatshirt, willing it to ring. I was hopeful. I knew that JD would be the right donor. I wanted to tell my mom this, but if I started to talk to her that way I wouldn't be able to hold back the flood of fear and anxiety.

The phone rang in my pocket and we both jumped. It was John. "Hi, honey. No he hasn't called yet. I'll call as soon as I hear anything."

"That was John," I said stupidly when I hung up. We continued walking. We had already walked several miles and I wondered how long it would take to get back to the car. I wanted to be home before John got there. Especially if we had some news.

"Where do you think you and John are going to take your first vacation once he gets well?"

I knew she had a whole arsenal of safe conversation topics ready to fire. "I want to go to Bhutan, but maybe our first trip should be somewhere easy."

"Maybe Mexico or Hawaii," she said. "Wouldn't that be nice to just lie on the beach and read a book?"

"Yeah." I couldn't picture us shouldering our backpacks in the Himalayas, John's sunny disposition on display. I couldn't even imagine reaching for his hand along the cool sheets of a hotel bed. I could hardly visualize us skiing again—my shorter turns weaving around his long sweeping arcs, watching him take up the entire slope.

The dogs ran in and out of the puddles next to the trail. Annie's long hair turned dark with puddle water.

I let my mind grow quiet and just watched, taking refuge in my own thoughts. I differed from my mom in this way. She found solace by talking because it kept her from her thoughts. When I needed safety, I ran towards my thoughts. I created elaborate fantasies that offered escape, or I noticed the details around me, wrapping my jagged heart in the green flicker of leaves unfurling on the maple trees.

I had learned to make small talk, and even to open myself to the occasional "heart to heart" with my sister. But it wasn't easy. Writing was different. It was like a stethoscope to my chest, noting the timber of each beat.

"Maybe we should turn around."

"Just a little further." Mom wanted to stay out as long as we could. Once back at the cars, our time together would be over. She wouldn't be able to wrap her arms or her words around me like a shield against the news. She was stalling.

When we finally did turn around it was nearly halfway back before JD finally called. "Hello?" I said, automatically reaching for my mom's hand.

"Kim, I have good, but cautious news."

"Okay. Tell me."

"While my right lobe is not suitable, they think the left lobe is. This is good because it's an easier surgery." We already knew his right lobe, the bigger one, had two arteries instead of one, which could be problematic. I knew that, but was disappointed that one road had closed.

I raised my eyebrows at my mom, who mirrored back my expression. "When do you find out for sure?" My heart lifted a little.

"Maybe by Monday, but Tuesday for sure. I just got out of the CT scan and they have to compare it to John's anatomy to confirm. But the technician said it looked pretty good, not that it means anything until a doctor looks at it."

I listened. It all depended on the results of the CT scan. They needed to be sure his left lobe was the correct size. It seemed so possible all of a sudden, like I had rubbed Mentholatum on my nose and could breathe again. This was what joy felt like. "Thank you so much, JD. You're my hero."

"If not, then it's God's will." He sounded a little like a preacher. "Okay?"

I nodded. "You're still my hero, no matter what. Have you called Angie yet?"

"Not yet. I love you."

"I love you too." I stopped on the path and filled in the missing details for Mom. Her arched eyebrows framed her open and fragile face. It was her son making this sacrifice for me. Mom stood a little taller, trying to look brave, her eyes shining with pride and fear.

"Can I hold your hand?" I asked.

"Oh, honey," she said placing her hand inside mine. We started walking again. "I just know this is going to work out."

"I have to believe that."

"Do you? Do you see John living through this?"

The dogs were out in front of us, running helter-skelter from
bush to tree, sniffing frantically, having caught the scent of a
squirrel. "Yes," I said, "and no." I knew I shouldn't be talking like
this. I had promised myself just to visualize the outcome I wanted,
as if my fears might conjure up the demons. "Yes. I can see us
getting through this. But, I've also thought about the alternative.
We made a will, and we've talked about what would happen."

Mom briefly squeezed my hand and continued with her
breakneck speed.

"I just can't go there," I said.

"That's why you must always imagine him living through
this."

I smelled the tender new daffodils rising from the dark earth
beside the trail. Last season's dead leaves had nearly shriveled,
making way for the new arrivals. Soon this walk would be choked
with brambles and dandelions and other suburban weeds, so I
made sure to drink in the newness while it lasted. "I know. You're
right."

"Now, when are you going to call John with the news?"

John was more cautious.

"But that left side could be too small," he said when I called
him.

"My brother is 6'8." He's a giant," I said into the phone while
herding the dogs around my legs. "I'm sure his left lobe is big
enough."

"So we have to wait the weekend to find out?"

"Don't worry." Damn, I felt cheated by his lack of optimism.
Something had shifted in me, and I didn't want caution. This
would work. "Come on. This is as close as we've gotten."

"I know." He was silent for a moment and I thought we had
lost the connection. "God I hope he's the donor. I don't know if I
can wait any longer. I don't even know if it's too late already."

I stood my ground, hanging on to my hopeful confidence.

"It's not too late. It's not. We've done our part, and it's up to the surgeons now."

Hanging up, we walked back to our cars. I felt swept along by a swollen stream. It was finally going to happen, this nightmare would end. I looked at my mom and held her gaze. "I just know he's going to be the donor."

Mom, the pragmatist, reminded me of the obvious. "We still have to wait out the weekend."

I passed my hand in the air between us as if swatting a fly. "No problem. They already told him to keep the week of May 19th available. I just feel it deep in my bones that he's been chosen and this is just a formality." I unlocked the car and loaded the dog. I wanted her to believe it too. "I'll call when I hear something."

Mom hugged me hard as if trying to keep all the pieces from flying apart. I appreciated this, but knew it wasn't unnecessary. It would be okay now. John would live.

Just like dying people claim their past lives flash before their eyes in the final moments, I saw my future life with John flicker in my mind, like a sappy Hallmark card of two black and white figures running down a beach, her hair flying behind them, his eyes full of admiration. Just a few more days and that would be us.

"I love you no matter what," Mom said into my shoulder.

"I love you too, no matter what," I patted her back as we hugged, consoling her. I had enough to go around now.

26

The Ones We Can't Save

In spite of our best efforts on the hill, we can't save everyone. One day several years ago, a call came over the radio that a ski instructor was unconscious on a run near where I sat eating my lunch in the patrol shack. I grabbed the defibrillator, known as an A.E.D., and rushed out. CPR cannot restart the heart of a cardiac victim; it only keeps the organs perfused until an electric shock can reorganize the cardiac rhythm. Under the best circumstances only 30% of patients receiving CPR live, even in cities like Seattle where a high percentage of lay people have CPR training and great access to medical care. Nationally, the statistic is closer to 8%.

When I approached the scene, the instructor lay on his back on the slope. Two students huddled nearby, their arms hugging their chests. I immediately started CPR, while Greg, another patroller, readied the A.E.D. Only when a patient's heart creates a certain rhythm, ventricular fibrillation, also known as v-fib, can the defibrillator restore it to normal. Any other abnormal rhythm cannot be shocked.

After less than a minute of doing chest compressions, we stuck the defibrillator pads on his chest. I leaned back from the patient so as not to interrupt the machine's test. The machine blinked. *Analyzing rhythm.* I scanned the slope and spoke into my radio, informing Dispatch of the situation. We had a Code 1—a medical emergency. And we needed all the resources we could muster. A helicopter was on its way and would land right on the slope beside us, whisking the patient to the hospital within minutes.

The patient, a man of perhaps 60, was a weekend ski instructor, and his class stared into space as we conducted our efforts. They'd come up to learn to ski, never expecting their instructor to collapse on the hill. I watched a young woman stand alone beside the edge of the run. She'd taken off her skis, and now she stared at the snow.

Death's transformation can be a terrible thing to witness. A person never quite recovers from seeing a body cross over into death. I'd been watching John slowly fade, his skin yellowing, his eyes receding into bony sockets. Unlike the ski instructor on the hill, John had gradually grown weaker, giving me time to adjust. I even had a chance to say goodbye and mourn the loss before it was real. But to see a vigorous man change so quickly horrified the senses, etching the image of death into one's minds.

The robotic voice of the A.E.D. squawked. *Shock advised.* The patient was in v-fib. Since we'd gotten here within minutes, perhaps he would live. Studies have shown that a patient receiving CPR and defibrillation within five minutes of collapse have a much greater chance of survival. After ten minutes, the chances lower dramatically. A patient without intervention after fifteen minutes has no chance at all. For every minute that passes, the patient's chance of survival is reduced by 10%.

On the scene of a Code, time races. Greg pressed the shock button on the A.E.D. and I watched the patient's body rise and fall. Then I checked his pulse. Nothing.

We continued CPR while the A.E.D. recharged. We shocked another two times before I heard the blades of the helicopter chop the sky. The victim's face had turned a pale gray, and his lips splayed open, revealing a white, lifeless tongue. After nearly fifteen minutes of pounding on his chest I was getting fatigued. But I couldn't imagine stopping.

A paramedic arrived on the back of a snowmobile, his orange crash cart strapped to the rack on the back. I cut open the victim's sleeve, readying his arm for an IV. Layers of Gore-Tex and wool caught in my trauma sheers, and I snipped cleanly through them. When a patient's heart doesn't respond to defibrillation, we can administer powerful drugs like epinephrine and atropine in order to restart the proper rhythm.

Relieved by the presence of the medic, I continued CPR compressions while he readied his needles and tiny bottles of drugs. Dispatch came over the radio, telling us the helicopter was circling the valley and would land momentarily. I concentrated on my task, the heel of my hand pressing the sternum. With each compression, my hands sunk a little further as if the ribs were growing soft, unable to withstand the rigors of death and pressure.

The medic injected the long needle into the crook of the man's elbow. Working quickly, he pushed atropine into the port, and we all watched the A.E.D. monitor, hoping for a blip in his pulse. Again there was nothing. The medic tried two more times.

The young woman near the edge of the run took a step back and brought her hand to her face. The medic dropped the empty vial of atropine onto the snow and reached in the cart for more, running his fingers along the labels, looking for something that wasn't there. "You can continue CPR," he said.

The helicopter whirred overhead and lowered onto the slope, sending frozen pellets of groomed snow flying into our goggles and the grooves in our jackets. The medic closed his crash cart to protect it from the snowy onslaught. The fine snow particles covered the patient; his eye sockets were caked in white.

A flight nurse in a blue one-piece jumped out of the open helicopter door, lowered her shoulders and hunched towards us. She gently touched my arm, signaling me to stop. I compressed the patient's chest one last time, the soft give in his sternum having become familiar now. I rocked back on my heels and sighed. She would gather him up now and take him to the hospital, where they could save his life.

"How long have you been doing CPR?"

I shrugged. I wasn't sure.

Greg answered. "Fifteen minutes."

The nurse glanced over her shoulder at the pilot and shook her head. "We can't take him."

I stared at her. I didn't understand. Surely they could help this man. Certainly with more drugs and a skilled surgeon, someone could do something for him. Even if they couldn't, they could harvest his organs.

"We can't transport them," she glanced at me and then back at the patient, "when they're dead."

When the helicopter took off, I put my goggles over my eyes and covered my face, as much to protect myself as to hide my tears. For another moment, the charged scene was chaotic with the burst of wind caused by the rotor wash. Plastic wrapping from the A.E.D. pads went fluttering away, the patient's hat was blown into the woods. I let it go. He wouldn't need it anymore.

Greg and I hoisted the body into the toboggan. Someone had to bring it to the base, where the medical examiner would decide where to take it. Unnaturally heavy and awkward, we covered the body with blankets so we didn't have to look at the eye sockets still rimed with snow.

Not everyone lived. Not even when medical attention was quick and just, arriving within the short window of time.

I tried to push away the memory of the man we couldn't save as I waited for word from JD, hoping the doctors would choose him, praying he could save my husband's life.

Not everyone lived.

Dear God, how I wanted to be wrong.

~~~

"Kimmy," JD said when I answered on the first ring.

I knew what he would say just by the tone of his voice. "No," I said, trying to push the words back into the phone all the way to Rochester and into the doctor's office.

"I got the results of the CT scan." His voice sounded sugary sweet, like a parent breaking news to a child.

He'd probably found a bench outside the doctor's office. Or maybe he had waited until he got back to the car. Maybe he was sitting inside the Beetle, his knees pressed against the dashboard. "Okay," I said. *Let him go ahead and say it.*

"My left lobe is not large enough." His voice mimicked the words of the doctor.

I fell to my knees on the carpet and put my head in my hand. "Oh no." The truth of his words lay there in front of me like a limp bird. I wanted to cradle it and see if it would live again. I wanted to make him take back the words, say that he was just kidding. That he could, after all, save my husband's life.

"Bimp, are you okay? I'm so sorry."

I held my head in my hand and shook my head. "It's not true. You have to be the donor." I had built a wooden structure around myself and now it was crumbling.

"Kimmy. My left lobe isn't big enough. I am not a suitable donor. I wish that I was."

"Okay," I nodded, tears streaming down my face, unable to control my words enough to even have this conversation. "Okay." I wanted to get off the phone now, wrap myself in a sticky cocoon and never wake up.

JD continued to talk, explaining the test results.

"Maybe I just can't do this anymore," I finally said. For the past few months, every new donor was like a scaffold that I could build on. If not that one, then there would be another one. A whole list of waiting donors pointed like an arrow in the direction of travel. I knew where I had to go. With each rejected donor that arrow grew shorter and shorter until there was just one left. I'd tried again to get the nurses to agree to a blood test for me, but they'd refused, having decided that no matter what I couldn't be the donor.

"Yes you can. You can do this."

"John is going to die and I can't tell him," I started to cry hard, rocking back and forth on my knees. "I can't." The room whirled around me; my tears coming hard now, creating a wet spot in the carpet at my chin.

"Kimmy. Don't talk crazy."

"I can't do this anymore JD," I sobbed. "How can a person go through so much heartbreak? How can God expect me to accept all this?" I knew now that I had put too much hope in this one. How could I be punished for hoping? Isn't that what He wanted me to do?

"This may sound crazy, but this is all part of God's plan."

"Are you saying God wants John to die?"

"None of us can understand how He works."

Maybe he was right. Maybe John wasn't supposed to live. Not everyone lived through cancer, no matter how hard their wives prayed and pleaded with the nurses. I had tried to assign meaning to every step, creating an elaborate story about how this would go. As if this had all been a plot line filled with tension and conflict and would eventually resolve. I imagined he would be saved.

"Don't go yet, Kimmy. Whitney has already called the Mayo Clinic. He had a blood test a few days ago and his numbers look better."

"I just have to be alone for a while." I didn't want to hear about Whitney right then. That wasn't part of the story. The Mayo Clinic had already wasted time on him and I knew they would never choose him. It didn't work that way. "I'll call you later."

"Will you? Do I need to have Mom come over to your house?"

"No, no, I'll be fine."

The earth shifted beneath me as I hung up the phone. John was outside watering the plants. I knew he couldn't hear me, so I howled. I crouched on the carpet in our living room and held my hair in tight fists while rocking back and forth. The room moved around me like I was at the center of a vortex. The phone rang and I ignored it, taking comfort in sinking back down into self-pity. I couldn't move my head or my hands. The tears poured from my eyes and my nose ran hard. My body heaved and bucked and sobbed all the tears I'd held back since the first time the doctor said, "Its cancer." This was it. It crushed me like an avalanche, pressing against me like a living thing.

I didn't notice the sunlight streaming into the room, making a rhombus shape of bright light on the carpet. I was suffocating, choking on my own tears. My forehead pressed into the palm of my right hand, I wailed, wondering if I could just quit. Simply put down this burden once and for all. Human life could just be too heart wrenching to bear. This was too much to endure, too much to carry. If only the doctor would have chosen me. Even after two attempts, the donor team still wouldn't consider me as a candidate. My frustration sat in my abdomen like a razor blade. If only I could just kill myself, directing the doctors to use my liver for John's benefit, I would have gladly done it.

The phone rang again. I didn't answer it. One of my family members was likely trying to get hold of me, trying to wrap his or her arms around me. It was selfish for me to want to give up. Realistically, John would live the rest of his life with the guilt that his life caused. I would save him, but he would be ruined. Who was I kidding here?

I rolled over on the carpet and positioned my torso in the light coming through the window. I looked up at the specks of dust floating above me and blew a hard breath to see them nudge out of the light. No matter how hard I blew the specks floated this way and that, hardly concerned by my bleating. I took another full breath in and let it out slowly. I would not be the one to save him. Maybe there was another donor out there, or maybe the doctors would get him moved up on the deceased donor list, or maybe God would perform a miracle for us.

Here was a moment that I just had to get through. If I could just get through it when things were so bad then maybe I could see through to a clearer time. In another fifteen minutes the skies might clear and my heart might be lightened by the new moment. Wasn't that how alcoholics got through the darkest cravings, just one moment at a time? When you think you can't go another moment without taking a drink, just give it that moment. See if you can get through it. And then manage the next moment and the next. I had tried to get through this nightmare fifteen minutes at a time. Right now I just needed to get through the next five minutes, or the next fifteen seconds. I would take this one moment at a time. I needed to do the next right thing for John, do the next right thing for myself and survive the onslaught of uncertainty and disappointment.

I ran my fingers across the carpet, noticing the wet spot made by my tears. The world shifted a little bit. Not new and sparkling necessarily, but alive at least.

I checked my pulse to verify the beating of my heart. I was still alive.

We were both still alive.

~~~

The sun was going down on the lake, burning the windows of the houses across from us, and leaving us in shadow. It had been two days since the news of JD's rejection. The water, calm now, buoyed one lone skier who sliced fissures through it, spraying out beside him.

The leather couch was sticky beneath my thighs, and when the phone rang, I answered it slowly. John and I had just sat down on the couch. I had poured myself a glass of wine and put my feet up on the cushions. Two days earlier the world collapsed around me, and today I woke up to it. John had looked to me for a new direction—something to pin our hopes to. But I couldn't. Numb, I looked forward to twilight when I could crawl back into my cocoon, shaking with fear.

"Hello."

"Hey Kim, its Whitney."

He had tried to call me earlier, but I didn't answer. He still thought he had a chance as the donor. I didn't want to tell him yet that I'd given up hope. I thought he'd hear it soon enough from the Mayo. "Hi." I took a large sip of wine.

"Well I just got off the phone with Barb at the Mayo Clinic," he said, his voice plucky and upbeat.

"Yeah." I was weary.

"And I look good."

"Did you get another blood test?"

"Yes. And all my numbers are in the normal range."

I was silent for a moment. "What does that mean?"

"Well." He let out a short laugh. "They asked me if I could be out there Monday for the surgery on Tuesday."

"What?" I looked over at John. He was leaning forward in his chair, staring at me.

"They chose me, Kim."

"For sure?"

"Yes," he laughed again. "This is the real deal. The moment we've been waiting for."

I nodded my head at John and smiled, leaning forward to clear my mind. John looked puzzled. I held my index finger up to hold off his questions, then raised my thumb high in the air, feeling a throat-numbing happiness. He frowned; he was pushing away the urge to feel hope again.

Whitney gave me the details. I committed them to memory, knowing I'd repeat them over and over again later. All the while I looked at John, smiling and nodding ridiculously. Finally, I held my hand over the receiver and whispered. "Whitney's it. They want to do the transplant next week."

I was nearly screaming when I hung up the phone. All the hope had rushed back in like a tsunami. But instead of the damaging waters coming back onto the shore, it was hope flooding back into my parched heart.

"They're choosing Whitney. After all this time and all those negative blood tests." This moment froze in time, stretching out before us. "He's lost fifteen pounds and his triglycerides are normal now." My voice rose to a falsetto. I wanted to get it all out so John could believe it too. He pressed his lips together as I talked.

I held John's hands over my face, tasting salt and pencil lead from my tears and kneeled over the coffee table. I felt happiness as sharp and quick as sunlight glinting off a window. We were cry laughing, saying *Oh my God. Thank you God. Thank you Whitney. Oh my God.* We held each other, my face against John's neck, my tears making him wet, my hand resting on his shoulder.

"I'm going to live," he said. "We finally got there. The transplant. They'll get this cancer out of me. They'll take it all out."

"Yes," I said, my face still buried in his neck. "You're going to live." I pulled back and looked into his eyes. His long wet eyelashes turned them a deeper blue. I smiled, a little surprised that the muscles in my cheeks still knew how. It seemed so long since I had felt real joy. Like pressing my face into a strong wind, I had to turn my head to breathe. When was the last time? I couldn't ever remember feeling this way.

I must have felt this much joy on our wedding day. Perhaps then, I decided. Yet today, something had been peeled back in my heart. The pain and fear and utter loss of hope had changed me. It carved out a deep hole in me that now filled with this new feeling. It was the same painful place in my chest, just below my sternum, that now brimmed with a joyful froth.

I couldn't say that the pain was gone, the raw nerves within the hole still twittered. Yet now it was filled with a balm so soothing that I wanted to jump in and swim around in it.

"Of course," John said, his eyes looking past me now to a place far away. "I have to get through the staging surgery." He looked into my eyes again as if fingering the painful hole in my chest.

"You will," I said, trying to hold in all the joy. I had already begun to mentally write an email to our friends—telling them how long I'd waited for this. I just wanted this triumphant moment to go on a little longer. "Let's just enjoy this."

"But I have to think of the next step."

The momentum of the past year was catching up to me. I had always pointed the way forward, moving us in the direction of the next step, asking myself what the next right thing was. Now when I wanted to stop time and enjoy this triumph, the tide pulled back at me.

"I have to get through that or all bets are off."

"We will." I felt that protective barrier rising up around me. It would give me strength to keep us pointed in the right direction now. This was what we had been worried about all year: that the cancer would spread before they found a donor.

"I just hope we aren't too late."

"We aren't." I wasn't worried this time. Perhaps I was just reluctant to let go of this new joy. "This time I'm sure. The cancer hasn't spread."

27

A Good Look Inside

I read the instruction sheet the attendant had given me. "It says: Remove all jewelry before surgery." Reaching across John's chair, I smoothed down his gown and pressed it over his bare knees.

John fingered his wedding band, pulling it off and slipping it back on. "What should I do with this?"

"I'll keep it."

He placed it in my hand and closed my fingers around it. I slipped it on my thumb. He looked at it and smiled. "It fits. You can keep it on there, in case."

"Just for now," I said. "You'll get it back after the transplant. On Wednesday, when you get out of ICU."

Dr. Heimbach knocked on the door and walked in. In a few hours she would place her scalpel on John's sternum and cut straight down. She gave us the visual by tracing her index finger along her own chest while she talked. Her finger made a branch to the right, towards her hip. "The next day, provided John's cancer-free," she said as if today's findings were just a formality, "we'll cut from the corner out towards the left." A circle drawn around the ensuing scar would look like a peace symbol.

"When will I find out the results?" John asked.

"Immediately." She looked back at me. "I will accompany him back to his room, and I will have the results then."

"I'll be waiting." John and I had a plan. But when it came right down to it, I wasn't sure I'd be able to hold up my end. If Dr. Heimbach found cancer, I was supposed to be brave and stoic and postpone my emotional breakdown and simply tell

John like a big girl that he would die in a few months. I was supposed to tell him as soon as he woke up.

Dr. Heimbach nodded gently. "I know."

One of her colleagues told us she was the best in the world. She had been called a remarkable surgeon and brilliantly talented. In that moment before John's staging surgery, those hours compressed into a speck of glacial ice, I placed all my faith and trust in her.

She didn't have to say that her findings today would determine everything—we already knew that. She didn't have to tell us that all the stent changes, radiation, the tortuous wait in Michigan for the first staging results, the long list of donors that had to be sifted through, the staph infection, the pancreatitis; all of it had been leading toward this one moment—we already knew that, too.

We also knew that either he got to live, or he didn't.

I couldn't imagine her peering into his abdomen: her gloved fingers poking into the lymph nodes with a microscope between her eye and his tissue, and hearing her utter the words, "Uh-oh." I wouldn't allow myself to see her silently stitch him back up and wonder when, exactly, the cancer had gotten away from them. From us.

Or maybe those images did creep in, like water seeps through cracks in the ice before it refreezes. My experiences in the mountains prepared me for this day. I'd brushed up close to death. I'd heard the black hole of oblivion whisper into my ear. I knew what I had to do. I pushed out those seeping images and focused on the critical task. I could finally rely on what I knew to be true: get through the crisis; you can always panic later.

~~~

"As soon as they wheel me back in," John said again, "I want you to just blurt it out—did it spread or not—okay?"

We had been over this before.

"I mean it. I need to know right away as soon as I open my eyes." John's voice wavered a little as he spoke.

"The surgeon already told us that we'll know right away one way or the other."

John's family members had arrived, so we snatched some final minutes together before the orderlies arrived to get him. "Now don't worry," I said, knowing the next few hours had become like a crucible, distilling the whole long wait of the past year into one crucial diagnosis.

"I'm scared." A shaft of morning light shone across his face, illuminating tiny beads of sweat on his lip. He reached for my hand and held it tight.

"I'm not," I lied.

All the other rejections were nothing now. All that mattered was this. Right here. I couldn't keep my hands from shaking.

Whitney arrived with his mother and girlfriend. "Hey Whit," John said. Whitney stood aside, his face slightly pale. He held a travel coffee mug in one hand and a leather messenger bag hung on his shoulder as if he had just stepped out of a café. John's other family members filtered into the room.

John's mother walked over and rested her hands on his. "How can we ever thank you?"

Whitney could have let the first rejection from Mayo Clinic sideline him. He could have said, *Well I tried.* But instead, he persisted. He'd lost weight, lowered his triglycerides and sacrificed the next few months of his life in order to save John.

"They're here for you," John's sister, Kathryn, said.

John looked at me as I leaned over to kiss him. "What was that poem?"

"'Do not go gentle into that good night;'" I whispered into his ear. "'Rage, rage against the dying of the light.'"

When I raised my head, he was smiling. The orderlies transferred him to a gurney. "It's going to be fine," I said.

"No stalling. Just tell it to me straight as soon as you see me."

~~~

My mom and I worked together on the one thousand-piece puzzle in the waiting room. It had been nearly four hours since they took him back, and I was getting antsy. Greg joined us at the puzzle. It was another hard one, this time the blue-gray water and the cloudless sky blended together. We hadn't yet finished the edges.

I twisted John's wedding ring around my thumb, feeling the smooth inner band rub against my knuckle. We'd bought it on a trip to Mexico before we got married—a silver trinket that cost less than a cup of coffee. The sides had already begun to dent, and if I pressed hard, I could feel it almost give way as if held together by the thinnest of membranes. Our third anniversary was coming up and I'd bought him another wedding band—a real one engraved with our wedding date and the words *In sickness and in health*. It was still at the jewelers waiting to be picked up.

The clock ticked audibly on the wall above the door. I concentrated on the puzzle, quietly asking Greg if he had any more edge pieces on his side of the table.

"There he is," Kathryn announced. I looked up to see John's feet disappear around the corner. The gurney carrying him turned the corner near the waiting room. John's other sister, Amy, walked next to the Dr. Heimbach, who pushed John's gurney down the hall. I stood up and quickly followed.

"We got a really good look inside," Dr. Heimbach said to me as I walked up.

I tried to quiet my vibrating body so I could hear every word, feeling like a refrigerator humming loudly on a hard kitchen floor.

"There is absolutely no sign of the cancer spreading."

"Oh." I looked at Amy. My body felt two sizes too big, and every organ was suddenly swimming around in the cavernous space. I touched John's gurney to steady myself. "Oh," I said again. I scanned my brain for the appropriate response. I knew I needed to say something, to ask questions and pretend like a wife who had things under control.

Dr. Heimbach looked back at John on the table. "I wanted to tell you right away."

After a moment, I cleared my throat. "How does everything else look in there?" I asked her, knowing John would ask me a million questions. She told me about the damage to his stomach and pancreas from the radiation and said it was no wonder he had so much pain. She made a round shape with her hand as if holding onto a large mug of coffee. "Was it charred?"

"Severely burned. Yes."

I looked at John while she told me all this. "Anything else?"

"He's lucky," she nodded again and smiled, this must be the easy news to share. "He's very lucky."

It felt like a warm blanket had been thrown around my shoulders. "Thank you."

~~~

John woke up as the orderly pushed him into his room. He saw me at his side and before he could ask, I told him. "You're fine." I wanted to spit it all out quickly, but my mouth ran dry. I was going to cry. "It hasn't spread," I managed to say. "The transplant's a go." My voice quavered a little as I said it. I should have kept my mind in the moment. I would later return to it like a talisman, over and over again. But instead, I remembered that day spooning his turns in España, how the light made the ridges seem like billowing sheets. It wasn't over yet. We'd been given a reprieve.

John opened his eyes wide and his body relaxed into the bed. He raised both his fists in the air, letting the sheet drop around them. With tears in his eyes, he brought his fists to his ears. "Thank you," he said. I touched him, feeling his warm arm in my palm. The room was dark except for the gray light from the window. His tears caught the light of the glow in the room and fell down his cheeks like pearls.

It's okay to be happy now.

~~~

I pulled the letter out of my purse and began to read it. John had written similar letters to his children, Evelyn and Andrew, but I didn't want to read those just yet. Maybe I'd never have to. It was six pages, written in John's neat cursive. He had told me to read it only if he died, but I couldn't help it.

Dear Kim, he'd written. *The last few years with you have been my best.*

I closed the letter and returned it to my purse, guiltily wondering if by reading his letter I was somehow jinxing it. Instead, I wandered about the waiting room, wondering what my next steps should be. The fish tank hummed quietly, the fish mouthing the glass between us. Magazines lay in messy piles on tables scattered throughout the room. This was a room a visitor could sleep in, and it felt lived in. A stack of puzzle boxes lay crooked in the corner and I ran my finger along their spines, wondering if I had the energy to start one. I'd spent the last year of my life waiting, and I wasn't sure what came next. How do I write myself a new story?

Instead, I decided to crochet another ski hat. Settling into a chair, I wondered who I'd make it for—by now everyone I knew had one of my hats. My left index finger had grown a callous where the yarn pulled across it with each stitch.

The letter was still in my purse and I straightened it as I extracted the yarn. I didn't need to read it—I knew what it said. The first few pages extolled his love for me, how he wished he had more time with me, that he was glad to have spent a few years together. In the second half of the letter, he'd more than likely offered advice—details about running Crystal after he died, how to access his life insurance policy, that kind of thing. I still couldn't bring myself to read any of it.

This hat would keep me warm in the mountain next season. The thick wool slid across my index finger, leaving a mark. I imagined myself standing at the top of the King, John at my side.

We would look down into Pinball and feel the upslope wind. I would adjust this hat, pulling it more tightly over my ears as my body cooled. John would look at me and raise his eyebrows. "Should we ski it?"

I'd pretend to consider it and point out our line. "Jump onto that spine, then turn and point it through the slot."

John would agree by leaning forward with anticipation. "Then turn hard left to scrub some speed."

"You'd have to watch out for the rubble. That could be a real bummer."

I imagined John's smile. "Maybe we should try Hourglass instead."

We'd both push back from Pinball and slide down the ridge towards the easier couloir. He'd stop at the top and tell me to go first. The sun would be behind us by then casting long shadows on the snow, illuminating the spray of each turn. I would carve across the chute, knowing he was watching me, scattering snow and laughing all the way down.

That was a vision I could tell myself.

~~~

"Whitney's surgery is going well. They're almost done," his mother, Sharon, said. Understandably, her voice was a little shaky. She must have wondered why her eldest son would agree to a risky surgery to save my husband's life.

"Wonderful," Carol said, no doubt joining Sharon's vision of their sons lying unconscious, the skin of their abdomens held open with clamps, their insides glistening. Whitney's liver would be cleaved in two, each blood vessel carefully sewn together behind the scalpel.

I worked the hook into the stitches in my lap, forming a circle that would be the top of the hat. Once the liver was extracted, the surgeons would put it on ice, inspect it and start in on John. There was no pattern to follow. First, the old liver came out, and with it the gall bladder, the bile ducts, and perhaps a portion of the pancreas. It all depended on what it looked like when they got in there. The new one must be reattached precisely, which sounded simple until I stopped to realize the connection points are no bigger than the piece of yarn in my fingers. The surgeons would then sew the artery and veins first, and then relocate a portion of the small intestines as the new bile duct.

Whitney would awaken depleted, his body quickly working to make up for the loss, while John would feel better than he had in almost a year. Like the nose in Woody Allen's *Sleeper*, Whitney's liver would grow back in three weeks, in his body as well as in John's.

It was almost ten a.m. and John's part of the procedure would start soon. I imagined the two of them, donor and recipient, side by side in the operating room, with the doctors alternatively working over Whitney while others prepared John to receive the new liver. Once Whitney's right lobe was out, one surgeon stayed back with him to stitch him up and the other two moved over to John. Circles of bright light would illuminate each body. The doctors—gloved, gowned and masked like Halloween caricatures—would speak in clipped verse asking for scalpel, suction, scissors. One surgeon would lift her mask slightly, breathing in fresh air. Another would straighten his back for a moment, coaxing the blood back into his tense shoulders.

It was a long surgery.

~~~

While Whitney rested in post-op, Michelle and Sharon left for breakfast, their vigil complete. I imagined the liver, a dark triangle, being passed across the room towards John's gaping abdomen. This was the hard part.

"Hello?" I answered my phone. "This is Kim."

"I have some news about your husband," the nurse's voice was chipper. "The surgeons have started on him."

"When did his surgery begin?" I looked at Amy and gave her a thumb's up sign.

"About two hours ago. I just heard from the surgeons and John is doing really well." The others studied my face, looking for cracks.

"I will call you when I hear anything more," the nurse said.

~~~

Earlier, before the surgery, someone had asked John if his last will and testament were in order. It was a strange sort of question—one that lingered in that quicksand between hope and despair. Of course we had done the will. In John's letter to me—the one neatly folded in my purse, the one that might, as it turned out, be his last words—he tried to distill the ensuing years down into a potent liquor. I hoped that I would never have to hold the letter in my shaking hands and read the words for some deeper meaning, or some lost translation that could offer me solace after his death.

I watched the fish swim in the tank. The sound of heels pounding down the hallway floated past the room, barely registering. It seemed I too was suspended in water, as if I'd warmed up the narrow space around my body and didn't want to move around and get cold again. But I knew I'd have to come up for air sometime.

Scott, the Mountain Manager at Crystal, once had a dog named Goose who had been attacked by a moose as a pup and had lost his ability to walk in a straight line. He could only walk in circles. His balance and coordination had been put askew and so he had learned to navigate the base area around Crystal Mountain in large, looping arcs. Sometimes, I would see him carving turns in the playpen area, kids dodging him, laughing at his strange, confused gait.

"But," Scott had once told me. "Somehow he always made it home at night."

Now, sitting in the waiting room, I imagined Goose making curlicues that eventually spun him home. He'd double back on himself and get turned around, but eventually head off in the right direction again, determination in his eyes. I'd call to him to follow me, but my path was too straight for him and eventually he'd arc away.

It had been like that for John and me, too. It hadn't been the straight line we'd hoped to take—the one that other patients with shorter waiting times and fewer complications seemed to have. But somehow here we were.

Somehow we'd made it.

~~~

John and I were in this very room almost a year ago, I realized, as I stood in the recovery room and watched my husband's chest rise and fall. We were on a tour of the ICU as part of his weeklong orientation to the transplant list. That week had been interrupted by the staph infection. We had returned in September to finish up some of the tests for listing. Now I couldn't remember if we were here when he was so sick or was it later just before the radiation. It all seemed so hazy and far away.

What we did remember was that John hadn't liked it here. He had seen a patient with a breathing tube taped to her mouth and an enormous IV strapped to her neck. She had looked anonymous as they wheeled her in through the double doors as we were pushed aside and had our backs to the walls. From our perch against the wall, we watched the nurses move efficiently through the round room, attaching orders to clipboards and placing IV bags on silver trays—their center station a hub with the rooms spreading from it like spokes on a wheel.

Now this was John's room and he was hooked up to the machines. He had begun to wake up and the large rectangular machine behind him rhythmically filled his lungs with air. Once he woke up, he wanted the breathing tube taken out immediately. He'd given me these instructions before the surgery ever started, and I knew it scared him more than the surgery.

His eyes opened and he motioned me with his hand. His arms were strapped to the bed, and I held his hand tightly. "I'm right here."

He shook his head back and forth slowly and pointed to his mouth. I asked the nurse to unstrap his arm. He pointed to his mouth again, shaking his head, his eyes wide. "Just breathe normally," I said. "Can you take the breathing tube out?" I asked the nurse.

"I've called the respiratory doctor. He'll be here soon and will assess."

John moaned through the tube; it sounded almost like a scream. He pointed to his mouth again, making a complicated motion with his hand like he was rolling a cigarette and then cutting it in half. The nurse calmly handed him a small wipe board and a dry erase pen.

John wrote on it in small, strange letters, "the tube has a flap on it that is blocking my windpipe, and I can't breathe."

I watched as his lungs filled. "Hold on, honey," I held his hand again. "The doctor is on the way." I watched the machine carefully to make sure his lungs inflated.

When the doctor arrived a few moments later, I explained the problem. Closely watching the machines, he held a stethoscope to John's chest. Like the nurse, he was measured and calm.

I wondered if they would spring into action if John stopped breathing or his heart stopped beating. Would they arrive with a crash cart, nurses and doctors running in from the adjacent rooms? Since John was already monitored so heavily, a life-threatening situation could be addressed quickly. He already had an IV in his neck where they could administer drugs, his vitals bleeping away on a monitor above his head.

The doctor assembled the implements to remove the tube in John's chest. It looked complicated. He explained to John that this would be uncomfortable and asked him to take several deep breaths. John struggled to inhale with the machine's timing, while I stood at his feet and held his toes in my hands. "Look at me John," I said.

The doctor pulled out the inner tube, making John convulse. He wouldn't be able to breathe until they finished. The nurse suctioned the open tube, and I imagined it rummaging around in his lungs. They had to get any fluid out since John wouldn't be able to cough for some time. John's legs stiffened and his toes arched forward like a ballerina's.

"Just hold on." I willed the nurse to finish the suctioning quickly. It took a full minute—a long time to hold your breath. Then slowly he pulled out the second tube. John's legs jumped around on the bed, and I tried to hold down his ankles. I talked soothingly to him, knowing he probably couldn't hear me, imagining he only heard the slow slurping sound of the tube sliding forward through his trachea.

When John gulped the air hungrily, I exhaled as he filled his lungs. I had been holding my breath, too. As John's breathing evened out, his eyes went around the room, focusing on the doctor, our family members, and to me, and smiled.

"I get to live."

~~~

Running the shaver across John's head, soft clumps of hair fell onto his shoulders. It was hot outside on the deck of our Rochester apartment. John wanted his hair short—just like Whitney's. A sheet laid across his lap like a bib to protect his incision from falling hair. I evened it out, stepped back and looked. "There you go."

He rubbed his palm across his head. "I love it."

"Here's the mirror. Have a look at it first."

"I don't need to. It feels perfect."

I went into the kitchen and opened the freezer to pull out two ice cream sandwiches, one for John and one for Whit.

"I think Whitney has the best scar," John said. Both men sat on the deck with their shirts off and their faces lifted towards the sun.

Summer was just around the corner. In a few weeks residents near Soldier's Field would be readying their driveways for the fireworks, clearing away weeds so they could park more cars.

"It's in the shape of a J," Whitney said, tracing his index finger along it.

"It looks like you've been in a bar fight," I said. His scar was red and raised, just beginning to heal.

"Or like you've saved someone's life," John said.

It was true. Whitney had saved John's life. Sitting there on the deck, the guys eating ice cream sandwiches, I sniffed the air. It was the smell of our old lives, like newly cut grass, but sharper, more like fresh cut limes. The laughter of children riding their bikes around the cul-de-sac rose around us. Two men, one holding a cooler, both carrying fishing rods, walked across the grass towards the pond. And if I inhaled deeply, opening my nostrils fully, I was sure I could detect the distinct scent of fresh snow.

Epilogue

A few short months after his transplant, John was back on the slopes. A new ski run at Crystal, named Whit's End, now commemorates the selflessness of the donor Whitney Meriwether. The short pitch underneath the Northway Chair is steep and unforgiving, much like the wait for organ donation. Whitney looks forward to the day his skiing skills match the difficulty of the run named in his honor.

As I write these words, John is on the eve of his three-year transplant anniversary. Without the expertise of the doctors and surgeons at Mayo Clinic, he would not be alive today. Every year thousands of patients die waiting for liver transplants before a suitable donor can be found. Living donor liver transplantation is becoming more widespread in the United States, and yet, it is not without risk. Our nation has seen two post-transplant donor fatalities in the three years since John's surgery. From our perspective, the donor process often felt cryptic and slow, but we are now grateful for the care and diligence shown by our team of doctors.

While organ donation is on a slight incline, the need for organs has risen sharply. There simply are not enough deceased organs to go around. And yet one donor can save eight lives. In John's case, waiting for a deceased donor simply would have been too long; the cancer would have spread before he rose to the top of the list.

John and I have returned to Crystal, and every day I gaze across the ridges and peaks, grateful for their rigid lines and harsh lessons. The mountains do not forgive nor relent. They simply are. Against this world of white ridges and black rocks, sparkling snowfields and detonating bombs, I can only slow down, breathe, and live fifteen minutes at a time.

Acknowledgments

Words cannot express my gratitude to the doctors and surgeons at the Mayo Clinic who saved my husband's life, namely Dr. Glenn Alexander, Dr. Gregory Gores and Dr. Julie Heimbach. The donor, Whitney Meriwether, risked his life so that John could live. I will never forget the day you called with the "good news". You are amazing.

This book bloomed in the hands of my editor, Lynn Price, at Behler Publications, who believed in the manuscript, carefully polishing it and pushing me to excellence. Thank you, Lynn, for trusting in this project. Thanks also to my agent, Kit Ward, for her encouragement and expertise.

Writerly friends, Sharon Rice and Natasha Cottingham, offered valuable encouragement and feedback that propelled me forward, for which I'm deeply indebted.

Special thanks go to John for his support and reassurance. Your love, strength, and the simple fact that you are still in my life bring me joy every day; I love you.

Mom, your love and support during the darkest moments provided a sturdy framework against which I could rest. Thank you for reminding me to live just fifteen minutes at a time.

To Dad, who first introduced me to skiing, thank you for teaching me to catch snowflakes on my tongue and find answers on the slopes.

To my stepdaughter Evelyn: every writer needs a cheerleader just like you.